THE GENUINE LIFE,

OF

ROBERT BARKER,

DICTATED BY HIMSELF WHILE IN A STATE OF

𝕱𝖔𝖙𝖆𝖑 𝕯𝖆𝖗𝖐𝖓𝖊𝖘𝖘;

And commencing from the earliest Period of his Recollection, in the Year 1732, till this Publication took place, in the Month of November, 1809:

CONTAINING, A CLEAR ACCOUNT OF HIS REMARKABLE

TRAVELS, VOYAGES,

DIFFICULTIES, SUFFERINGS,

AND

OTHER UNCOMMON EVENTS,

DEEMED MOST WORTHY OF OBSERVATION

THROUGHOUT THE WHOLE COURSE OF HIS NATURAL LIFE.

LONDON:

PRINTED BY GALABIN AND MARCHANT, INGRAM-COURT,

FOR THE AUTHOR.

1809.

ADVERTISEMENT.

DURING my unhappy long period of 54 years melancholy darkness, without beholding the face of any mortal being whatever, the greatest pleasure I could find was in recounting up the whole tenour of my days, from the earliest part of my recollection to that or this present time; and, by so doing, from time to time, became enabled to retain many strange and uncommon events in mind, which might have otherwise been forgotten, if not for ever buried in lasting oblivion, though not altogether unlikely to become, hereafter, improved on by those possessing far superior genius and talents for the beneficial good of all the human race in general.

THE

GENUINE LIFE, ETC.

AGREEABLY to the information received from my parents and others, I was born at a lone farm-house, situate on the very summit of Cowbrew, one of the highest hills in the parish of Wiggan, Lancashire, from thence a most delightful prospect of the surrounding country may be taken, as it is situate close on the left-hand side of the main road, leading from Wiggan to Preston, about a mile and a half from the former and seventeen from the latter, at that time belonging to the Reverend Robert Harvey, my mother's brother, and from thence baptized in Wiggan-church, on the 12th of January, 1729; but to whatever might duly occur, happen, or take place, in that farm, I am a perfect stranger, from being too young to observe any thing of the kind previous to the time wherein my parents removed from thence to the Roundmore, another farm belonging to Squire Standish, about a mile farther from Wiggan, on the same side of the aforesaid road, and not much, if any, more than a mile from Standish-hall, the country seat and residence of their new landlord: and here it was the first accruing transaction of my life, whereof I have still some faint recollection, commenced, through the indiscreet folly and weakness of two thoughtless girls, namely, my own sister, and also Williamson, from the Bordered-house, another farm lying something farther from Wiggan, close to the opposite side of the road, neither of them being ten years of age, yet ventured on taking me from the house, while seated on a small chair, and, moving across the yard, placed me on the ice, where a whole dike had been frozen over, in order to please themselves by sliding the chair to and fro, with me in it; but, instead of enjoying the pleasure expected from such hazardous play on the ice, it gave way and let them both in to the waist, from which they were providentially relieved by the family, who, on hearing their cries, came and dragged us all out of the ditch; and is here given, by way of caution, warning all other children to avoid hazarding their safety with playing on the ice, where there is so much real danger to be apprehended, for, if the water had been deep enough, we should have all three inevitably perished therein; and, with respect to its having been so long retained in mind, I suppose that to have proceeded from hearing it so frequently repeated by my play-fellows and others during a period of some years after, and that being the only thing which I am still able to recollect during the length of our stay in that farm, which in course proved of very short duration; but, whether through that of my father having been brought up to the making of white cloths and checks, with the whitening business, in the parish of Billinge, near the chapel, three miles from Wiggan, in the direct way from thence to Liverpool, where, as he grew up, his parents thought fit to have him frequently brought into the company of various sporting gentlemen, while amusing themselves with the diversion of shooting, coursing, setting, hunting, and the like, which he, through habit, time, and practice, became excessively fond of, and more so of shooting than all the rest, and he was said to have become a very good marksman, and that being made known to his landlord, and other gentlemen, from the lips of their own servants, he afterwards became frequently prevailed on to join with them in those kind of amusements, and at length to decline both the farm and cloth business, but whether through their advice, or that of such farm being disposed of in a long lease to Mr Ralph Balding, of Wiggan, one or both I cannot truly pretend to say, though it happened to be let to him, as above, much about the time my parents moved from thence to the brick, or bowling-green, house at Standish, situate a mile farther from Wiggan, close to the right-hand side of the said road, where the bowling-green became very much frequented by gentlemen throughout most part of the summer time, and the house with gentlemen and their servants from Adlington, Rickington, Parbut-hay, and Standish-hall, with many other sportsmen of less note, residing within some few miles round during winter: and here the first religious opinions of good and evil were instilled into my innocent mind, by the moral precepts of the most kind and tender parents, whose sanguine advice having been duly attended to, had the desired effect, by taking such firm root as could not easily be removed from the innocent mind of one so young,

while hoping to enjoy most heavenly delight in the blisful realms above, proving likewise useful in preparing me to hear religious disputes, arising from the different opinions of others, while in company I could not always shun, but without losing any sight of, or even departing from, those whosesome instructions which had first been so cautiously inculcated by my parents, as both thoughtful and thoughtless, discreet and indiscreet, people used the house, some taking no small pleasure in training me up to all that was upright, just, and fair, while others took no less pains in teaching me how to become idle, weak, and useless, if not injurious to myself and parents, who first perceived it from an accident which I still remember to have happened in the presence of some few neighbouring servants and others, while passing through the kitchen with an egg, which happened to drop from my hand, and thereby caused some little amazement while viewing it lie burst on the ground, till recovering therefrom, and, on holding up my head, said: " Pray, mo-
" ther, shall I go to Dutton and get it mended?" meaning the cobler that mended our shoes, and thereby causing all the company to either laugh or smile, except Mr. George Plesenton, butler at Standish-hall, who, being of a serious turn of

mind, rather approved than disapproved the innocent words he heard me utter, and soon procuring another egg, he, from that time, seldom or ever beheld me, in or out of doors, without presents of fruit, sweetmeats, or other agreeable things, most pleasing to children of that prattling age, and, when forgot, halfpence supplied their place, wherewith he mostly sent me out to purchase for myself, unless he was going the same way; advising me to choose what I liked best, while paying for it with a secret kind of pleasure in his looks, thereby inducing me to run at his heels from place to place, till observed by others of another cast, as may be seen from what happened while viewing me at play with a favourite kitten, claimed by my sister as her own, though absent from my father's yard, wherein I then was, separated from the public road by a low brick wall, over which three men were leaning, with a penny in the hand of one, saying: " Here, look what I have for you, in case of " putting little pussy in the ditch," which was about two yards across, with a foot-path close to the wall, reaching near the kitchen at the farther end; but, with respect to the temptation so held out, that proved more than I could withstand, so, through fear of missing the bribe, I most reluctantly put little pussy in the ditch, where, observing her to swim quietly away, and those hardened wretches laughing heartily thereat, while desiring me to meet her round that way and turn her back, which I did, from time to time, both to and fro, from side to side, agreeably to their harsh commands, till poor little pussy became entirely deprived of life therein, for which I alone was blamed, instead of those hardened wretches who had led me to the thought of committing such a naughty crime, in order to afford themselves nothing more than a scene for laughter, which, however, at length subsiding, and their selfish amusement coming to an end, the person, from whom I had received the bribe, sent home for another kitten, and, on giving it to my sister, appeared to satisfy her parents, to whom she had, by reason of her loss, complained; and so the matter ended, with partly shewing the natural temper of some few individuals seeming intent to cultivate and mould my early disposition into a shape much like their own, as appeared from their uniformly persevering on one and the same point, step by step, from time to time, and place to place, as though in a seeming kind and friendly way, enticing me from home to play with children wholly disapproved and likewise suspected by my parents, though having selected other children for me to associate with, meaning John Tovey, son of the curate, and Joshua Marsden, son of the parish-clerk, both near my own age, and likewise training up in a very pious way, all having proper leave to meet, associate, and freely play together, in the habitations of each other, a thing which often happened, as I had become exceedingly fond of running to the house of Mr. Tovey, that having been the usual place of rendezvous, unless when stopped and prevented by those designing people, with trifling presents, tempted me to go and play with many other children, which, though so very unpleasant to my parents, yet frequently taking place, I soon became acquainted with most parts of the village and likewise the company to the bowling-green, with playful children like myself, as a thing most wilfully contrived by those designing tutors, if their own weak and silly actions do not make them to appear undeserving of that name; one of them taking place at the gate of such bowling-green, while I and another child, like myself, stood viewing two fat pigs lay wallowing to cool themselves in a dirty hole, on a most delightful summer's day, which being observed by two of those silly tutors, who both came up together, with each a kind of switch and a bit of sugar-candy in his hand, saying: " Here, look at this, which you may have for " going with these sticks and driving away those " stinking swine from that mucky hole;" which proved sufficient enough for us to hear; we, therefore, took the bribe, and sat off running both together; but the other child, having no shoes nor stockings on his legs, getting the start, soon became a yard or two ahead, and I, unwilling to remain behind, continued swiftly running on, till, happening to hit my toe against a stone, it threw me down flat on my face, half covered with the filthy soil drained from my father's stables, and was removed from thence into the house by a neighbouring spectator, where, being unable to explain the matter right, I was there blamed and chided for playing with that child against the will and instructions of my parents, whilst those principally concerned therein were by no means suspected in the least, though laughing slily at each other, to see how well their ungenerous scheme had succeeded; but, without desisting from those base designs, as afterwards appeared from that of their contriving how to keep me longer away in rambling to a greater distance, by sending other children with me to the parsonage-house, and from thence to both the Workington and Jolly mills, each lying about a mile from the village; and, as you descend to view the adjoining parts, my father and the butler took me with them both to Standish-hall, lying about a mile on the other side, where, being noticed by the ladies, they entertained me with plumcake, tarts, sweetmeats, delicious fruit, and other good things, then filled my pocket with trinkets of various kinds to play with; and frequently diverted myself elsewhere, and so filled my head therewith that I could think or talk of little or nothing else. They, ere long, sent me on a visit to the rectory, by the consent and approbation of my parents, where, being caressed and entertained in like manner as at Standish-hall, wherewith my innocent mind was so taken up with future hopes of pleasure and delight, as to ere long find my way alone to both one and the other, even before I had sense to know the danger of passing close by a deep pond, as well as over a narrow wooden bridge, crossing the mote to Standish-hall, yet continued pursuing those former visits occasionally, till a pretty little boy, with whom I used to play, happened to be deprived unluckily of life, by driving the ducks about the public road, wherefrom he was supposed to have followed through a narrow path into the pond opposite the bowling-green, from whence he was brought out some hours after, and laid on a corn-chest in the stable, belonging to my parents, previous to the coroner's inquest being taken, for his play-fellows to come and see, by way of caution, warning them to keep at a proper distance from the water-side, through fear of meeting with a similar kind of fate, and had no trifling effect on me while thinking on his loss, and how it came; yet could not refrain from pursuing my usual visits to the rectory and Standish-hall, nor yet from rambling about elsewhere, at the instigation of those weak-minded tutors, who, instead of resigning their silly tricks, contrived another still more base, vile, and obnoxious, than either of the former, which they absolutely put in force, close to the blacksmith's shop, then belonging to Alexander Shaw, at the four lane ends, and, to the best of my recollection, near a hundred yards beyond the bowling-green, where too I had been led and properly enticed by another child some years older, than myself, with a view to see the axletree of a cart besmeared with tar and grease, in order to make the wheels go swiftly round; and, when the job was nearly over, behold, the smith was suddenly called away, and followed by the other child, leaving me alone to see it finished by the driver, who, observing no other person near, held out a penny, saying: " I will give you this, to put " your hand in there;" and, having no better sense than to accept of his bribe, I soon became elbow deep in a pitcher of tar and grease. He stood by my side, saying: " Now, if you will put in the " other arm, and wipe them both upon your " clothes," said he, " the penny is your own;" then leaving the place, and me busily employed there, he continued briskly driving along the Preston road; and, before I had moved from the spot, many other boys appeared, coming over a stile at no great distance from me, all followed by Mr. Tovey, then master of the grammar-school, who, on observing me in that dismal kind of plight, ordered some of them to conduct and see me home, while he went on before with the unpleasant news to my parents, who having surveyed my clothes, and learned how they came into that situation, they seemed to be alarmed, through first suspecting that some kind of underhand play had been going on, at the same time expressing their wish to sift that and other matters to the bottom, and, with such intent, the blacksmith was shortly called on by my father, who, being wholly innocent thereof, gave in the farmer's name, to whom the cart belonged, a person well known to him, therefore continued walking on to his house, near the Seven Stars, where, finding him quite ignorant of the matter, and his man being out, they agreed together concerning the business, accompanied each other to the public house, and there found him much disguised with liquor, through having been some time enjoying himself and others with half-a-crown, which he had received from a near relation of my parents, who, upon farther inquiry, proved to have been the principal cause of the dirty action, while on a visit to them from Wiggan, though not altogether alone, as there were others of as light a turn of mind as himself, according to the driver's information, at the same time viewed the whole process from the window of a public house nearly opposite to the blacksmith's shop, and, on the above account being found really true, our relation was accused therewith; but, instead of denying the charge, he turned the whole affair into a laughable kind of joke, saying: " the " accusation was, in reality, very true, as he had " contrived a plan, and should have no small plea- " sure in seeing it properly executed;" and going on, said: " he had long wished to furnish m " with a complete suit of other clothes, as I had

" already worn my frock and petticoats for some
" months too long;" then desired to have them all
got ready by a set time, which he appointed, and
charged to his account, as he intended to pay
them another visit at the Red Lion, near the
church-gate, to which said public house he well
knew they were intending to remove, previous to
the time appointed, where and when he should
discharge the tailor's bill with pleasure, in case
the above proposal was accepted of; and, that
being done accordingly, he then set off on his return to Wiggan. However, long before the time
arrived, I and my brother, a boy near four years
older than myself, got astray, with various other
children, to a brick-field, near the free-school,
having at that time one side thereof lying open
to the public road, where, observing a spade on
a bank, near the brink of a perpendicular precipice, leading into a hole from whence the clay
had been taken, having at that time four or five
feet of water collected underneath; when, thinking myself able to use the spade like others, I
took it up, and, placing the edge to the brink of
the precipice, I, with endeavouring to set my
foot thereon, slipped headlong into the water below, which a person, then moulding bricks at
some distance therefrom, providentially observing

came time enough to draw me out while living; some part of which I well remember to this very day, in particular, that of endeavouring to set my foot upon the spade, and, likewise, admiring the water trickle from the bottom of my petticoats to the ground, while on the way home with my brother, who was severely reprimanded for leaving me in so much danger, while he himself had strayed away for the sake of pulling black-berries at some distance from the place: this is here mentioned by way of caution to children, really wishing them to carefully avoid such dangerous holes, and all deep waters in particular, through fear of experiencing such disasters as I then did, which would have put a final end to my temporal existence, if timely assistance had not been near; however, the long-wished for time at length came, wherein our relation from Wiggan returned with a select party of his own choosing, who all seemed to appear well pleased with the clothes, by finding them made and prepared according to the instructions he formerly gave, except the shoes and hat, that having been made cock and pinch, with a broad gold lace round the edge, as also a new wig, coat, waistcoat, breeches, stockings, and buckles, all being of a shining white colour, for which he seemed to pay with no small degree of pleasure: it being on the 5th of November, in particular, above all other days in the year, when upwards of a chaldron of coals were burning in the open street, within about a hundred yards of the door, affording me great delight in viewing it and my new clothes; but, considerably more so on hearing them order me to join the numerous multitude of people throwing squibs, crackers, and other combustible things, near the bonfire, which, together with the smoky vapours arising from the burning coals, soon changed the colour of my new clothes from a clear white to that of a most disagreeable swarthy-coloured hue, to the no small diversion of the by-standers, and more so to the visitors of my parents, who seemed to have purposely fixed on that day in order to amuse themselves with such unnecessary, fulsome, kind of delight, as the more black and dirty my clothes appeared, the more pleasure it seemed to afford them; which my parents, though highly disgusted therewith, could not prevent without considerable loss, or disadvantage to themselves, as most of the party were men of property, and excellent customers to the house, yet appeared to find more pleasure in promoting such weak kind of buffoonery than seeking after real wisdom, judgement, and understanding, whereby far greater pleasure and happiness may be obtained; and, though I was not desired to quit those smoky vapours till after the setting in of night, yet my parents thought fit to pass it over, without notice, rather than presume to offend those whimsical gentlemen, whose perpetual good-will and esteem seemed to considerably promote and increase the business of their house, and would have actually been far more acceptable to my parents and others, if those fanciful tricks had not been so frequently carried on with so much weakness and folly, from time to time; as another commenced on the following day, by some of their party, who, taking me into the outhouse, and there rearing up a hunting staff slantways to the wall, over a quantity of loose straw, then shewing me how to lay hold with my hands, and twist my legs round, instructed me to swarm up with my back underneath, even at the same time persisting in my so doing, till I had reached the top several times; and, on finding myself thus able to swarm up and slip down without danger of dropping on the straw, it seemed to become a new fangled sort of play, which I was frequently seen practising, both in and out of doors, whenever their hunting-staffs fell in my way, till I became more dexterous at it than any other child in the village. But this was not all, as one or more of these tutors were, generally, advising me to clamber up the fruit-trees and others, in the orchards, lanes, and adjoining fields, till I became so very bold and fond of running headlong into those dangerous ways, that no one of my play-fellows, throughout the whole place, dare venture to imitate the example which I had so daily set before them, and became well pleased in finding myself more expert and capable of pursuing those dangerous adventures than what other children of my own age were; and, with respect to the acquiring of dishonest achievements from the farther advice and instructions of those inconsiderate tutors, I cannot recollect any thing of the kind to have successfully taken place till the month of January following, when a main of cocks, which fought in the cockpit-yard, a little beyond the stables, having rooms in-doors for the purpose of cutting them out, and I being called to see the manner of it, and the method of heeling them, and then they were taken from thence to the cock-clod, from time to time, till I had beheld various battles fought; and, at length seeing a beautiful cock lying dead thereon, I still remember having told those gamesome gentlemen; saying: " It was not " fair to let them kill each other with swords on "their legs unknowingly;" but that being taken little notice of, I was brought again and again, till a dispute happening to arise, (I think it was from the counting out of a cock) and increasing to high words became followed with blows, wherein several of each party were engaged so near the spot where I stood as to be entangled with their feet, and so greatly bruised in various parts of my body, legs, face, and arms, as to bear visible marks thereof for a month or six weeks after, and became so very much alarmed at it, as to run from large multitudes of people whenever I saw them collecting together; and, since then, never have been fond of mixing with crowds of any kind: however, at the commencement of the next ensuing spring, some few of those restless tutors, taking me into one of the adjoining meadows, began beating on a thick, high, and close, blooming May-thorn hedge, where they continued so doing till a blackbird came out, flying from one of the highest bushes, which they told me, had just sprung up from off its nest, wherein there were young birds, fledged, and fit for taking, they having raised it therefrom with a long forked branch of a tree, seemingly brought for such purpose; adding that, if I could devise how to get up and bring the birds down they should be my own; and the more to incite a desire for my so doing, one of their party lifted me up in his arms till the nest came in view, seemingly four yards high, though scarcely discernable, from the numerous green leaves wherewith it was surrounded; and, no sooner found me desirous enough to obtain the prize, than I was set down close to those branches spreading wide from the bottom: while lifting them up, he bade me to creep under, saying: "That was the only way to come at the nest;" which, being truly desirous of, I undertook the job, and scrambling up the tree body, with much difficulty, till getting sight of the young birds, where, from finding myself unable to bring them down, by reason of both hands being found necessary to prevent the sharp-pointed thorns from hurting my flesh, I told those below of it, who soon removed the obstacle, by tying a hat to the end of the forked bow, brought with them for that purpose; and, raising it to that part of the bush wherein I then was, ordered me to put in the nest and birds altogether, which, having made a shift to perform, I descended to the bottom, exhibiting many visible scratches received from those sharp-pointed thorns on both hands and face, whereat they smiled, on expressing much delight on finding me so well pleased with the young birds, which my sister engaged to bring up, but failed therein, as only one out of three or four was reared, yet gave pleasure to all parties concerned, by becoming a very good singer, and proved the first instigation of my rambling along the fields, hedges, bushes, and trees, in search of bird's eggs, with the shells whereof I have long furnished the walls of my sleeping-room, greatly admiring their different sizes and colours, while hanging by strings fastened thereto; but that was not all, for they took me with them to the river and neighbouring ponds to fish, furnishing me with a rod and line as my own, and continued persevering in their design till I had become able enough to catch roach, gudgeons, numerous bleaks, and other small fish, thereby greatly adding to the danger attending those rambling ways, whereof I had already become too fond, as appears from the result that afterwards happened. In a large pit or pond, then belonging to Mr. Taylor, at that time residing just opposite to our own door, who, for some reason or other, best known to himself, ordered his pond lying on the left-hand side of the Preston-road, near about a quarter of a mile from the village, to be drained, or laid dry, which, when coming near to the bottom, many from the villages went to view the pit, and, amongst the rest, two of those tutors with me at their heels; where, perceiving numberless small fish swimming about in the water below, too far distant for me to reach with a line from the bank, and, being desirous of fishing therein, I, by the consent and approbation of those tutors, ventured into the mud, where, happening to slip down, I could not avoid sliding on the slippery mud into the water till I was up to the arm-pits, at which one of those tutors became so alarmed as greatly to bemire himself in extricating me from that dangerous situation, yet were, nevertheless, both highly blamed for their indiscreet and neglectful conduct, in suffering me to venture on the mud, by several gentlemen from Standish and Revington Halls; but, whether really caused by such reproof, or that arising from a proper remorse of conscience, I cannot exactly say, from not being able to recollect any thing like sorrow to have been visible in their looks till then; and, from this time, nothing material occurred till that of corn-harvest, when they took me with them to view some reapers at work in a close, about half a mile from the village, through which I had not passed till then; and observing it to appear like something novel, I strayed, from both them and the reapers, to the side of a hedge, where, discovering some few nuts scattered here and there, apparently ripe enough to drop from the husks, I continued on picking them along the hedge-side, till I got near the stile, when my tutors coming up and observing what I had been at, said: they would take me to a place where I might soon pull a far greater plenty of nuts; then, crossing the stile, continued moving on through a pleasant path, from stile to stile, from one close to another, till we came to Bradley Hall, situate near about a mile from Standish, and at that time farmed by Mr. William Simson, a person well known to me, by frequenting our house occasionally; and, after causing me to be well entertained in-doors, sent one of the family with me into a very large orchard, well stocked with great variety of delicious fruit-trees, where the first thing that attracted my notice happened to be a full-grown peacock, spreading out his beautiful wide tail in the sun, which afforded me great pleasure and surprize, having never beheld any bird of the kind till I saw this, spreading out his long and broad tail to the sun, near a considerable quantity of filbert-trees, pretty well stripped of their nuts, except here and there one would be perceivable under the lower branches; and, while I was diligently seeking for them, my tutors arriving soon filled my pockets with palatable fruit; then taking me to an open part of the orchard, and from thence pointing at a large wood, seemingly three or four hundred yards from the house, saying there was an immense quantity of nuts still growing in that wood, which, by reason of their not ripening so fast as those growing on hedges, had not been at that time pulled, which induced them to agree on bringing some other friends with them, in order to spend a day or two at that kind of amusement ere long, which would, if I thought proper to accompany them, afford me a convenient opportunity of clambering up those trees and pulling quantities of fine nuts from the top boughs; which said harangue so filled my little mind with a desire of pulling these nuts, that I could not think of waiting the time, but, on the contrary, began to plan how, and in what manner, to come at them without delay, and was not long at a loss, for, on our return home, I found a particular companion there, waiting to play with me, who, on being acquainted with the desire I had of going to pull the nuts then, he became equally desirous of going with me to the

No. 2. Life of Robert Barker.

wood, notwithstanding it was such a dangerous undertaking for two children of our age to venture on, while the certain result thereof never entered the brain of one or the other till too late to prevent the frightful confusion attending it; nay, so very intent were both of us upon the diversion, that we played truant the next morning, and eagerly set out together, (with a pillowcase ingeniously taken away to hold the nuts,) even without properly satisfying ourselves at breakfast, yet happened to find the direct way for Bradley-wood. Had we not been seen by the servant-maid, from an upper window of the house, while passing through the farm-yard, the most likely result of such rash and thoughtless undertaking might have proved fatal to us both, as, on observing plenty of nuts aloft, I mounted a pretty high tree, and there continued, filling my pockets, while the other child contented himself with pulling those he could find on the lower branches, and thus continued on, from tree to tree, emptying my pockets into the pillowcase, occasionally, for several hours together, till we had got into the middle part of the wood, without looking back or once thinking of the way out, through eagerly pushing through the brambles after the plenty of nuts we saw before us; and that without tasting any thing more than nut-kernels and blackberries, of which there was plenty; and in that manner continued on till the pillowcase was full, then, with pleasure, sat down together and shelled them, in order to make room for more; however, we, on filling it up a second time, found nut-kernels and blackberries insufficient to satisfy our craving appetites, on which we tied up the pillowcase and sat out on our return to Bradley-hall, as we thought; but, instead of hitting on the right way, found ourselves entirely bewildered together, without being able to find any way out of the wood, and continued wandering to and fro therein till the dusk of night began very visibly to approach, and brought with it uncommon apprehensions of both dread and fear, which highly increased by hearing the sound of two voices, at a considerable distance from each other, echoing through the wood, which we took for kidnappers in search of rambling children strayed away from home by night; and, in order to evade being taken away from thence to America, and there sold for tobacco, as we had been previously and confidently informed was the practice, we, in the greatest panic, crept under a close thicket of shrubs and brambles, lying flat on the ground, with the nuts at our heads for a pillow, trembling close together, while hearkening to both voices, which, from the night being very calm and serene, became louder as they approached nearer, till we at length plainly heard both our own names distinctly called, which, instead of alleviating the fears wherewith we had been struck, only served to raise them up to a higher pitch of terror, for we still thought they were kidnappers, and even such as were in the regular scent of the bush under which we then lay, as appeared from their both coming in a direct line toward it; and, when within a few yards, my companion pricked up his ears, and, in a low whisper, said, " I never heard any voice so like that of my cousin William before; I hope it is himself, instead of any kidnappers whatever; and shall venture to peep through the leaves;" which being accordingly done, he soon got the glimpse of him, while brushing close to the bush, and loudly called out, saying, " Here we are cousin William; here we are, both safe, under this bush;" then creeping out, after each other, soon banished all fears of being sent to America, through so unexpectedly meeting with two real friends instead of kidnappers, meaning his own cousin and William Simson, the farmer, who conducted us both safe, with the bag of nuts, to Bradley-hall, where, after having been furnished with a sufficient repast, we were then conducted safe home by his cousin William, who, agreeably to the information received from the people who met us on the road, they were sent in search of us to Bradley-hall, and so on from thence to the wood, accompanied by the farmer, according to the information of his servant-maid, who saw us making directly for it, after having past through the farm-yard, and was not unlikely to have been the providential means of preserving both our lives, as we might otherwise have perished with cold and hunger. But my rambling companion had no sooner got home to his parents than he was properly chastized for it, while I entirely escaped from correction, by some of those tutors which, though highly displeasing to my parents, they could not evade or prevent without offending those perpetual customers; therefore, in order to break me from those rambling ways, I was sent to reside with farmer Williamson, at the boarded house; and, likewise, ordered to attend the school of Mr Grimshaw, at the Round Moor, having previously been under the tuition of Mr Colderbank, usher at the free-school; who, having a penetrating judgement into the natural temper of children, and through well knowing the variety of characters wherewith I was daily surrounded, thought it much better to lead than to drive, and, by adopting that plan, generally found me one of the first scholars, when not opposed and withheld from coming to school by those weak or evil-minded tutors. And Mr Grimshaw, a person standing on the very best terms of friendship with Mr Colderbank, from whose regular information he had previously obtained some knowledge of my natural disposition, as also of the manner in which I had been so frequently prevented from accompanying Jackey Tovey and Joshua Marsden, in whose company I took so much delight, either in or from school, by sending idle boys to purposely obstruct me therein; and, when that failed, would now and then personally do it themselves, by leading me into some unnecessary kind of amusement or other; and, for those same reasons Mr Grimshaw pursued the same plan as Mr Colderbank, the usher, had done, which always drew me to school with far more pleasure than pain, and would have undoubtedly had a much better effect if those indiscreet gentlemen had not thought fit to interfere with me, as heretofore mentioned, and would have, according to my own weak ideas thereof, proved the best method of withholding me from those rambles, if my tutors had only thought fit to decline those fanciful tricks into which they had led me, for no other reason but that of causing laughter and amusement to themselves and others, which would have in course been far more to their own credit to have wholly resigned, or never have put in force, to the prejudice of an innocent child, wholly insensible of the numerous evils likely to spring out of so many wandering habits; and how far they did so will hereafter appear, as when the long winter nights set in, the young people and children began to entertain each other with numerous tales and stories of apparitions, hobgobblins, ghosts, spirits, giants, fairies, kidnappers, witchcraft, conjuration, magic-art, and such like wonderful things, to pass away the long nights by the different fire-sides of each other; and whether the following dream principally came from hearkening to those fabulous tales and stories, or from a supernatural cause, I dare not presume to say, though I have at times thought it to have proceeded from the latter; and whether really so or otherwise, I leave that matter to the due consideration of the candid reader, as my bodily frame actually was greatly agitated, and no less terrified therewith. Near about that time, while sleeping above stairs with my clothes on, at about midnight, though company were enjoying themselves in the parlour and kitchen below, whom I past in my sleep without any one observing such hasty movement to have been caused by the effect of a dream, wherein I thought myself intermixed with a great number of the inhabitants viewing Rivington Peak, one of the most lofty mountains in all those parts, apparently situated about ten or twelve miles from thence, will change itself from the shape of a mountain to the figure and shape of a most frightful large man, terrible to behold; it will seem to look round every way, and delivering himself in a loud voice resembling thunder, but distinctly and properly understood by the people, will he seem to command the other adjoining mountains on each side to form themselves into the like figure and shape of men as he had just done, which they all seem to quickly obey, and soon appear like a mighty large, but frightful, army of ten or twelve miles long; and bowing low on each side to their chief in the centre, will throw up their long arms into the clouds while receiving orders from thence to march, which seem to have been no sooner given than all began to move in regular uniform order towards the village, as though intent on crushing both church, buildings, people, and houses, quite level to the earth with their feet, which seem to throw the whole multitude into such a terrified sort of panic that induces them to separate from each other while flying in various directions for the preservation of their own lives; which uncommon fright seemed to have roused me from the bed at the time of passing the company below into the street, and continuing on for about two hundred yards to a stile in the main road, where happening to awake from my dream, with those frightful monsters seeming to follow in my thoughts, so increased and continued the panic, that instead of going back I turned along the Wiggan road for near a hundred yards to the left, where I knocked up Mr Harvey, a baker who served our family with bread, under whose roof I was sheltered till the next day; but without being able to otherwise explain the matter, when desired, than by telling my parents, that I had been greatly frightened, as well as many other people in the village, by seeing Rivington Peak, and the other adjoining mountains, turning themselves into men a hundred times bigger than any giant I had ever heard tell of in all my life before, as though intent on coming to crush both houses and people under their feet. Those amusements gradually diminished as the length of the days increased; and, in the month of February, when the cock-fighting commenced, in order to view, without the danger of going in the crowd, I climbed up a fir-tree in the churchyard, from the top of which I could see numerous gamesters laying wagers for and against many a fine bird that laid dead on the sod; and, at other times, from that tree-top, saw various dogs, thrown dangling up in the air from the horns of a bull, to the height of a story or more, where, in the time of the hurry and confusion, one of the dogs happening to seize him by the nose, and sticking fast to his hold, got thrown, belly upwards, between the horns of the bull, which made him to loudly roar; as he moved close to numerous men that appeared desirous of preserving the dogs, and one of them being more bold and venturous than others got tossed, and so gored with the horns of the bull, as to be carried off the ground in a dangerous state, which put an end to their rough and unpleasant diversion of that day; and now my restless tutors were so frequently dragging me into the fields, seeking for various nests of different sorts and kinds of birds, as also to fishing in the ponds, rivers, and brooks, as thereby to induce me to waste more than half my time from school; but that was not all, for they had formed both new and dangerous projects of their own, to instruct me in one of which was that of teaching me how to stand on my head, at the tip end of an antient stone cross, with my feet erect in the air, at some considerable height from the bottom, which said cross had formerly been erected in front of the church gate, and at no great distance from our own door, where, though in danger of losing my life, or meeting with broken limbs, by tumbling from it, yet their inconsiderate designs were not given up till I had become expert and dexterous enough to perform the task with ease and pleasure, though I never saw any other boy in the place shewed courage and spirit enough to follow the example; and, with respect to another bold and dangerous project, which they had actually contrived and prevailed on me to practise, though it might have most likely put an end to my existence, if kind Providence had not thought fit to interfere in my preservation. The experiment was to have been tried and put in practice on the cross post of a sign, projecting from the second story of a house near the stone well, having a painted bull made of a two-inch plank, with the feet mortised into another, and secured to the outer end thereof with nails, about four or five feet beyond the upright post, supporting it, which they, with the offer of a small bribe, had prevailed on me to climb up, at such time proposing to double the reward if I would get astride on the back of the bull; and they seemed to find great pleasure in seeing me prepare for it, when got on the cross post, which was luckily prevented by Mr. George Pleasenton, who happened to be riding past at that very moment of time, and, observing the danger, called to me, saying, "he "had something very good for me, and a most "valuable secret to disclose, if I would come "down immediately, even without attempting to "get on the back of the bull:" and those words coming from the lips of a gentleman, whom I held in such uncommon esteem, had the desired effect; so I slipped down the post to the bottom without farther delay, and presenting myself before him, he turned to my tutors, saying: "Gen- "tlemen, I became very much alarmed for the "safety of this child, on first observing him pre- "pare to get on the back of the bull, which I "well remember to have been thirty years there, "but how much longer I cannot pretend to say; "though well convinced of its having been so

"much decayed, through time, that they proba-
"bly would have tumbled down both together;
"therefore hope you will never induce him to
"attempt any thing of the kind hereafter:"
then looking at me, said; "here is a penny,
"and I will give you another whenever we meet,
"if you will now promise never more to attempt
"to get on the back of the bull;" which, having
heard me readily assent to, while observing my
tutors looked ashamed of the action, he bid them
farewell, and rode off: which said lucky affair I
have since looked upon as the immediate interposition of divine Providence in bringing him that
way, as the same bull was blown to the ground a
few weeks after by a gale of wind, and the bottom part of the legs, where they gave way, near
the mortise hole, was found so very much decayed
and rotten, through time, as would most likely
have made it come down with me while endeavouring to get on his back, in case the trial had
been made; yet this fortunate escape proved
in no ways detrimental to their future designs, as
I was not long after taken up the winding stairs
of the church, on to the lower and upper leads,
and there brought to an ornamental kind of
stone figure, projecting from the wall of the steeple, at some trifling height above the lead works,

and there instructed how and in what manner to clamber over it, on to the battlement of the steeple, in their company, having one before and another behind, where, having a much better prospect of Rivington Peak, and the other adjoining mountains, than from below, I could not view them without trembling, from having had my late dream revived fresh to my mind, while moving round the battlement with them; and though it was a place I had never thought of, or seen, till brought up with those who, after affording me a clear prospect of the surrounding country, instructed me how to get down by the way I came up; and they following, accompanied me down the winding stairs into the body of the church, and so on from thence into the house, while continually discoursing of what we had seen, helped to increase a curious desire which I had previously conceived, of viewing it again the first convenient opportunity that offered; and at times followed others to the church top, but without venturing any higher, through fear of having been left behind after the doors were fastened below, till it so happened that plumbers from Wiggan being ordered to come and repair the lead-work on the roof, when observing the church-doors remaining open for some considerable part of the day together, I embraced that opportunity of venturing to satisfy my curiosity, by clambering up to the battlement of the steeple, to view the aforesaid mountains; and, reflecting on them for some considerable time, without being able to satisfy myself concerning how or in what manner they seem to have been so quickly changed into living beings of their own size, forming a mighty large army, appearing so frightful and terrible to behold, while threatening destruction to both town and country, as represented to me in my late dream, which I hoped and thought such kind of phenomenon never could or would happen to affright the human race; however, being at length tired of viewing them, I walked round the battlement to the other side of the steeple; and whether it proceeded from a curious desire I had of trying my skill, or that of obtaining a more extensive prospect of the country, one or both, I cannot justly say, though true it is, that I ventured on the top of the outside stone of the battlement, not more than five or six inches wide, (if so much,) just as Mrs Tovey happened to pass the church gate, directly opposite from whence, unexpectedly seeing me stand erect, in that dangerous situation, gave a loud shriek, which caused me to slip off while turning my head aside;

and that being observed by her, she, without stopping to behold the result of the fall, ran hastily to my parents, in a fright, telling them she had just that moment before seen me slip from the battlement of the steeple, on the outside, where I must have certainly been dashed to pieces on the ground; however, they, on recovering from the surprize, caused by such unwelcome news, came to the foot of the steeple, in expectation of finding me dead, but that not proving the case, they entered the church, and there found me in very good health, without having sustained the least kind of injury whatever; as, instead of slipping on the outside, it was only to the lead-works, inside the battlements, near fifteen or twenty inches lower down; but the real truth, as it came from my lips, was wholly disbelieved, through the mistake of Mrs Tovey, who had positively said, that she actually saw me slip outside of the steeple-wall, which produced a report concerning that of my having fallen astride upon the ornamental figure projecting from the outside wall, upwards of two feet below the stone whereon I stood. And here it may not be amiss to shew the difficulty of removing such like mistaken ideas from the public mind, when received from the lips of such a respectable, well-disposed, woman as Mrs Tovey really was. — It of course caused a mistaken report, which soon spreads through a village, concerning that or other things; though all I could say or do, to establish the real truth, proved of little avail; as the report was spread every where, and was generally mentioned by all sorts of people, with so much confidence, as to have the same notions in mind when I arrived to years of maturity, without being able to convince them concerning the mistaken error of judgment which they had conceived, though widely differing from the real truth; and does not appear altogether unlikely but that it may have been handed down, from father to son, and continue to be spoken of, at times, by their offspring, in Standish, to this very day; and let that have been how it may, nothing very material occurred from that time till the young people began to amuse each other with their usual tales and stories in the following winter, during which I experienced another frightful

dam; therein thinking myself very boldly assailed by an ugly fiend, of nearly my own height and statue, but somewhat more bulky, appearing neither black nor brown, yet of a most disagreeable, swarthy coloured, hue; having two wings like those of a bat; as also arms, with long talons, resembling birds claws, with horns on his head, and a long tail trailing on the ground, by which sad, frightful, and disagreeable looking fiend, I seemed to have been most boldly seized, with such determined resolution, as, notwithstanding all my strength, courage, spirit, and resistance, he still seemed to have thrown me flat on the kitchen floor, with both arms fast round his waist, which, from my appearing unable to extricate myself from his clutches, I seemed to lay hold of his naked breast with my teeth, and tearing out a mouthful of the most noxious flavoured matter ever tasted by mortal, continued so doing, and spitting it in his face till both his strength and courage seemed to visibly fail, which having observed, I, with a more than common exertion of bodily strength, seemed to have got the upper hand, by quickly turning the ugly fiend underneath me, then, kneeling on his breast, seemed to pull one arm from the shoulder joint, and likewise the other; both of which seemed to resume their joints and become useful as before, though not appearing strong enough to defend himself against the continual exertions I seemed to make use of in order to master him, and, at length succeeded, by hearing a most dreadful kind of unpleasant yell sent forth, while he remained shuffling towards the fire-side, and, at length, getting into a hole, under the grate, where, setting my foot on him, he sunk into the earth, and disappearing, gave me no small pleasure in finding myself victorious and clear of such a powerful adversary. When, near about this time, a young gentleman of the place, who had formerly been apprenticed out from thence to a surgeon and apothecary in the city of London, and returning from thence at the expiration of his time, married a very amiable young lady of a reputable family, within a few doors of our house, which she frequently using, occasionally, soon found the loose manner in which I had been trained up, where, from those rambling kind of habits, which I had so unhappily acquired, to have been solely owing, and weakly imagining himself not only capable of weaning me therefrom, but likewise forcing me to attend the school in a far more regular way; and how far he succeeded therein will appear in the experiment, as he began with threats; telling me, that as my bringing up was then left to his future care and management, by the consent of my parents, unless I thought fit to cautiously pursue his advice and instructions in every point, I might expect to be severely chastised before all the scholars, whenever he found me idling about during school hours, which I, however, thought little or nothing of, till he caught me at play with a party of boys, when I ought to have been at school, and hastily dragging me from them, I was hurried away into the master's presence, giving him to understand, that the future management of my conduct having been committed to his care by my parents, he wished to have me chastised for neglecting school, contrary to his orders: however, Mr. Colderbank, through well knowing how and in what manner I had been led into such neglect of duty by those weak-minded tutors, who still continued encouraging me therein, thought fit to excuse himself from it; whereat the doctor seemed offended, as appeared from his telling the master, that it was only for want of proper school discipline that such neglect of duty had been caused; as, also, that I could not be made a scholar without it. And as he had heard that necessary point of duty resigned by the person to whom it belonged, he would take it upon himself, and chastise me whenever he discovered me neglecting school at the time I ought to be there, and performed his promise accordingly; for, happening to catch me at play some time after, I was dragged into his house, and there well disciplined with a small stick, which he seemed to have ready prepared for such purpose, and was soon after exposed with it in the presence of both master and scholars, accompanied by many threats of laying it on my back with redoubled force, when appearing defective in like manner any more; and how far his well meant design was thereby obtained, will soon appear, as I from that time viewed him in the light of the greatest enemy I ever had, and even considered him as the worst of all men, and one I ought to avoid. I kept such a very watchful eye on his person, as to fly swiftly from the place wherever I saw him appear; and, having a good pair of heels, prevented his catching me for some considerable time after; nor could he have succeeded then without bribing one of my companions with a trifle to stop and detain me till he came up; and that having been accordingly done, I fell into his hands again, at which he seemed to rejoice, while dragging me along into a new built stable of his own, where, having given me a severe drubbing, he tied both my hands fast to the ring of a manger in the stall where his horse usually stood; saying, he was just then prevented from giving me another flogging at school, as intended, through a country patient that he was obliged to visit without delay, so found himself under the necessity of leaving me there till he came back, in order to secure me elsewhere the next day; then locking the door I heard him ride off, and began endeavouring to extricate both hands from the cord, with the help of my teeth, and, after excoriating the skin from several fingers, succeeded, though not without causing visible marks of blood to appear on various parts of my hands. When looking round for a way out, without perceiving any, except a hole over the cratch, leading into the loft above, through which, having struggled, I got among the hay, where seeing the window or door, through which it was easily thrown from the carts, open, I took a peep every way, and, on finding that the coast was clear, without any individual being in view, I, on laying hold of the lower edge with both hands, and hanging down at full length, with my feet, dropped near four yards to the ground, without having sustained the least kind of injury whatever; and thus finding myself at liberty once more, instead of going home, made the best of my way to Bradley-hall, and so on, from thence, to the boarded house on the following day; where, being welcome to farmer Williamson, as before, I attended the school of Mr Grimshaw, at the Round Moor, which my parents hearing of, became very well satisfied with the change, as plainly appeared from my having been allowed to remain there as usual, even till the very unexpected news of the doctor having precipitately gone from Standish; which was said to have happened from the circumstance of a human corpse having been scratched up from under the mould in his garden, by the dogs, greatly mangled, and supposed to have been taken out of a grave in the church-yard, to practise on; a thing so highly obnoxious to the inhabitants, as to have (according to the reports of those times,) proved the sole cause of his having hastily removed from Standish, without taking leave; and, whether really so or otherwise, I cannot pretend to say more than what came to my knowledge from hearsay alone, having never seen the body, or hole from whence it was taken, by reason of the uncommon aversion I had to the doctor, and every thing belonging to him, which rendered it nearly impossible for any one to have otherwise brought me on his premises than by great force; though I can truly say, that, from the time he confined me in the stable, on those premises, I never saw him after, though I returned to Mr. Colderbank, at the free-school, with no small degree of pleasure; and have reason to believe the affair would have been of some advantage to my future education, through the aversion I had conceived against those companions for holding me till the doctor came up; as, without which, his design would have been rendered abortive; however, in the course of that summer, my father removed from thence to the Red Lion, in Wiggan, then belonging to Mr Locker, his stepfather, having become so through a marriage with his mother; and, if memory does not fail, I saw them both there, nearly about one year after, when they came to execute and make over the title deeds of that house to Mr John Walmsley, who made the purchase with intent to pull it down, and rebuild the same for a woollen-draper's shop. And here it may not be improper to observe, that I came there with no small degree of pleasure, by reason of the usher and approved master in the free-school being my uncle, through a marriage with the sister of my own mother, from whom I in course expected some kind of indulgence; and now having to reflect on one point, that is to say, whether it would or would not have, according to the ideas of others, been necessary to acquaint me with the strict discipline of a school-where I was placed to acquire the future part of my education; and think it would have been far the best to have previously acquainted me with the correction I had to expect, which, together with a little private indulgence from my uncle, would, I am persuaded, have had a very good effect, by reason of my first approaching him with great satisfaction of mind: so that by viewing the loose manner of my bringing up, some idea might have been formed concerning the two extremes; that is to say, whether mild, or coercive, means appeared most likely to agree with my natural temper and disposition; a thing, when hit on, though very difficult to discover in the minds of so many different sorts of children, yet is, in such case, and will be, according to the weak ideas I have formed thereof, of credit to the master and advantage to the scholar. Neither may it be altogether improper for me to shew how, and in what manner, I was, from the earliest part of my recollection, trained up to speak the truth on all occasions, without fear of blame or correction of any kind; though for a lye, or even the shadow of a lye, I was severely chastised by my parents, tutors, and others, in the most severe manner; which, through habit, time, and practice, at length brought me to freely speak the truth, without any fear of danger, and was in that state of mind sent to Wiggan school, as a perfect stranger, without having any companions, or even likely to have any, but such as might become afterwards collected from the other scholars; neither had I received any kind of information, whatever, concerning the discipline I might expect from my uncle, in case of playing truant; which, since I have arrived at sufficient years of maturity, I have reflected on with much regret, by reason of having lost sight of that education which might have turned out to my future advantage through life; and from nothing more than want of foresight enough in my father and uncle, to have privately acquainted me with the proper rules I had to observe in order to avoid correction; but, in such a kind and friendly way as to have appeared most likely to gain him my good-will and esteem, by which I might have become a regular scholar, without having any reason to complain of the discipline due to myself any more than to others, when neglect of duty required the same to be inflicted on them, as appeared from that of my regularly attending school during the period of six weeks, or two months, when happening to accidentally meet with two of my late tutors, who innocently detained me walking with them during school-hours, in the afternoon, which I verily believe to have really been the case, from having since heard them frequently express their sorrow for it, by candidly telling me of their not having conceived the least kind of idea whatever, or ever once thought of the certain result that followed such detention, a most unhappy affair, which a little foresight alone might have easily prevented; for, on attending school in the morning of the following day, I soon became publicly horsed and severely whipped by my uncle, which put an end to all hopes of reaping any beneficial advantage with respect to my future education, while continuing under his tuition, through the uncommon disgust I had then taken to his person; even more so, if possible, than what I had formerly conceived against the Standish doctor; nay, such was my fear, dread, personal rage, and indignation thereat, as to swell my little head and bosom with internal thought of contriving how to quit the school for ever; and at length concluded with a most determined resolution of never more returning into it again, unless from being overpowered and forcibly carried in by the main strength of others, in which uncommon state of mind I left the school, with the intent of not returning to it. During the next morning I betook myself to wandering about the streets in search of idle company to play with; however, not finding any, I returned to dinner, and then to the streets again, during the afternoon, with no better success; but, on coming home, after school-hours, I was unexpectedly followed into the house by my uncle, desiring to know the reason of my having been absent from school during the whole day, and that in the presence of my father; to which I freely answered, saying, it was because he whipped me severely on the day before, that induced me to resolve on never coming to school again. Never coming to school again! replied my father, somewhat hastily, What do you mean by that? Never let me hear another word of the kind issue from your lips, through fear of gaining my displeasure, and lifting up a small stick in his hand, while assuming a very stern look, as though inclined to lay it across my shoulders in case of not repenting of the words I had said; but to no purpose, for, on being interrogated concerning them again, and still persisting therein, I, at length, got a severe drubbing from him, without having been prevailed on to comply, or even making any promise of attending the school again as usual, either with their blows, threats, or otherwise; and, on this, finding me so steadily resist all they could say or do, in such a stout, obstinate, manner, it was at length agreed for my father to see me off for school the next day, which seemed to place me in a most dreadful situation, between two inevitable extremes of danger; namely, that of being horsed at school, and likewise flogged at home, thereby setting my little brain to work in devising how to evade the impending danger wherewith I had to contend. At the time appointed, which being at length arrived, my father took me with him, past the Eagle and Child, into the Millgate End, a pretty long street, leading to the school directly, where, making a stand, he, with a stern look, commanded me to go freely on by myself, and take care not to let him hear any farther complaints concerning my absence from it, lest I might in such case have reason to experience far more severe treatment from his hands than what I ever had before; which, having heard, I seemed to obey, without making any reply; while moving up the rising ground, towards the summit of a hill, being the highest part of that street, near a hundred yards from the spot

No. III.

OF

BARKER'S

GENUINE LIFE,

INCLUDING,

BOTH TEMPORAL AND SPIRITUAL

CONCERNS:

WITH HIS EXTENSIVE

VOYAGES, LOSS OF SIGHT,

AND FIFTY-ONE YEARS

Travels with his Spouse

THROUGH VARIOUS EUROPEAN NATIONS,

WHILE STRUGGLING UNDER A MELANCHOLY

𝔖tate of perpetual 𝔇arkness.

———

LONDON:

PRINTED BY GALABIN AND MARCHANT, INGRAM-COURT,

FOR THE AUTHOR,

And may be had of Mr. HUGHES, Bookseller, Stationer's Court, Ludgate-Street; and of Mr. BROWN, Boston, Lincolnshire, and all other Booksellers and Newscarriers.

———

1810.

whereon he remained viewing me, till shaded from his sight by the summit of the hill; and all those unlooked-for disasters that continually pursued me after this change in the conduct of my beloved parent took place, may be far better conceived than described, and, likewise, more edifying to pass over, with outmentioning, till the everlasting Giver of all blessings, out of his infinite goodness and mercy, thought fit to interfere in my behalf, when near about twelve years old, while exerting my whole strength and abilities in throwing a pebble-stone over the house of a school-master, residing nearly opposite the Roebuck public-house, to a greater distance than many other boys that were present, of nearly my own age; one of them, for his diversion, while seeing my arm extended, with a stone ready to fly from my fingers, gave my elbow a check from behind, which caused me to break the school-master's window, which the school-master observing, threw up the sash, and beholding my companions running away in every direction, while I alone continued on the spot, which he observing, instantly directed his discourse to me, saying, "Pray, do you know who it was "that broke my window?" "Yes, sir, it was I

"did it; but not wilfully, and intend to pay for
"the mending of it with the first money I get:
"you may believe me." "And do you really in-
"tend to pay for it?" in a kind of surprize, replied he: "Yes, sir, said I, and will perform my
"promise when able." "Nay, then, if that be
"the case," said he, "you are not wholly deser-
"ving of the evil character which common report
"has charged you with, and here is a penny for
"telling the truth;" which having let fall to the
ground, he pulled down the sash; and this circumstance coming to the ears of my parents, who
had long been and still were very unhappy on my
account, yet knew not how to reclaim or bring
me to a proper sense of the danger of those most
wicked habits with which I had been so long involved, had now some small hopes of success, and
therefore put me to the school of Mr. Duckworth,
which happily changed the former scene to another
far more useful and agreeable, by enabling me to
see through those unnecessary follies into which I
had been so imperceivably drawn by others, while
too young to distinguish right from wrong, or
good from evil, regularly bringing me to a far
more enlightened sense of gratitude remaining
still due to my indulgent parents, for having so
cautiously inculcated those Christian principles of

religious virtue into my tender mind, when first able to receive and retain them, without which others of such a pernicious kind and evil tendency might have taken root therein as for ever to have blasted all my future hopes of peace in this mortal state of life and that which is to come, likewise by enabling me to become most thankful to the supreme Power above, for having wonderfully supported me through so many difficult passages in life, before and since I lost my sight, as, by duly reflecting on them towards the latter part thereof, all the whole seem to have no small resemblance to a long dream, which, in order to place in the best manner I am able, hope the insertion of a prayer may be in no ways found displeasing to the candid reader, as it was most humbly offered up to Almighty God, our heavenly father, by me in a fervent manner, with a real desire of being heard, while a grandson of mine was preparing his pen to commit the following lines to paper from my lips, while in Boston, upon the 6th day of October, 1801, which is as follows:—
Lord, I beseech thee to enable me to give up myself: time, and study, towards the attaining of thy divine will and pleasure; and that I may not only understand right, but, also, become enabled to so publish and make it known to the world as

to thereby promote the gospel, peace, and unity, amongst the inhabitants of the earth, and that it may spread from nation to nation, and to the uttermost parts thereof, to the downfall of Satan's agents and abettors every where; and that universal peace may over-spread the face of the whole globe, to the honour and glory of thy everlasting kingdom, through the merits of our Lord and Saviour Jesus Christ, for whose sake I most humbly pray that these things may, in spite of all the infernal opposition of Satan, most rapidly increase now, both henceforth, and for evermore; and that the produce of the church may become so very numerous, and powerfully elegant of speech, as to therewith convince the philosophers of every kind, whether Pagans, Turks, or others, concerning the existence of their own immortal souls to all eternity, after the dissolution of this mortal frame, whereby they may become induced to extend the eloquent sound of their voice in preaching and explaining the sweet sense of the everlasting gospel to their numerous auditors of every kind, through which the whole inhabitants of the earth may ere long become like unto rivers of water, clear as crystal, intersecting it in all parts, while their works spring up on the bank, like fruitful trees, yielding their delicious fruit continually, and the eloquent sound of their voice hail the internal minds of each other as the leaves do their external wounds, preparing all for the reception of that new name, called wisdom, which is no sooner imprinted in the heart, mind, and forehead, of each individual, than it becomes well understood as a perfect, sure, and true guide, leading them into the new Jerusalem, brought down from heaven by the holy spirit, where there is no night, because, the glory of the Lord is continually shining there and affording sufficient light for them to clearly see their way to that everlasting peace which all hope to enjoy in the blissful realms above, through the merits of our Lord and Saviour Jesus Christ, whose everlasting grace, with the love of God, and fellowship of the Holy Ghost, be with all the human race, both now, henceforth and for evermore.

After apologizing for this digression, permit me to return to the subject concerning that school wherefrom I was seldom or ever known to remain one hour absent, though frequently enticed thereto by others, and may be justly said to have learned more in the space of one year than what I had really acquired during the course of my whole life before, through being very attentive thereto, without ever joining those idle companions during school-hours; and there it was that kind Providence thought fit to interfere in my behalf a second time, in bringing Mr. Holland, shipwright, of Liverpool, from thence, to build vessels in Wiggan, a trade which I had often expressed a wish to learn, and was, accordingly, bound apprentice to him, when near about thirteen years old, which proved another mark of divine goodness visibly displayed in my favour, through inducing me to constantly attend the working-hours, from five in the morning till seven in the evening, with no small degree of pleasure, a thing found both useful and necessary, in withholding me from the company and conversation of those loose-minded playfellows, with whom I had so long associated, and lately engaged with their idle tricks, after school-hours, which now diminished through want of rest at the usual time of leaving work, and, by agreement, allowed to diet with my parents at home, while Mr. Holland continued in Wiggan. All the connexions which I usually had with those my late companions shortly became reduced to now and then a time by chance, arising from their own advice and appointment after leaving work on Saturday night, in their nocturnal depredations, while stripping the neighbouring orchards of their rightful owner's fruit; and, though

I very seldom or ever made free with any more than what filled my pockets, others, to my knowledge, carried them off in bags, though easily screened from blame through the general bad character which I bore; and one or other of their party, in order to clear themselves, endeavoured to lay the whole blame of those nocturnal depredations on my back, as the greatest part of the inhabitants were ready enough to believe any report of the kind, though ever so false; and one of those appointments having, by some means or other, come to the knowledge of my father, he cautiously endeavoured to prevent the same from taking place, by means of a lock which had usually been made use of, in order to prevent a Jackass from straying too far, by fastening it to his feet with a chain and heavy log of wood annexed thereto, which he thought fit to place and lock fast about my ankle, telling me, that I must assuredly expect to keep it for a companion till the next day. Just as the family were going to rest, and finding myself alone, I took off one of my shoes, where, finding the lock very wide on the leg, I forcibly shoved it over the heel, and joined those nightly marauders, while converting the property of others to the gratification of their own palates, for the last time, through the kind interposition of divine Providence, visibly enabling me to decline their company, when employed in those obnoxious depredations; for, ever after, as my father had been so highly offended at the late night's work as to watch my going in doors on the Sabbath-day, and soon followed with a horsewhip in his hand, apparently intended for my back, which, becoming sensible of, and in order to avoid the blows, I swiftly ran from the kitchen floor into a long dark pantry, made so by another building having been erected above the window, at the distance of eighteen or twenty inches from the wall, and divided in two parts, near the upper end, by a wooden lattice-work, to keep the beer and liquor separate from the provisions, up which I clambered to the top, and finding a beam run across higher up, quickly placed myself lengthways thereon, with the skirts of my coat turned over both thighs and back, to avoid being observed from below; and, having got flat on my belly, when he came in to search for me, without discovering any glimpse of me, he called for a light, and with it carefully examined the window, shelves, walls, corners, and other parts of the place, but to no purpose, in the presence of my brother, sister, and mother, to whom he at length turned in a kind of astonishment, saying : " Did not we all see him enter into

"the pantry, at this door, from whence there is
"no other way out; and, as he cannot be found
"therein, what can we think of such a most ex-
"traordinary concern? For, true it is, that I
"never believed in witchcraft, magic-art, or con-
"juration, but now cannot rightly tell whether or
"no this graceless child has not been concerned
"with some infernal spirit or other, which has
"rendered him invisible enough to pass us unper-
"ceived; and, if really so, all manner of beating
"will be of no farther use; I shall, therefore, re-
"sign him up to the divine will of heaven, which
"is stronger than the devil, and alone able to
"work a change in him;" when, throwing down the whip, he left them apparently in the greatest perturbation of mind, and was soon followed by the rest, seemingly no less affected with astonishment than what he himself really was; for I had paid due attention to every word that past, and received more beneficial good from it than from all the chastizement ever given me before; as, from that very time, I began to view him in the light of a most kind and tender parent, who had suffered much on my account, for which I ought to make the best return I could, by shewing him all the dutiful respect and gratitude in my power, for ever after, and, with such intent, came down

from the beam into the kitchen, where, finding him out, I addressed myself to my mother, in the most respectful terms I could, saying: " I hope " you do not, after all the unlucky failings which " I have been guilty of, suppose me weak enough " to have connexions with magic-art, or infernal " spirits of any kind whatever; for, I have distinct- " ly heard every word my father said, while in the " pantry, and, as he has laid aside the whip, so " will I endeavour to lay aside my folly, by never " attending those boys in their nightly excursions, " from that time for ever after;" then, begging her to accompany me into the pantry, with a candle, and there shewed her the beam whereon I had been concealed from their sight, making her sensible of it by means of dust from the beam sticking to the front part of my waistcoat, breeches, and stockings, in such plenty, as if the same had not been removed from thence before since the building of the house, seeming, from its appearance, but little less than a hundred years old, whereto my parents had withdrawn from the public business till a new house had been finished and made ready for their reception near the Roman Catholic chapel; during which they seemed to become very happy in finding me to strictly keep the promise I had made; but, with respect to playing at cards with young neighbours, in the evening, a diversion much practised in Wiggan, and what I had, through time and habit, got excessively fond of, and, without thinking any harm therein, continued pursuing that amusement till after we had removed to the aforesaid new house, where the diversion continued increasing as the autumn approached; and there it was that kind Providence again thought fit to interfere in my behalf, by losing all the pence I had, while amusing myself thereat; and being unwilling to decline the diversion, forgot the promise lately made to myself, by recollecting a fruit-tree, containing plenty of winter fruit, after all those growing in our own orchard had been removed away from thence; and, without reflecting on the consequence, ran hastily to the bottom, fronting a ditch, so very wide and deep as could not be got over without great danger, whereupon I got over a few wooden pales, into the adjoining orchard, and filled my pockets with the winter-fruit. I then returned to our own, which was well fenced in by others on each side, and, on looking up from thence towards the outhouse, being the way I had to go, beheld something appearing small, but of a shining white colour, near the outhouse, through which I had to pass, without having any other way out, which seemed to appear larger, as I approached nearer, till it resembled the size of a small house newly whitewashed, and, when I got directly opposite, it, consequently, threw me into a most terrible kind of fright, attended with a violent sweat, wherein I past through the stable, into the house, and went to bed, without ever attempting to renew the play: however, that was not all, for on dropping into a profound sleep, I thought myself to have been resolutely seized, in the open yard of that same house, by a most frightful kind of gigantic fiend, appearing at least twelve feet high, every way proportionably made to his height and stature, nearly resembling that small fiend which formerly seemed to have attacked me in the kitchen, when at Standish, with respect to his figure, shape, make, and colour. and from whose talons I thought myself to have struggled much, with intent to extricate myself, without effect, as four others, appearing nearly of his own height, shape, make, and colour, approaching, seemed to force me to obey, and forced me on his back, and, with wings outstretched, seemed to raise themselves to a considerable height above the houses, and, in that most terrific situation, I thought myself to have been conveyed through the air with great velocity for some time, till observing flames of fire issue from the earth, seemingly at a great distance, it helped to increase the terror I was in, by taking them for hell, the place of punishment, due to me for the crime I had been guilty of: then praying to God for mercy and forgiveness, while lifting up my eyes to heaven, I seemed to behold a most glorious bright angel, with expanded wings, hovering just over my head, as though purely come to extricate me from the power of those frightful assailants, who appeared to separate from each other, as I was conveyed away, and, in that joyful ecstacy of deliverance, awoke from my dream; and, on going into the orchard, on the following day, I there found two sheets, hanging on a line to bleach, between the fruit-trees, which explained the mistake I had laboured under concerning them; but, with respect to the crime so hastily committed, that stuck close to my heart, from believing it to have produced the dream, and must, with all other crimes of that sort, be resigned for ever, if I would wish to pass through life without incurring the danger of that everlasting punishment so justly due to them in hell: however, notwithstanding those ideas, card-playing still appeared to me as a harmless kind of diversion, whereat I frequently continued amusing myself during the winter; and, now and then, when bell or king pears were ripe in summer, then happening to lose all the pence I had, without having any left to purchase a kind of fruit I was become exceedingly fond of, it consequently, induced me, a second time, to forget the voluntary promise I had made, of never pilfering at all, and kept inviolable till strongly tempted thereto, while I was destitute of pence to market with, through the frequent sight of a beautiful tree well stored with those kind of fruit, close to that road-side we daily passed to and from work, having a perpendicular brick wall of near six feet high in front, but not more than two in the inside; and this wall I ventured to get over, soon after dusk, where, in moving towards the tree, strong imagination caused me to believe that others were following behind, when looking back, strong fear seized my person, through imagining the gigantic figure close at my heels, from whom I swiftly ran, brushing the trees without touching any fruit, circling to the wall, over which I tumbled, so very strongly impressed with fear, as to have been rendered unable to shake off the panic for some time after; yet this remorse of conscience brought me to a better sense of things, by convincing me that cards had proved the sole cause of my wanting money, as, if I had not lost it by cards, I might have had enough to purchase fruit, and other trifles, therefore I proposed to gradually decline that long habitual, but favourite, amusement, by endeavouring to cautiously avoid the house or place appointed for such kind of play, which, till then, I had freely attended, without ever desiring to avoid their company before; and, in this most sanguine design, I was again blessed with success, through the unexpected interposition of divine Providence, as manifestly appeared, by removing our seat of work to the village of Tarleton, where I became a boarder in a public-house, with two other apprentices, Mr. Holland, and one of his journeymen, where, seeing no cards, or people inclined to play thereat, I opened the family Bible, then lying in the window, and employed what spare hours I had therein, beginning with the first chapter of Genesis, and soon from that to the historical part, as my time and situation would allow, therein finding more peaceful content and satisfaction of mind than ever I had conceived any idea of before; and, while I was thus happily employed I regularly attended the place of divine worship every Sabbath day during our stay there of two years, or thereabout; and the agreeable life I spent gave me sufficient time to cautiously reflect on those early follies into which I had been so imperceptibly drawn by others, without reaping any advantage to themselves, or, probably, imagining any thing concerning those inevitable misfortunes which such misconduct was likely to involve me in, and was, during those times, most generally employed in secretly bewailing the loss of my own education, peace of mind, and numerous blessings which I might have otherwise enjoyed, as also in praying to almighty God for assistance from above, whereby I might become enabled to carefully avoid doing any thing of that kind, to the injury of my offspring, or to those of any other person whatever, throughout the whole course of my natural life.

And I must now beg leave to give some account of a dream, which I experienced, previous to the time of leaving Tarlton, wherein I seemed to behold a gigantic fiend, resembling those by whose means I had been forcibly conveyed into the air at Wiggan, swiftly approaching at some distance, as though intent on seizing me again; and, on perceiving no way to escape, I seemed to pluck up my spirits and run to meet him, with an intent to fight; however, instead of waiting for the result he opened his wings and flew to the water-side, where he continued watching me go to work, from behind the bank, and remained peeping at me there and elsewhere, as though having some future desire or other upon my person, till I awoke: however, the intended remove from thence to Liverpool took place some short time after, and Mr. Holland, having no wife, put me to board in a private family, where I continued steadily employed, without gambling or neglect of work, during the remaining part of my apprenticeship, which being at length expired, I returned to Wiggan, where, having spent a few days, and taken leave of my friends, I set off for Bristol, through Namptwich and Market Drayton, to Madeley Wood, where, on crossing the river in a boat, with Mr. Nash, barge-builder of Broasley, I was engaged to work for him in his yard, nearly adjoining to the ferry, and continued very happy under his roof for several months, till prevailed on, through his advice and persuasion, at the request of Mr. Harwood, barge-builder, of Shrewsbury, to join him, where I had the satisfaction of going from one beautiful seat to another, while building, repairing, and beautifying, various pleasure-boats, kept for the amusement of opulent families, situate in Shropshire and Montgomeryshire, without leaving Mr. Harwood till I had assisted him in building a new barge for Mr. David Morgan, of Landderinyea, on the river Virnew, a rapid stream descending from the Welsh mountains, having been induced to such a hazardous undertaking, in consequence of a large fall of timber, from whence the high price of land-carriage, over those mountains reduced them to near three parts less value at the spot than on the river Severn; however, when such barge was finished and launched from the building-ground, we left her on the rocks, nearly opposite to the spot whereon the antient castle of Mathravel once stood, for want of water to carry her off, though descending abundantly from torrents of rain, then falling on the surrounding mountains, and thereby enabling Mr. Harwood to fall down the rapid stream, from below those rocks, with two floats of timber, which he had prepared, on his own account, and lost them both on a shoal, fronting an island some miles lower down, from the want of room for the plank logs to pass on either side: however, no lives being lost, we removed from thence to Shrewsbury, and there parting by the consent of each other, I took a passage for Bristol in a trow belonging to the owner, Russel of Broasley, and sailed down the river in her to Frommilled, near ten or twelve miles below the city of Gloucester, where, coming to an anchor till the spring-tides put up, afforded me and the rest on board a most unexpected opportunity of viewing his Royal Highness the Prince, and the Princess Dowager of Wales, who condescended to indulge the inhabitants of those parts with the sight of their royal presence, while regaling themselves on the river in Lord Berkley's pleasure-boat, lying at a small distance from the vessel wherein I then was, on a most delightful serene day, viewing the royal pair, with numerous inhabitants collected on that occasion from the surrounding parts, many of whom appeared not a little surprized at the sight of a comet, to my ideas, passing over the royal pair in a horizontal direction, near a bow-shot in height from the boat, exactly resembling the shape and make of a serpent, nearly about seven feet long, with a head tapering gradually from thence to the neck, then swelling thicker to the body, and diminishing therefrom to a sharp pointed tail, seemingly hot, as though just come from a burning furnace, without moving the head, body, or tail, as I could perceive, while passing smoothly through the air from the Welsh to the English side, which the people on board viewed in the light of a trifling phænomenon, of little or no consequence, settled that point, and we arrived in Bristol a day or two after, where, falling into work under Mr. Toms, in his yard near the College-green, where I had not been many days employed till observed and taken notice of by two worthy gentlemen, one of

whom was Captain Sanders and the other an owner of a large ship, lying within sight, as though ready for sea, whereat they pointed, and desired to know if I had any objection against taking a voyage in her to the coast of Africa, with such an agreeable tone of voice, and mild aspect in both their looks, as induced me to accept the offer, accordingly signed articles that very evening, and prepared for the voyage with so much speed, as to drop down into King's Road with her some few days after, where the captain, on coming on board, called the whole crew, consisting of forty-two, before him on the quarter-deck, saying: "My
" lads, we are now come together in order to
" conduct this ship, which is very well stocked with
" provisions of the best kind, and all manner of
" stores suitable for such a voyage as we are about
" to take, therefore hope you will continually en-
" deavour to promote perpetual harmony amongst
" each other, while I shall do all that lies in my
" power to preserve the health, strength, and vi-
" gour of the whole crew, therefore I propose to
" begin with consuming the best kind of provi-
" sions first, then we shall continually have the
" best, for, barring misfortunes, we have more
" than sufficient for the voyage," or words to that effect; which being approved, they unmoored

ship quickly after and sailed down Bristol Channel with a favourable gale, on a voyage wherein I was a stranger, consequently stood in need of instruction concerning the variety of business I had to transact, which was, however, rectified; for the worthy commander and his mate began with shewing me where to erect a barricado seven feet high, just behind the main-mast, with spike-nails at the top, pointing up, and two port-holes for swivel guns, to hold men slaves in awe, upon the main deck, having, likewise, a platform six feet wide, to be erected fore-and-aft on each side, between decks, with ledges in front to support and prevent the slaves feet from moving while the ship heeled, as they were put to rest in two tier, one lying on the platform and the other on the deck underneath, in three apartments, separated from each other by as many bulk-heads, namely, one for the men before the main hatches, another for the boys under the main hatches, and a third for the women and girls, under the quarter deck, separated from the steerage by a grating bulk-head; but the other two forward are made strong enough to prevent any danger of their being knocked down by the men slaves forward; and the whole being nearly finished during the outward-bound passage, of near about three months, to Malembow, on the coast of Angola, where, by the time of receiving one half the cargo of slaves in the vessel, a youth of about nineteen or twenty years of age, being sent on board from the factory, positively refused to receive any kind of sustenance whatever; neither could he be induced to eat or drink, by fair or foul means, during the period of several days together: this circumstance being made known to the captain, at the factory, about five or six miles from the ship, who sent an interpreter on board to know the cause, it appeared, that he had been laid hold of and carried off by three or four ruffians, dependent on a Pagan priest, during the dusk of night, and sold for a slave to Captain Sanders the next morning, for no other reason but that of separating him from a beloved female, to whom the priest had taken a fancy, and rather than submit himself to be cruelly separated from the idol of his heart, parents, relations, and friends, he had resolved to perish and die, by refusing to taste any kind of food; yet, if the captain would promise and agree to send a person with a message from him to his parents, acquainting them with his miserable situation, he would, in such case, gladly eat and drink till they came to his relief, from well knowing how they would rejoice in having the agreeable opportunity of exchanging him for another of their own, which being made known to the captain, a black person was dispatched with the message, who, accordingly returned with his father and another slave, which the worthy commander accepted of in exchange for the youth. He left the ship with his father, greatly rejoiceing at such a happy deliverance: and now it may not appear wholly improper to furnish the candid reader with some little idea concerning the irreligious ignorance of those Pagan blacks, who made no shew of any Sabbath on that or any other day set apart for divine worship of any kind, as we could perceive, yet those irreligious customs were adopted and followed by the Europeans; but with no other view, except that of getting in their different cargoes, and leaving the coast with all the expedition imaginable, in order to avoid sickness, which they are so liable to in those warm climates: though our people came off very well, having lost no more than two, namely, the chief-mate and one seaman, while the crews of two other ships lying there had both their numbers greatly diminished through it. Having at length procured a plentiful stock of wood and water, to supply the crew and slaves therewith, throughout the middle-passage, and then taking the advantage of a tornado, meaning a very strong gale blowing hard off land, we sailed therewith and soon got wafted into the trade-winds, where, standing near three weeks on one tack, with upwards of 400 healthy young slaves on board, and allowed only two hot meals a day, namely, at eight in the morning and four in the afternoon, forming different messes, while feeding out of wooden crews, made open at the top like buckets, without handles, and supplied with four different kinds of food, changed every day, beginning with horsebeans, then supplied with rice; thirdly, pease and wheat on the fourth, while keeping the men slaves confined two and two together, by the right hand and left, as also by the right leg and left, with hand-cuffs and shackles, without shewing any displeasure thereat till the ship got on the other tack, when the humane commander, on account of their submissive behaviour, ordered the hand-cuffs and shackles to be knocked off, and the whole number of the slaves to continue on deck, from six in the morning till seven in the evening, at the same time mixed old salt junk with their daily food, which caused them to visibly fatten apace, while it caused them to exhibit bright shining skins, through constantly rubbing them with palm-oil, so that by the time we arrived at the island, off St. Christopher's, about six weeks after the ship's departure from Malembow, they were considered as the finest cargo of slaves ever seen there. The officers of the army wearing black crape round their arms, by way of mourning for his Royal Highness the Prince of Wales, lately deceased, caused me to recollect the fiery comet seen passing over the boat while in Frommilled, but without being sensible whether or not phenomenons of that sort have any malignant influence over the human species; though such as are acquainted with antient records may, probably, assign many reasons for things which I have no pretensions to; however, we only remained a few days at Old Road, to procure a supply of water, and then sailed again from thence for New York, where, having arrived in the space of a week, or thereabout, we continued tideing it up the river, till we had got about three miles above West Point, and came to an anchor directly opposite to the house of Colonel Corbin, to whom the cargo was consigned, and shortly advertised for sale on a particular day, which, being arrived, the planters came on board, and finding the slaves arranged fore-and-aft, on each side the deck, with the value of each placed on the breast, they had nothing more to say or do, but either leave or take them, all at that price, which made a quick and expeditious sale of it, through each planter marking those he wished to have, by fastening coloured tape to the wrist, and in such a hasty manner as to have cleared the ship of slaves by three o'clock in the afternoon, there and then paying ready money for them in the cabin; during which time many of the crew had been amusing themselves with observing the men, women, boys, and girls, titter and smile at each other, while leaving the ship with their new masters, after having been so long apart from each other on board, and comparing them all to as many young people of both sexes sweet hearting together at country fares in England. At this time, Captain Sanders and another gentleman, concerned with him, appeared on the quarter-deck, in discourse with each other, saying: The whole cargo of slaves, to the number of 402, had gone off at the average price of 36 pounds, sterling, per head, one with another, wherefrom some idea may be formed concerning the profits arising from the beneficial but dangerous kind of trade, when compared with the value of them in Malembow, where each prime slave then sold at the rate of 45 bars a head, by way of exchange, and bartering them for European goods; meaning such as common English spirits

No. 4, Barker's Genuine Life.

Robert Barker unluckily venturing to undertake that unfortunate voyage wherein he suffered much, and lost his Sight, during the prime of life.

coloured with molasses, slight-made guns with varnished stocks, cutlasses, knives, powder, and lead, which they cast into ball and smaller shot with very broad shallow pans, made of brass or copper, for them to extract salt from sea-water, through boiling it in them, whereto I may likewise add Guinea-cloths, with flowered chintzes, of very slight make; blue linen covers, cloths, worstead caps, beads, small earthen pitchers, basins, and other trifling articles of painted or flowered earthenware; but, with respect to their real value in England, I can form no proper idea; however, allowing each bar to be worth five shillings, for which they passed in Malimbo at that time, then, and in such case, every prime slave cost seven pounds five shillings, which, being deducted from thirty-six pounds, which they sold for in America, there will remain a clear profit of twenty-four pounds fifteen shillings, out of which the expensive charges of fitting out the ship, with the purchasing of provisions and stores, ought to be accounted for and deducted, if not settled and paid for out of the profits arising from a full cargo of tobacco, brought home in her; for, when the slaves were all gone, my orders were, to knock down the barracado, bulk-heads and platforms, clearing ship fore-and-aft, in order to caulk the sides and decks, and, by covering the gratings with platform-boards, make all tight for the homeward-bound passage, by which time both the hold and between decks were stowed chock full of tobacco, with which we dropped down the river to New York, and, sailing from thence, crossed the Atlantic ocean, with a very strong but leading gale, which never left the ship till we came to an anchor in King's Road, near about one month after, wherefrom we had not arrived many days in Bristol till I expressed a wish of going home, which the captain hearing of, paid me, and, after wishing each other all the happiness which this world could afford, I took leave, and returned into the employ of Mr. Alexander Leigh, of Wiggan, the chief proprietor of that navigation, where, having continued for some considerable time in his employ, I built two new vessels for a company of merchants trading in the coasting way, and then returned to Bristol again, with an intent to undertake a second voyage to Guinea, but without suspecting any reverse change of luck to have happened through it, though I lost my sight therein, through the cruel treatment of the chief mate and doctor, yet really wish to avoid inserting the particulars, if such voyage had not opened the way to a scene of far greater magnitude and consequence to the world than what I am able to explain properly without giving a place to that voyage, which is as follows: after having helped to lengthen the Thetis snow, in the Limekiln-dock, bound on a voyage from Bristol to Andony, on the coast of Guinea, from thence to Antigua, and back to Bristol, I sailed in her under the command of Captain Fitzherbert, Robert Wabshutt, chief mate, and John Roberts, doctor, in the month of December, 1754; but, on going down to Pill, where the vessel lay waiting for a wind, how great was my surprize on seeing her so exceedingly deep laden as to have only two feet eight inches clear from the gunwale to the water edge. This staggered me much, not knowing what to do, being very unwilling to proceed in her, yet ashamed to return to Bristol, as I had made a fair agreement: however, consulting within myself, I resolved upon the voyage, notwithstanding the difficulty and danger of the passage through the channel in winter; and although the ship's company, who came down the next day, going on shore in the evening at Pill, in order to bid farewell to England, (some discourse arising there, over a pot of beer, about the vessel,) declaring she was not fit to go such a voyage, at that time of the year, and murmured among themselves, saying: The vessel was but small; not one hundred tons burthen; 'too deeply laden, and would not be able to bear the weather; neither could she contain a sufficient quantity of provisions for a slaving voyage; and that, when at sea, the officers might live well enough, but the foremast-men must be in want through the shortness thereof. Whereupon they all refused to go the voyage, and absolutely determined on returning to Bristol. But I, being then resolutely bent on performing my contract with Mr. Blake, sat still and said nothing; till, having heard their final determination, I spoke in the following manner: 'We are going into a fine-weather country, and, 'with a fair wind, shall be soon out of danger; 'and it will be a cowardly action to return before 'we have performed our contract, whereby the 'owners and merchants will be greatly injured and 'damaged by the detention of the ship and cargo 'for want of hands.' And, in order to induce them to go on board, and proceed on the voyage, I farther said, 'That, in case it should happen, du-'ring the course thereof, we should be short, or in 'want of provisions, I would be the first man who 'would seek a proper remedy and redress.' This had its desired effect; for, through my earnest entreaties and persuasions, they were prevailed on to proceed on the voyage, all of them going on board the same night.

The next morning, early, being the 22d of December, 1754, we loosed our fasts, and dropped down into Kings' Road, where we came to an anchor till ten o'clock; when Captain Fitzherbert coming on board brought John Richardson with him, who was shipped by Mr. Blake as third mate, and then weighed anchor, and sailed from thence, with a fair wind, on our intended voyage.

John Richardson was born in Deadman's Place, in the borough of Southwark, and of good parentage. His father, while living, belonged to the clothworkers company; his mother is now a widow, eighty years of age, who, since her husband's death, followed the business of selling small beer in casks, whereby she gained a comfortable subsistence for many years; but, by supporting her son John in his extravagance, ruined herself, and is, at present, kept by the parish. I have been with her several times, to be rightly informed of John's character and behaviour before he sailed in the Thetis this voyage, who told me as above; and farther declared: That, when a boy, he fell into a lighter, whereby his skull was fractured; and, as he grew up, gave himself over to lewd women, and, by intercourse with them, frequently contracted the foul distemper, and was salivated three or four times, which affected his brain to so great a degree, that, upon drinking a small quantity of strong liquor, he was deprived of his rational faculties, and acted like a mere madman; and farther said: That she, by the interest of friends, got him a midshipman's birth in his majesty's service; but, while in such service, when on shore, he was several times sent to prison for quarreling and making riots and disturbances in the streets of London; frequently drawing his sword, and playing other mad pranks, putting her to great expenses before he could be released; and, when on board any of his majesty's ships, behaved so very badly and inconsistently with his office, that he was at last discharged from his majesty's ship, Princess Louisa, as incapable of doing duty. The truth of this can be proved by his mother, now living in Deadman's Place, and Mr. Birdlecomb's widow, a sawmaker, in Moorfields, and by the ship's books at the Navy Office.

I hope the candid reader will pardon this digression; for, as Richardson was a chief instrument towards my misfortunes, I thought it incumbent on me to shew his character; and beg leave to insert another of his weak or flighty transactions before I proceed to my sufferings, whereby unprejudiced people may, in some measure, account for the reason why he, through his unhappy temper and ill conduct, should be the author of great part of my misery, although, in the first part of the voyage, he lay under divers obligations to me.

Now, as this Richardson had some knowledge of Mr. Blake, he resolved to, and did, go from London to Bristol on foot, in order to make application for a birth in some ship belonging to him, and ordered his mother to send his chest and clothes, &c. by the carrier, but, before their arrival, he came on board the Thetis, as already mentioned, and went to sea without them, almost naked, though they were expected in three days time at farthest. Whereupon I, taking compassion, gave him part of my bed and liquors, and supplied him with several other things absolutely necessary, he being quite destitute, and unprovided for a Guinea voyage.

N. B. His chest, clothes, &c. with thirteen shillings in money, arrived at Bristol within three days after we sailed, but were all lost or embezzled through his indiscretion and carelessness, as his mother has since declared to me.

But to proceed.—We had moderate weather about three weeks, notwithstanding which the ship's decks were never free from water; and, if the weather had proved any ways boisterous, the ship could not have lived, but must have inevitably foundered, or been lost. However, at the end of three weeks, it pleased God to conduct us safe into a smooth sea, with fine weather, when Mr. Pope, our second mate, falling sick, died in six or seven days after, and Richardson succeeded him in that birth.

Pope's clothes being sold at the mast, Richardson came in for part; and what with his promotion, and being better supplied with apparel than usual, it so elated him, that he grew ungrateful, forgetting my favours in his distress: he became very insolent, and, provoking me daily, caused my resentment, and obliged me to absent myself from his company and conversation, and consequently from giving him any more liquors, which he was excessively fond of and much addicted to. Upon this he embraced all opportunities to injure me, as will now appear.

In a few days after Mr. Pope's death we caught a shark, part whereof was ordered for our mess, to wit, Richardson, me, the boatswain, the cooper, and a boy; but, having no butter, vinegar, nor pepper, to eat it with, (shark being very dry fish and good for nothing without those ingredients,) I desired one of my messmates to get some of the captain; who all answered it would be in vain, as they were well assured he would not grant any;

upon which I replied: That, as those things were under my care, we would go down and take some; but, on reflection, thinking it might be deemed wrong by the captain, and suspecting some evil design against me, I did not go, nor suffer any one else so to do, and for want thereof the fish was thrown overboard undressed. However, my suspicion was not ill-grounded, for Richardson went immediately to the captain, and told him that I threatened to break open the hatches and take what I pleased; but the captain, who well knew I had plenty of my own, and finding no grounds for so base an assertion, took little or no notice thereof, looking on it as the effect of Richardson's rancour and malice.

Some short time after this affair happened, the platform, over that part of the hold wherein the liquors were stowed, being broken open, and several of the ship's crew getting drunk, gave reason to suspect there had been an embezzlement in the cargo, as they had no liquors of their own; whereupon the captain ordered me, and Wabshutt, the chief mate, to search after such part as might be hid or secreted, which we accordingly did; and, finding a two-gallon cag, almost full of English brandy, hid under some junk on the platform forwards, we brought the same to the captain, when he ordered the people aft, who, upon examination, confessed that several of them, together with Richardson, broke open the platform and stole the liquor, being persuaded and instigated thereto by him; whereof the captain was so sensible, that he immediately divested Richardson of his office as second mate, and turned him before the mast, not thinking it safe or prudent to trust him in any capacity above a common man; and, at the same time told me, he was convinced that Richardson's story, concerning my breaking open the hatches, was a malicious design and plot contrived by him against me.

Nothing more material ensued during the remainder of our passage to Andony, where we arrived in the month of March, 1755; and, the weather proving very fine, I was all such time fully employed at my own business, viz. caulking the decks, making bulkheads, barricadoes, &c. for the reception of slaves, and doing other necessary things in the ship; so that, in short, my work was completed, except caulking the sides, which is never done till about a week before the ship's departure from the coast.

On our arrival at Andony, we there found the Anne Galley, of Bristol, captain Robe commander, at an anchor, who had taken most part of his cargo of slaves on board, but was then on shore himself at the factory at Amdony; a negro town of trade up the river, thirty miles distant from the place where the two vessels lay at anchor, about a musket-shot asunder.

Our ship's company were at this time all hearty, and in good spirits, when captain Fitzherbert entreated me to go with the boat's crew to cut firewood, for cooking the slaves victuals in the middle passage, although not my business. However, having completed all my work, as before mentioned, and having but little to do on board, being desirous of obliging the captain, and doing every thing for the benefit of the ship and cargo, I consented, and went with the crew in a small boat called the yawl: the captain, on the same day, going up to the factory at Amdony, with the pinnace, in order to purchase slaves.

We went on shore and cut a boat-load of wood that day, but could not get on board with the same till the next morning, and were obliged to dress our victuals on the coals, and lie on the beach, and all night exposed to the wind and rain.

Upon going on board in the morning, we acquainted Walshutt, whom the captain had left in charge of the ship, with the hardships and inconveniences we endured while cutting wood; and that it was impossible for us to labour all day without a kettle to dress our victuals in, and proper covering, and other necessaries, for shelter from the weather in the night; begging him to supply us therewith; which he utterly refused, saying: Nothing could be spared; so we were obliged to go on in that manner, exposed to all weathers, till the third trip.

Coming back over the bar, in order to carry the third load of wood on board, we met the Anne Galley's boat, who had got a pitch-pot for us to boil our victuals in, together with some bread, a piece of salt beef, two quarts of English spirits, and an old sail-cloth for our shelter, which would keep out no more water than a basket, although there were then several tarpaulins lying useless on board the ship that would have been very serviceable, and have made a tent, whereby we might have been screened from all weathers; and, by this boat, Wabshutt sent orders for us to return on shore with the wood, and stay there till we had further directions from him, and cut more wood, and lay it up in cords; during which time he would supply us with necessaries by the pinnace.

These orders were thought mighty extraordinary, especially as captain Fitzherbert, before he went up to the factory, had directed us to cut the wood and bring it on board directly, as soon as the weather permitted and we could get over the bar, (the sea frequently running so high that no boat can pass it for ten days together,) therefore we all agreed to, and did, return to the ship, and delivered this third boat-load of wood; but, upon coming alongside, Wabshutt was very angry with us for disobeying his orders, and, as soon as the wood was taken into the ship, he immediately sent us on shore again to cut more, and insisted on our staying till we heard farther from him, asking how we dared to disobey his orders? although I acquainted him with the directions given by captain Fitzherbert.

In our passage to the ship we consulted with each other what was the best method to be taken, and (considering the difficulties and hardships we underwent while on shore, for want of proper necessaries, to the great prejudice of our healths, in a very sickly country, as Guinea is well known to be, and that the negroes might steal the wood away as fast as cut and corded, and perhaps do us a mischief, which is frequently the case,) we all agreed to go up to the captain at the factory, and acquaint him with the whole affair.

It not being my business to cut wood, the captain sent me down in the yawl in order to do my duty on board the ship, but, being got down to the river's mouth, we found our pinnace and the Anne Galley's long-boat at the watering-place, filling their casks; when Charles Cooper, who was second mate in Richardson's room, desired me to shew him the wooding-place, saying, it would be his business to cut wood in my room; whereupon dispatching the yawl away to the ship, I went with him in the pinnace to the wooding-place, which took up so much time as prevented our getting over the bar before dark; therefore we agreed to lie alongside of the Anne Galley's long-boat till the next morning.

About ten o'clock that evening it thundered and lightened exceedingly; and a tornado coming on obliged us to shelter in a creek, and it was well we did; for, the Anne Galley's long-boat being heavy, her people could not weigh the anchor soon enough to prevent the boat's driving on shore by the storm, where she was stranded, and greatly damaged, the crew narrowly escaping with their lives.

This misfortune was unknown to us till the morning; when, walking on the sand we met the people, who informed us of their disaster, and shewed us the boat half full of sand, almost irrecoverable, desiring me to help to clear her, and if possible, to repair the damages she had received. Upon which, being always very willing and desirous to give what assistance lay in my power to persons in distress, I went with them and helped to clear the boat from sand, sending our boat in the interim on board the Anne Galley, to acquaint their people with the long-boat's mischance, desiring them to despatch the carpenter on shore with tools and proper materials.

The Anne Galley's carpenter being sick, and not able to work, the people carried his mate on board our ship, to be there in my room, while the long-boat was repairing; but Wabshut was so much offended at my staying on shore without his leave, that he swore, whenever I came on board, to blow my brains out, notwithstanding they acquainted him with the great necessity there was for me.

I continued assisting the Anne Galley's people and repairing the boat three days; when, about ten o'clock in the evening of the last day, being asleep in the tent, we were surrounded with upwards of one hundred negroes, armed with pistols and cutlasses, who stripped us all stark naked, cut the tent and boat to pieces, and robbed us of every thing we had, which they took into their canoes, and carried the same clear off.

While the negroes were busy about their plunder, we had an opportunity of escaping, and ran down to the sea-side, where we continued till four o'clock the next afternoon, exposed to the weather, stark naked, it raining very hard all that time, when our boat passing by took us in, and we went up in her to the factory, where captain Fitzherbert received me very kindly, pitying my misfortunes; and captain Robe, in consideration of my loss happening through the service I endeavoured to do him in saving his boat, made me a handsome present of several things very profitable in that country.

Now, the Anne Galley's people having acquainted captain Fitzherbert with Wabshutt's threatening to blow my brains out, upon the account before-mentioned, he wrote a letter to Wabshutt, wherein he desired him to take no farther notice concerning that affair, as I had been helping the distressed, which was no more than my duty.

This letter I delivered to Wabshutt himself, and he seemed to be satisfied; but, from that day, he laid his schemes for my ruin, as I have all the reason in the world to imagine.—And now he began

For, at this time, the second mate being employed in the pinnace to fetch wood and water, and the boatswain in carrying goods up and down to and from the factory, and the cooper also employed there, we had no other officers left on board but Wabshutt, (the chief mate,) the doctor, (his crony,) and myself, when it was my right to mess with them, which they would not suffer, as it might defeat their hellish designs then hatching against me; so I was obliged to mess with the foremast-men.

We had now no more than three messes, and one piece of meat a mess, which, according to the custom of Guinea voyages, should be chosen by each mess in their turn; but, instead of that, Wabshutt and the doctor constantly took the smallest piece and brought it themselves for the mess I belonged to, which occasioned a murmuring among my messmates, who several times said it was wholly through me that they were served in such a manner; and that they could plainly perceive the mate and the doctor were absolutely determined to oppress me; but I bore it with patience, seeing into their drift, hoping for a remedy when the captain came on board.

Captain Robe, of the Anne Galley, having completed his cargo, came on board his own ship, and sent his carpenter to beg some of our tools, all his own being taken away by the negroes, when we were repairing the boat, as before-mentioned. The carpenter and boatswain came both together, and presented me with a two-gallon cag, and a gallon stone bottle of neat brandy, in return for two young parrots which I had before given them: the cag I put into my chest; the bottle I kept out, and made some toddy for the carpenter and boatswain, and my messmates, to drink at parting; and, having good store of tools of my own, spared so many as the carpenter had occasion for. We sat over the toddy about an hour, when the carpenter and boatswain of the Anne Galley returned on board their own ship, at which time Wabshutt went with them in order to take leave of his friends, and took my messmates to row him back.

"Unhappily for Richardson, I left the bottle of brandy near the combings, where we sat while drinking the toddy, forgetting to put the same into my chest; when he, in a clandestine manner, unknown to any of us, got the bottle, and drank so much, that he intoxicated himself to a degree of madness, which soon after appeared; but, not suspecting what had happened, I did not miss my brandy till next morning, having put the bottle into my chest soon after drinking the toddy, without ever examining or looking into it, which if I had done I could easily have accounted for Richardson's following behaviour.

Wabshutt had not been gone long, before Richardson, coming forward, directed his discourse to me, as I sat on the gratings, thus: " Carpenter, will you make your fortune?' 'How?' said I. He replied, 'Let's take the vessel.' I asked him, 'What shall we do with her?' His answer was, 'I know where to carry the vessel, and how to dispose of the slaves.' Upon this, being astonished at his folly and rashness, I told him he was either drunk or mad, and bade him go about his business, and not trouble me with his nonsense. He then went aft, but, in two or three minutes, coming again, he asked me to lend him my knife, which I did not choose unless he would tell me for what; his answer was: No harm; and, on delivering the knife, he went with it in his hand upon the forecastle, where he stood five minutes, looking over the bow of the ship, without saying or attempting any thing as I could perceive, for my eyes were fixed on him all the while, fearing some mischievous trick in his mad frolics. Coming from thence, and going aft, he threw the knife down at my foot as he passed by, which I immediately put into my pocket, and, presently afterwards, being still sitting on the gratings, ruminating on Richardson's bad conduct, I heard him, on the quarter-deck, speak to the doctor as follows: 'Doctor, you are no more doctor here.' To which the doctor replied, 'Why so?' Richardson answered, 'I am commander of this vessel;' and, speaking to the people on board, said, 'Lads, will you live or die?' One of whom answered, 'Live;' Richardson replied: 'Then cut one of the cables, and slip the other; loose the topsails and hoist Jolly Roger.' This discourse alarmed us all, and, upon my going up to the barricado-door, Cooper, the second mate, and John Bray, a lad, came and asked me if I was any ways concerned with Richardson, for they suspected me by seeing us talk together; I answered in the negative, and acquainted them, before all the rest of the ship's company then present, with the conversation between Richardson and me, as before related; and, moreover, told them such proceedings were quite disagreeable to my inclination, and that I would be the first man to secure Richardson, or any other man who dared to attempt any thing to the prejudice of the ship or cargo.

About an hour after this affair happened, Wabshutt came on board, when he was made acquainted with the whole transaction; and I informed him of the discourse between me and Richardson; upon which he ordered a pair of shackles; and the same being immediately brought by Henry Curry, an assistant to me, Wabshutt himself fixed and bolted them on Richardson's legs, and then, before the ship's company, cleared me from the imputation of having any concern with Richardson in the above proceedings; and likewise declared, there was not the least foundation for cause of suspicion against me.

But, to return.—Both Wabshutt and the doctor still continuing to bring our mess the least pieces of meat, as usual, for about ten days afterwards; and the doctor's bringing a piece, the bone whereof weighed upwards of four pounds, and the meat not one, occasioned a general discontent, put my messmates quite out of patience, who plainly told me, that they should not have proceeded on the voyage had it not been for my promises at Pill, and insisted on my making the same good; therefore, being under a necessity of so doing, I, taking the bone and meat in my hand, went to Wabshutt on the quarter-deck, and spoke in the following manner: 'Mr. Wabshutt, this is not a fair way of 'proceeding; for some people to have plenty while 'others starve, (shewing him the bone and the 'meat:) it is five pounds, I believe; but upwards 'of four pounds are bone, and only one pound of meat to serve five men twenty-four hours: we have made a proposal, which we beg you will agree to, and it is this: that you allow five pounds of beef to a mess on beef-days; and, on pork-days, four pounds of pork; and four pounds of bread a week to each man, and water to drink; and, if provisions fall short, give us less, but all alike, with which we will be content; and let every man in his station do his duty to the utmost of his power; but, if you will not give your consent to these proposals, we must be obliged to go where we can get provisions, and not be forcibly starved by you.' To this he made no reply, and we were obliged to rest satisfied with the morsel we had got; a small modicum to feed five hungry appetites twenty-four hours; and this practice still continued for five days longer, although there was plenty on board at that time. Therefore, I am convinced that Wabshutt's and the doctor's bad treatment, in regard to provisions, was done with a view to compel me to commit some outrage, whereby they might have it in their power to put their villainous designs against me into execution, which they had been contriving ever since my complaint to the captain at the factory, and which, I believe, was partly the cause thereof, and partly through my application about the bone and meat; for now begins the scene of my misery.

At the end of the last-mentioned five days, Wabshutt said, the captain had sent for me to the factory, in order to clean the bottom of the pinnace, and give her a new coat; whereupon I took all necessaries for that purpose, together with some goods of my own, intending to traffic therewith in the country; and Wabshutt wrote a letter to the captain, and delivered it to the boatswain, who was patron of the boat, which I imagined to be an account, or bill, of particulars concerning the goods or stores we were carrying to the factory; not having then the least suspicion of any plot or scheme laid to ensnare me. But how great was my surprize when we came there! for the captain, on reading Wabshutt's letter, instead of giving directions about the boat, immediately clapped a pistol to my head, and ordered me to be put in irons and chained to a post, which was quickly done by John Bray, before-mentioned, without assigning any cause for so doing, although I, as well as several of the head negroes, who spoke very good English, divers times requested to know what offence I had committed to be thus barbarously treated; but the captain's answer always was, he had reason enough, and that was sufficient.

I remained confined in this dismal condition fourteen days, during which time I saw several of my goods and tools embezzled before my face, no care being taken thereof; and was likewise visited with a severe fit of sickness, insomuch that I was given over, and looked upon to be a dying man; and, notwithstanding the frequent intreaties of divers persons, especially several of the chief negroes, I could not obtain any relief or comfort, till, at last, I told the captain, before them all, that I did not expect to live, but should certainly die by his cruel treatment I therefore laid my death absolutely to his charge; whereupon, the captain, thinking me to be past all hopes of recovery, and that I could not long survive it, ordered Bray to loose me from the post, saying, at the same time: 'Take him to the boat, and carry 'him, shackled as he is, on board the vessel to 'Wabshutt and the doctor, and let them answer 'for his death, for they are absolutely the cause 'thereof;' and bade the people take special care that I did not fall overboard in the passage.

This confession of the captain gave me great reason to suspect the base artifices and villainy contrived and carried on by Wabshutt and the doctor, who had grossly imposed on him, through their monstrous lies and perfidy; and I am now fully convinced of their hellish design to destroy me, not only by reason of their future unparalleled behaviour, but also by what some of the crew have told me since we came home; for they have declared, that when I was sent to the factory, as before set forth, Wabshutt and the doctor wrote the captain word, that I had threatened to staple down the scuttle, and confine Wabshutt in the cabin, and take the boat, together with what goods I pleased, and leave the vessel in distress; and that, if he offered to stir or make any resistance, I would blow his brains out with a harquebuss; and that Bray (a fellow entirely dependent on Wabshutt, and therefore obliged to say or do what he ordered,) confirmed the same to the captain at the factory, which was the sole cause of my confinement and ill treatment by the captain, he being, in all other respects, a good-natured humane man.

When the boat came alongside of the vessel, Wabshutt, with a smiling countenance, asked me how I did; ordered me to be taken on board and put on the main deck, where Richardson then was still in irons as I had left him, when Wabshutt himself, very officiously, knocking off the shackles from Richardson's legs and mine, coupled us both together with two irons, one above the other, me by the right leg, and Richardson by the left; and, to complete the matter effectually, confined my right-hand to his left with a pair of handcuffs, and then chained us fast to a ringbolt on the deck.

In this miserable posture we continued five weeks, exposed to the inclemency of the weather, without any thing to lie on or shelter us; and I, being reduced very low and weak by sickness, could not stand or help myself but was obliged to lie flat on the deck, in the midst of excessive heavy rains, which fall on that coast for a great many hours together; the water running in a continual stream under me, and round my sides; and, when those showers abated, the sun would shine out exceedingly hot, insomuch that it was like being in an oven, enough to kill any person under our circumstances.

During such confinement, Wabshutt took possession of my chest and effects, and sent them on shore, and what became of them afterwards I could never learn, except some things of little value, which he returned when he set me at liberty, and those were soon lost, partly for want of a chest to keep them in, and the other part thereof I was obliged to sell to get victuals; for, the sickness leaving me, my appetite returned, and, Wabshutt and the doctor still continuing their bad treatment, I must otherwise have, several times in the course

Calabui and Marcham, Printers, Ingram-court, London.

No. 5, Barker's Genuine Life.

BARKER and his Spouse in their present state of life.

of the voyage, perished for want; although, when we arrived at Antigua, there were near three months of the ship's provisions left untouched.

Captain Fitzherbert, being poisoned at the factory, came on board, and there died; when Wabshutt, succeeding in the command of the vessel, went up to the factory to purchase the remainder of the cargo, where he continued five weeks: in whose absence several of the lads on board, pitying my condition, acquainted me that Wabshutt and the doctor obliged them, among others, to sign the letter so sent to captain Fitzherbert at the factory, without letting them know the contents thereof; but they really believed such letter was the only reason of my confinement there.

Now, by the bad conduct, ill usage, and wicked contrivances, of Wabshutt and the doctor, the ship's company (consisting of twenty-two hands) were so reduced, through death, sickness, and desertion, that we had no more than three who were able to perform duty; and, while Wabshutt was on shore, the slaves broke open the gratings in the night, when two of the very finest took to the boat, and got away undiscovered, which is no wonder; for, the few people who were able working hard all day, it was impossible to keep a good look-out in the night; and, those two slaves leaving the gratings open, it is really surprising the others, near one hundred in number, did not all rise and cut the ship's company off, which was then very easy for them to have done.

Wabshutt, having finished the cargo, came on board; when, finding the crew reduced so low, that we had not hands sufficient to work the vessel, he and the doctor came to me and Richardson, saying, they would give us our liberty provided we signed a writing, promising not to prosecute them for their ill usage, otherwise they would keep us in irons till the ship arrived at Antigua. Whereupon, being glad of any opportunity to get discharged, and compelled also by necessity, we agreed to their proposals, and so were released from our wretched confinement.

However, this confinement was absolutely my ruin; for, being exposed to all weathers, and cruelly treated by Wabshutt and the doctor all that time, and no care taken of me, I contracted a very bad distemper in my eyes, which increased in so violent a degree as to deprive me entirely of my sight in about a fortnight afterwards: and I have ever since remained quite blind.

The ship's crew being reduced to the condition before related, we were obliged to go to Calabar, a fresh-water river, about thirty leagues down the coast, to wood and water, where we got the assistance of other ships to help us; and, about eight days afterwards, we proceeded to the island of Ponantipo, twenty leagues from thence, which we could not well have done without being assisted by some of the people belonging to the Eugene of Bristol, who attended us all the way with their long-boat.

At this island we were furnished, in three days time, with a large quantity of yams for our consumption in the voyage to Antigua, and then set sail with the assistance of our own slaves, there being no possibility of working the ship without them.

Upon the passage the people recovered apace, and grew hearty by eating the yams, which we had in plenty, being far better food than the ship's provisions; but Wabshutt and the doctor still continuing their accustomed malice, and having determined to make an end of me, absolutely refused me any allowance thereof, although great numbers, weighing ten or twelve pounds each, were thrown overboard in a morning, being grown rotten for want of use, giving me only the ship's provisions of about two ounces of meat a day, and four pounds of bread a week; excluded me from the slaves provisions, such as rice, yams, beans, &c.

which all the rest of the ship's company had plenty of, being their chief support.

John Richardson, soon after his release, was restored to his former post as second mate; but, about a week after our departure from Ponantipo, being in conversation with some of the ship's crew, he indiscreetly said, that, as the writing was signed by him while under confinement, it stood for nothing, and that he would prosecute Wabshutt and the doctor, when he came to England, for their ill treatment; which, coming to their ears, nettled them so much, that they determined to punish him farther, but could find no plausible pretence for some days; he, continuing to do his duty, and dreading his former sufferings, was become very cautious and reserved, evading many questions asked on purpose to ensnare him.

But all would not save him, and to pot he must go right or wrong; for, after he had again enjoyed his post about six weeks, and behaved extremely well during that time, Wabshutt called him upon the quarter-deck, and ordered him to sit down and help to mend the top-sail, when Richardson begged to be excused, saying, his bottom was so sore with the yaws, (a common and contagious distemper among the negroes,) that he could not sit, but was very ready to obey his commands in any thing else: upon which Wabshutt declared, if he could not sit to work, he was no ways serviceable to the ship; and, for that very reason, and no other, put him in irons again immediately, where he remained till our arrival at Antigua; and, at the same time, deprived him of the slaves provisions, allowing him no more than what was granted me, although Wabshutt well knew Richardson spoke the truth, and he had contracted such distemper, in doing his duty, by going among the slaves, and then was very ill.

Henry Curry, an assistant to me, likewise falling sick, and being unable to work, the doctor said it was the scurvy, and that he was lazy and slothful; whereupon both Wabshutt and the doctor beat and kicked him frequently, and forced him beyond his strength, till, at last, by their inhuman treatment, he was reduced so very low and weak, that he could not stand, his legs being swelled to a monstrous size.

In this condition he continued languishing for some days, till about five o'clock in the morning of the day on which he died; when, sitting near me, on the deck, and talking to me, he complained of his belly, and then laid himself all along. Shortly after, Wabshutt ordered to put about ship, and he, coming forwards and seeing Curry lie there, spoke as follows: 'Damn your blood, you dog, what do you lie skulking here for?' and then struck, or kicked him twice; I heard the blows given, and, immediately after, heard Curry struggle for breath. Upon which, Wabshutt went away and said no more; but, as soon as he was gone, Peter Bates, the cooper, who was standing by all the while, declared that Wabshutt had actually killed Curry by two kicks with his foot, for Curry never spoke afterwards; and his body was, by Wabshutt's orders, thrown overboard within two hours after he expired.

About a week after this melancholy affair happened, we touched at the island of Annabona, and there took in a large supply of goats, hogs, fowls, and other provisions: notwithstanding this, and the great plenty we had of every kind on board, Wabshutt and the doctor were still so cruel and hard-hearted, that they would give me no other, or more, provisions than as before described; which scanty allowance was always delivered on a Sunday, in order to serve me all the week: but, this quantity being so very small, I frequently ate the whole up by Monday night, and then was obliged to fast to the Sunday following; so that, when the vessel arrived at Annabona, I was almost famished, not having tasted one morsel of any sort of victuals during the space of five days; but, while we lay there, a canoe with provisions coming alongside, gave me an opportunity of gratifying my appetite once in the voyage; for, taking the shirt off my back, being the only one left, I purchased therewith two fowls, some cassavi-bread, a few cocoa-nuts, and a quart bottle of brandy, sufficient to have served me a week; however, I had the satisfaction of one meal only, for the rest was all taken away by Wabshutt's orders, who would have deprived me of the whole had he known it time enough.

My case was now deplorable indeed, being obliged to lie on the deck with the heavens for my canopy, and the bare boards for a bed, exposed to all weathers, which are, in that climate, very variable and uncertain; sometimes exceedingly hot, and then immediately excessively cold rains will follow; and I, having only a jacket and trowsers, was glad to herd among the goats and hogs for warmth; but, they being nearly expended in about a fortnight after we left Annabona, I lost my bedfellows, who used to lie round, and, in some measure, shelter me from the cold. This reduced me to a worse state than before; and, what with herding with them, almost starved for want of victuals and proper necessaries, and being always exposed to the open air, I was brought very low and miserable; insomuch that, with tears in my eyes, I begged of Wabshutt, for God's sake, to have compassion, and let me partake of the food given to the hogs, (after the slaves had done with the same;) but he, relentless, refused such humble request; expressing himself (in the hearing of the ship's company) thus: 'If the hogs have no victuals they will not grow fat, or be fit to kill: if I thought it would be your last you should have your belly full; but, if of any service, I would sooner hang you at the yard-arm than give you a morsel; and, were it not for the law when we come to England, I would hang you up directly.'

Much about this time a dispute happened between Wabshutt and the doctor, concerning a negro girl, purchased with the goods of Mr. Pope, our late second mate, deceased; which arose to such a pitch, that they determined to cut her in two; Wabshutt to take one half of her, and the doctor the other, although she was no property of either; and, many words ensuing, Wabshutt challenged the doctor to fight, which the doctor accepted, and went down from the quarter to the main deck with such intent, telling Wabshutt that he would fight him there, and not on the quarter-deck, as he was commander of the ship; but Wabshutt's heart then failed him, and he declined fighting. Upon which the doctor warmly told him, he was a rogue and a coward; that his villainy would soon come to light; for, as soon as we arrived in any English port, justice should take place: all his Wabshutt took in good part, not giving any answer thereto: however, the doctor resented it so far, that he would not mess or converse with him for near a week after; until Wabshutt, by frequent intreaties, prevailed on him to drink tea, when they made it up, and so the quarrel ended.

I was in hopes this difference would have been productive of some relief to my misery, which was now so extreme that I was even grown ravenous; insomuch that raw meat, or any thing eatable, my keen appetite devoured greedily like a dog; so that the very negroes, pitying my lamentable circumstances, took all opportunities to assist me, privately, with part of their provisions; but the doctor, keeping a watchful eye, detected several, and whipped them himself severely, which deterred all the slaves from any ways helping me.

The hogs and goats (my poor old bedfellows) being all killed, caused me to contrive some shelter in the night, which I performed by getting under a half tub, bottom upwards, where I lay crampt or doubled several nights; but was soon deprived of that privilege; for the doctor, finding me out, he, together with Jack Bray, shoved the tub, with me under it, from one end of the deck to the other, till they were tired, and then sluiced me with several buckets of water.

Being now in the midst of my calamity and distress, Bray, in a sneering manner, said: 'Carpenter, if it were my case, as it is yours, I would jump overboard and end my misery.' I answered: 'That I was more willing to die than live in such a perishing condition, but would not be accessary to my own death.' Upon which the doctor, who was then at hand, replied: 'You have no occasion to destroy yourself, for I will throw you overboard;' and, directly seizing me with that intent, both he and Bray, and another person whom I could not find out, carried me to the ship's side; and, putting my legs over the gunwale, the doctor called the boatswain to come and help; but the boatswain refused, saying, 'He would not be hanged for any body; and that, if the doctor and the others did it, they would all three be hanged on the ship's arrival in England.' These words terrified them, and saved my life; for they all went away, leaving me in that posture.

Soon after this, I intreated Wabshutt and the doctor to let me lie among the slaves; which was consented to, provided I would strip into buff as they were; whereupon I stripped immediately, and put my jacket and trowsers (being all the clothes I had left) under the boat's bottom; but was no sooner got down below, than the doctor threw them overboard, and ordered the negroes to drive me up, otherwise he would flog them in the morning. Upon this, I was forced upon deck, stark naked, about nine o'clock at night, when it rained excessively hard, and the air was very cold: what to do I could not tell; and, feeling for my jacket and trowsers, found they were removed; so I humbly supplicated the doctor, and begged his leave to shelter myself in the forecastle from the inclemency of the weather; but he, being inexorable, refused so small a favour, and absolutely swore I should lie upon the deck, naked as I was, until we got to Antigua; whereupon Charles Cooper (then chief mate) and Peter Bates, the cooper, being shocked at the doctor's barbarous and inhuman treatment, told him, That if he would not grant my request, and I should die on deck, in our passage, they would both of them lay my death to his charge when the ship arrived in England. To this he made no sort of answer; but, walking off, I went into the forecastle, and lay there all night quite naked, having no one thing to cover me or lie on except the bare boards.

It is an old saying, and a true one, that hunger will break through stone walls, which was verified in me; for, being in the forecastle by myself, and my week's provision quite exhausted, although this was but Monday night, it put me on a contrivance how to defeat the hellish designs of Wabshutt and the doctor, whose intentions to destroy me, at all events, were now too visible to admit of the least doubt; and, as necessity is the mother of invention, I was not long at a loss; for, ripping up part of the forecastle flooring, I soon got into the hold, where I found a way to a bread-but; when, drawing the staple with an old scraper and a shackle-bolt, I took out some bread, and then drove the staple tight into the same holes it was in before, to prevent suspicion: and, by that means, gathered flesh and strength, to their no small wonder and mortification, otherwise I might have been starved to death by inches.

In this naked condition I remained till the ship arrived at Antigua; and, during all that time, was obliged to go to the quarter-deck to drink water there; when Wabshutt and the doctor, for their beastly diversion, would frequently order the negro women and girls to haul me about, and take the most indecent liberties with me. However, being now grown healthy and strong, through the continual supply of bread, in the manner above set forth, I thought it no great punishment, except the indecency of the thing, and only mention this circumstance to shew how far Wabshutt and the doctor's inhumanity and brutality extended.

The day after our arrival at Antigua, his majesty's ship the Warwick, and four other men of war, anchored there, when Wabshut threatened to send me on board one of them, and have me tried for piracy, without accusing me of any one act whatever: but herein he was disappointed, for, before he could carry that design into execution, (if any such he had,) the men of war all sailed away.

We lay here a fortnight, when Wabshutt and Mr. Allen (the merchant to whom the cargo was consigned) made interest with the magistrates to have both me and Richardson put in prison, right or wrong. Till now, I remained quite naked, except wearing a pair of trowsers, which Peter Bates, the cooper, gave me on our arrival at this place; and Richardson still continued in irons, being reduced to a meer skeleton, through the cruelty and barbarity of Wabshutt and the doctor, who starved him in the passage: and, although both his legs were swelled above an inch over his irons, they would not suffer them to be knocked off, nor a larger pair to be put on, though they very nearly caused a mortification.

This fortnight being expired, Wabshut ordered Richardson's irons to be knocked off, and an old frock to be put on me; and, on the 24th of October, 1755, about nine o'clock in the morning, we were both carried on shore to the court-house, where we staid, by ourselves, till four o'clock the same afternoon; at which time, Wabshutt, Mr. Allen, and Mr. Warner, the justice, came there; when Mr. Warner directed Richardson to be unhandcuffed; and then, taking me by the hand, asked Wabshutt if I was the man whom he had declared was so great a rogue: his answer was, 'Yes.' Whereupon the justice said to me, 'Well, my lad, what do you think of being hanged?' To which I answered, 'If the law will condemn me, I am very willing to die.' Upon this he said no more, but sent for his brother Daniel, another justice, who soon came; when Wabshutt and the doctor, together with John Bray, Richard Belton, and Samuel Bendin, were sworn as witnesses against me. Wabshutt, on his examination, could say nothing. The doctor informed the justices of Richardson's discourse and behaviour to him on the quarter-deck, as before related, and nothing farther. Bray confirmed the same. Belton deposed as to Richardson's stealing the brandy, for which he was turned before the mast; and Bendin only confirmed the doctor's deposition. But, through the whole examination, my name was never once called in question; thereupon I thought fit to speak for myself, and acquainted the justices with the conversation between me and Richardson, about making my fortune, and his going to the doctor on the quarter-deck; together with his odd behaviour there; confirming what the doctor had before deposed; and then gave them an account of what happened concerning the small quantity of beef, and largeness of bone, brought by the doctor to our mess while at Andony; and was proceeding to acquaint them with Wabshutt's and the doctor's base dealings in getting me sent to the factory and laid in irons; and also designed to inform the justices of all their cruel, inhuman, and barbarous, usage to me during the voyage: but Wabshutt, stung to the quick, could bear it no longer, and, interrupting me, said, I had been in the rebellion in the north of England: this was enough, (although a base villainous lie intended to prejudice me,) for the justices would hear no more, and thereupon committed us both to prison, without any farther cause or inquiry.

While in prison, the jailer applied for my wages, but I could get no other answer than this: that I had been guilty of mutiny, and my wages were forfeited. However, I was very well satisfied with my confinement; for, reflecting on the dangers and hardships attending me in the passage from Andony to Antigua, and that I lived far better in this prison than on board the ship, I looked upon it as the direction of kind Providence to save my life: for, I am very certain, had I been sent on board the Thetis again, I should never have reached England; Wabshutt's and the doctor's malice being grown so inveterate, that they would have absolutely destroyed me in the voyage.

On the 11th of March, 1756, Richardson and I were taken out of the said prison, and carried on board his majesty's ship the Advice, bound for England, when captain Affleck immediately rated us both able; and I fell in with some Liverpool lads, who, commiserating my lamentable state, supplied me with a bed, and other necessaries, so that I was furnished with plenty.

In May following we arrived at Portsmouth; when, going on board the Torbay, where the Advice's men were then receiving their wages, commodore Keppel inquired how I came by my misfortune; and, on being acquainted therewith, pitying my condition, he recommended to the people, as they severally were called to the pay-table, to give something each man, whereby I might be enabled to prosecute the villains (meaning Wabshutt and the doctor) for their cruelty.

Having made a tolerable collection among the Advice's crew, I set out from Portsmouth, in the waggon, full of spirits, hoping to obtain satisfaction for my damages. And, coming to London, I had the good fortune to quarter at the Paul's head, in Doctors Commons, then kept by Samuel Collins, where I was recommended to Mr. John Lee, a proctor, who wrote to the merchant at Bristol, but could get no answer, as he frequently informed me. In this situation I remained at Mr. Collin's near five months, who supported me all that time; during which I wrote several letters to my landlady at Bristol, inquiring after Wabshutt and the doctor, desiring her to let me know what was become of them; but she never sent any answer; and, in the interim I made application to divers proctors, who would none of them be concerned, as Mr. Lee was already employed.

Finding no redress at Doctors Commons, I applied to Mr. Oakley, an attorney, in Wellclose-square, who gave me great encouragement, saying, he would cause the vessel or Wabshutt to be arrested as soon as they could be found; whereupon I set out for Bristol in October 1756, having only six shillings in my pocket, being all I could possibly raise for the support of myself and another person as a guide, trusting to providence for a supply on the road.

I arrived at Bristol in the same month, and, going immediately to my landlady, I asked her the cause of not answering my letters: when she answered, she did not think it worth her while, as she had heard I was going to turn pirate. By this, and upon farther inquiry, I found she had been biassed by Wabshutt, who was then a captain of a privateer, and spent, or caused to be spent, a great deal of money at her house, where numbers of seamen boarded, or frequented, when at home.

The next day I wrote to Oakley, informing him that the Thetis was lying with a broom at her masthead, as a signal for sale: and then I applied to the mayor and aldermen of Bristol, acquainting them with my misfortune, and in what manner it came; who said, they could take no cognizance of the matter, and I must seek a remedy at law;

but, lamenting my hard fate, they settled a pension of three shillings and sixpence per week on me for life, payable by the merchants hospital.

Five days after this, I received a letter from Oakley, with advice that he had sent down a writ, issued out of the Common-pleas, to Mr. Young, an attorney, in Corn-street, in order to arrest Wabshutt for my wages, who was then at sea on a cruize, which I knew nothing of when I wrote to Oakley; I, therefore, did not at that time mention him at all.

I staid at Bristol about a fortnight, and went from thence to Tarlaton, in Lancashire, among my old acquaintances, hoping to raise money, or friends, who would enable me to carry on a prosecution against Wabshutt and the doctor for damages; where I tarried till the latter end of February, 1757, when I received a letter from Bristol, informing me that Wabshutt was arrested, and had given in bail; and, if I had been there at such time, the affair might have been compromised. Upon this, I thought it most prudent to take Oakley's farther directions therein; for which purpose I set out; but, being short of cash, and falling in with some pack-horses, I took the opportunity of travelling all the way to London, by holding one of their tails.

Upon my arrival, Oakley informed me that, unfortunately, the writ expired three days before the arrest; so that all this time, expense, and trouble, were thrown away for no purpose, and I obliged to begin the suit again.

Being now reduced, and having nothing to support myself with, it put me on a resolution to print my case, and distribute them over the town; which had the desired effect; for, what by those cases, and the charitable donations of several Lancashire gentlemen and others, I gathered up a little money, sufficient for my present occasions.

Wabshutt being again arrested for my wages, by virtue of a King's Bench writ, about the middle of April, I sent a petition (with one of my printed cases) to counsellor Clayton, in Brick-court, Temple, setting forth my grievances, when he was pleased to order me to bring my attorney; whom I several times intreated, but he refused to go: whereupon Mr. Martin, jun. in King-street, Cheapside; at my request, went himself to Oakley and prevailed on him; when he promised to call on Mr. Martin in his way, but never did, and disappointed him twice, although Mr. Martin waited at home two days in expectation; neither did he ever call on the counsellor. This behaviour of Oakley's deprived me of my friends, who all deserted me, imagining some roguery; whereby I could get no one to assist me.

Easter-term being expired, Oakley told me the cause would be tried next term, then nigh at hand, and wanted my witnesses, but would never let me have any subpœnas; till a friend of mine, accidentally coming to London, and finding the dilemma I was in, advanced Oakley four guineas; and, pressing him hard, at last got the subpœnas; wherewith I immediately set out for Bristol, being supplied by my friend for the journey.

Arriving at Bristol, I received my pension, and got two of my witnesses served; but, Charles Cooper, the chief-mate, secreted himself, being induced and prevailed on so to do by Wabshutt, whereby I was deprived of the benefit of his evidence.

Soon after this, Mr. Young informed me that the trial was put off till Michaelmas-term: however, I brought one of the witnesses with me up to London, Oakley having ordered me to bring them at all events, saying, he could get their affidavits made before one of the judges, in his chambers, which would be good evidence at the trial; but, after keeping the man near a fortnight in town to no purpose, I was obliged to send him back again, Oakley not once attempting to get his affidavit according to promise; and the expenses of this transaction reduced me once more to the last extremity.

During the long vacation I applied to the shipwrights, both in his majesty's and the merchants yards, for relief, who assisted me very much, whereby I saved some small matter against the trial, well knowing money to be the sinews of law, as well as war, and that nothing can be done without it.

Michaelmas-term drawing nigh, Oakley told me the cause would then be tried, and my witnesses must be ready, but would not grant my subpœnas, therefore I was obliged to go without; and, on my arrival at Bristol, I could find only one witness, the others being at sea. This witness was the man that came to London with me before, whom I now brought a second time, daily expecting the cause to come on; when, in about a week afterwards, Oakley informed me the trial was put off again to Hilary-term.

These delays caused me to suspect unfair play; and that Oakley was not sound at the bottom: however, I determined, if possible, to keep this witness in town all that time, and he, consenting thereto, staid; which, with the great expenses I had already been at, soon exhausted my small substance, and put me on a contrivance to recruit; whereupon I published a ditty, setting forth the cruel hardships I suffered in the voyage, and the dismal situation it reduced me to, selling them in the most public places about London; and, by these means raised money sufficient to carry me through the cause.

This transaction alarmed the friends of Wabshutt and the doctor; for, some short time afterwards, Oakley sent for me to his house, when he informed me that Wabshutt had made proposals, and, therefore, desired to know what would satisfy me. I, being willing and desirous to see an end of the affair, agreed to take one hundred and fifty pounds, in full, for debt, costs, and damages; although my wages came to forty pounds, and my loss in the voyage to upwards of twenty pounds prime cost, besides the total deprivation of my eye-sight. To which Oakley replied, that Wabshutt had offered twenty-six pounds in the whole, so I might have eighteen pounds clear money, there being eight pounds due for charges. This offer I utterly rejected; when Oakley immediately said I was a very great villain; and, unless I would agree to take the same, he would secure me for the charges in twenty-four hours. Whereupon I went away directly to acquaint Mr. Martin, and be advised by him what to do; but he was, unfortunately for me, gone into the country, where counsellor Clayton had likewise been for some time; therefore, not knowing what step to take under these circumstances, or to whom to apply for advice and assistance, and, dreading a jail, where I might lie and perish, I was compelled, through necessity, to accept of eighteen pounds, and give a general release.

The latter end of February, 1758, this affair was settled in judge Foster's chambers; when Oakley, receiving a twenty-six pound Bank-bill, ordered me to execute the release, which I refused until the money was paid into my hands, having great reason to suspect him, after treating me in so vile and base a manner, as before related; and, I am very certain, had I not then received my money, I should have found a deal of trouble in getting the same out of his hands, and much doubt whether I should have recovered it at all.

Now, having gone through the whole narrative, I will conclude with a few remarks thereon, whereby the candid reader may judge what foundation or cause Wabshutt and the doctor had for their barbarous usage, and unparalleled cruelty throughout the voyage.

First: While under my afflictions, Wabshutt, several times, declared, that, when at Pill, I endeavoured to prevail on the people to turn pirates; with which he acquainted the merchant before we sailed from thence; but the merchant said, as he had advanced me twelve pounds, I must proceed on the voyage. This assertion is a most notorious falsity, and not a word of truth contained therein; for, on the contrary, had it not been through my prevailing arguments and entreaties, not one of the people would have gone the voyage, as they had all then absolutely resolved to go back to Bristol.

Secondly: Richardson's telling captain Fitzherbert that I threatened to break open the hatches, when the keys thereof were in my own possession, was so very absurd, that I heard no more of it.

Thirdly: Wabshutt lays the fault of the ship's not being wooded or watered, at Andony, to my charge; and told the people that the reason of our going down to Calabar was, my taking the boat away, when I went to make my complaint of his ill usage to the captain at the factory, as before related. However, this is another of his monstrous lies; for the boat's absence one day from the ship could never be the occasion of her not being wooded and watered, when she lay there near three months afterwards. But the truth really was, and is, this: Wabshutt and the doctor (by their cruel treatment and behaviour to the people, and not allowing them provisions and proper necessaries) had reduced the ship's company into such a weak and sickly condition, that there were not hands sufficient for that purpose: and this, and no other, was the reason of going to Calabar, where we got assistance, as already mentioned.

Fourthly: My being put in irons, at the factory, was solely owing to the letter sent by Wabshutt and the doctor to captain Fitzherbert; and it is now well known, that Wabshutt lays Richardson's proceedings to my charge, although no mention was made thereof before the justices at Antigua: and, when the matter was settled at judge Foster's chambers, the lawyers told me they were glad I got the money, for Wabshutt had so full a proof, by affidavits made at Antigua, that they were certain I must have been cast upon the trial. But,

Fifthly: How could it be possible for either me or Richardson, or any one else, to have turned pirate, when, at that time, there were not hands on board sufficient to work or navigate the ship, the major part being then on shore, some cutting wood, and others at the factory? Neither had we any artillery; and, besides, we lay within musket-shot of the Anne Galley, a large ship, far superior in force, mounting several carriage-guns, who could have torn us in pieces; and the wind blowing very hard, right on shore, we must infallibly have run on the bar and perished, had the cables been either cut or slipped; therefore I leave the world to judge of the possibility of so rash an attempt, if any such were ever intended, which, I am certain, never was; nor even one word mentioned, during the whole course of the voyage, except by Richardson, in his mad and drunken frolic, at the time he was put in irons at Andony.

Sixthly: After my giving the note to Wabshutt and the doctor, (the surgeon belonging to the Eugene of Bristol, then at Calabar, declaring my eye-sight was absolutely lost for want of proper care and assistance,) I could not refrain from speaking, and told them, That, notwithstanding the paper, signed by me, promising not to prosecute, yet my friends in England would certainly call the authors of my misfortunes to account, and oblige them to make satisfaction; which weak expression, I believe, was the sole motive of their future barbarous treatment: for, being terrified, and fearing a prosecution, they determined, at all events, to prevent it, by putting an end to my life, frequently telling me, they would take care to prevent an[y] trouble coming upon them, for I should not liv[e] till we got to Antigua; and, if I did, they woul[d] get me so secured, that I should never have th[e] opportunity of telling my tale in England; whic[h] plainly shews the intention to sacrifice me in th[e] passage; but the bread-cask defeated their de[-]signs.

Seventhly, and lastly: They were wicked aban[-]doned men in other respects, for the vessel mad[e] an exceedingly good voyage, having near 170 slave[s] when she arrived at Antigua, which was a ver[y] fine cargo for so small a vessel: yet the merchan[t] at Bristol told me, that he had lost almost seve[n] hundred pounds by the voyage. This I do no[t] wonder at, especially after having heard Wabshutt several times, brag, that he had purchased seve[n] hundred weight of ivory for himself, and but fou[r] hundred for the merchant: and he likewise bought on his own account, a great number of parrots and other things of great value; therefore, I am confident, some illegal practices were carried o[n] by him in conjunction with the doctor; for they had not wherewithal, between them both, to pur-chase near so much as they did upon their own accounts: besides, I have two reasons more to confirm my opinion; the one is, what the docto[r] said to Wabshutt on their falling out about the negro girl: and the other is, that Mr. Pope's father had no more than four shillings and sixpence, and his silver buckles, returned out of his whole effects; although Pope's clothes, instruments, and chest, (exclusive of his venture, which was considerable,) were sold at the mast for near fifteen pounds; and the negro girl was purchased with part of his venture. And then, again, captain Fitzherbert's widow informs me, that Wabshutt has made me debtor to her husband, notwithstanding I never received more than half-a-crown of him. Therefore, upon the whole, it is very easy to guess how, and in what manner, Wabshutt and the doctor purchased so much as they did; who, without doubt, are the only persons who were gainers by this voyage.

N.B. Captain Fitzherbert's widow lives near the Hotwells; and Pope's father is a basket-maker, to be found on Bristol-bridge.

What has been here related is real fact, which can be proved by living witnesses; and I defy both Wabshutt and the doctor, or their friends, to contradict the same, or any part thereof, by evidence.

And now I hope it may not appear out of the way for me to give some account of the only pleasure I enjoyed, during the most distressing part of that unhappy voyage, which, though in itself may appear very strange, yet is no less true, that I seldom or ever went to sleep without seeming to partake of great plenty of good food, even such as roast beef and plum-pudding, roast geese, ducks, fowls, capons, turkeys, and other sort of agreeable diet, which appeared very acceptable to my keen appetite, though nearly starved to death with hunger every time I awoke therefrom; and, whether such frequent dreams proceeded from that of continually devising how to obtain one thing or other to satisfy my keen stomach when openly awake, or from some kind of heavenly being or other, purely to hold up my spirits, without which I should have, most probably, sunk under the heavy pressure of those uncommon distresses, regularly attending me throughout that voyage, having likewise to add, that my continual spirits were so frequently increased and supported by those dreams as to continually think myself ordained and allotted to effectually call such hard-hearted wretches to account at one time or other, and, likewise, enjoy better days myself, on this side the grave; which said digression will, I hope, be considered as in some shape necessary by the candid reader, as I thought it really so, previous to that of entering on a different subject.

Concerning the Advice, of 50 guns on the main deck thereof, I happened to be left with a few bumboat-women, after the whole crew had been removed from thence to the Torbay; and the women observing me alone, while in such a helpless state of darkness, on board of a king's ship, where no more provisions was to be served out, humanely offered to put me on shore, if I thought proper to go in their boat; which kind offer was too gratifying to a person in my then situation of mind, without being able to devise how or in what manner I might either become enabled to obtain a support, or otherwise, on shore; so, after a short reflection, thought fit to prefer the latter, and most gratefully accepted thereof, and was, accordingly, put on shore at Gosport side, wholly resigned to the divine will of kind Providence, while the boat made off from thence for Portsmouth-point: and here it may not be amiss to mention the cause of it so happening for me to have been left on board alone, as it afterwards came to my knowledge while getting the ship's books examined, concerning it in London; and turning now to the point in hand, I found myself on a sandy beach, close to the water-edge, in a place which I had never seen or been at till then, and, consequently, no friend or acquaintance likely to afford me any kind of succour; though it appeared, from the ship's books, that I had been ordered to the hospital, and left on board through the mistake or negligence of those persons to whom such things were entrusted, as all the clothes I had on was a jacket, shirt, and a pair of trowsers, bestowed on me by a messmate, while on board the Advice, having neither stockings, shoes, hat, cap, or even a single penny in my pocket to purchase food in that strange place; and, with respect to the changeable vicissitudes of life, a thing weak mortal beings seem wholly unable to comprehend, yet my whole frame of mind has, since that time, been filled with most thankful gratitude to the heavenly powers above, for thus conducting me to the very spot where immediate relief was so appointed to be given by those of whom I had formed no idea, or even expected any thing of the kind to have been so freely granted, without applying for, which, truly, was the case; for, being wholly insensible of the proper direction where the most inhabited parts lay, I stood erect, listening to various kinds of voices, seemingly employed at some kind of work or other, but too distant from the place for me to understand a single word they said, yet thought fit to walk slowly on, carefully placing my feet step by step on the sand, for want of a stick to enable me therewith to examine the bottom, and, with the help of it go more freely on, which the person so employed happening to observe, without perceiving the unhappy state of darkness I was in, and mistaking my slow way of moving to the effect of liquor, said my good friend, take care, or you will be in the pot of hot boiling pitch; on hearing which I stopped without moving another foot, till he had discovered my real situation; when I heard him say, how came you here in that unhappy situation; with some bum-boat women, (replied I,) who have just landed me here from the Advice, in their way to Portsmouth-point. I see the boat making for the Point side, (said he;) but do you mean the Advice, of 50 guns, so lately returned from the West Indies? Yes, the very same ship, (replied I.) That is very well said; and, if you will sit down upon this log of wood, and wait till I have finished coating the bottom of this boat, you shall sleep with me to night, and be conveyed on board the Torbay, where the crew of the Advice are going to receive their wages to morrow. Now this most friendly, but unsolicited, humane offer, was of too gratifying a nature to be declined by a person in my then situation, as he did not only perform such promise of furnishing me with a bed, but also with a good supper, at his own house, near the Two Loggerheads, in Gosport, and afterwards carried me to the Torbay, with two or three other people, in the course of the following morning, where, being well-known to the people of the Advice, who freely entered into discourse with me, in the presence of that most worthy commander, commodore Kepple, who, on perceiving the natural cause of my unhappy misfortune, from hearing something of the manner in which it came, thought fit to humanely recommend me to the people of the Advice, as they came from the pay-table; ever since which I have revered him with uncommon esteem and gratitude, as well as thankful to all the people at that time belonging to the Advice, from whom I so happily received such kind and seasonable relief, as to be therewith enabled to most thankfully return with Mr. Fleming, that being the name of my truly worthy friend, the waterman of Gosport, under whose most hospitable roof I was likewise enabled to have necessary aid in procuring such articles of apparel, as appeared necessary for my journey to London, and was conveyed to Portsmouth-point in his own boat, and so on to the waggon by himself, in person, who saw me up, and the wheels in motion, before he took leave, in order to return back again. And here I have to give some account of a most strange and remarkable kind of dream, which I had experienced, while under the roof of my aforesaid friend, the very night before we parted from each other, wherein I thought myself placed, at full length, on a quantity of floating rubbish, consisting of various sorts of grass, rushes, and broken boughs of trees, intermixed with numerous prickly thorns, and confined together by nothing more than brambles, whereon I seemed to be greatly afraid of slipping through, into a kind of muddy water, resembling an open sea, appearing so extensive, that I could neither see the end nor side of it, though floating on the rubbish, which seemed to have been driven from the land by some heavy storm of rain or other, and collected there together from the mouth of some long, wide, and open, river, whereon I seemed to lie stretched out in very great pain, from sharp thorns penetrating through my clothes, yet dared not move from the spot, through fear of perishing in the muddy water underneath, while lying on that painful sort of couch, driving along to whatsoever place the wind and tide might carry it, continually wishing for the sight of land, but without venturing to stand up, or look about, through fear of slipping through; and I seemed to continue in that wretched situation for some hours together, till released therefrom, as I thought, by the rubbish grounding fast on a lee shore; when venturing to rise up, in order to get hold of a smooth bow, therewith intending to push away the rest; instead of so doing, I seemed to unluckily slip through to the bottom, where, standing arm-pit deep, with my back to the land, stretching out both arms over the prickly thorns and brambles on each side, devising how to extricate myself therefrom; and, while in that perplexing situation, seemed to feel the rubbish loosening from behind, and, on facing about, was most unexpectedly surprised with the sight of a beautiful young female, looking affable, mild, and agreeable, with both eyes earnestly fixed on me, while visibly employed hooking away the rubbish with a long stick, appearing so intensely bent on extricating me therefrom, as to have got the bottom of her own clothes entangled with the brambles, through venturing into the surf, which, having observed, and thinking myself able to clear away the rest, I hastily strung next through, and, having assisted in extricating her clothes from the brambles, wherewith they had been surrounded, she seemed to move gently up the rising ground, discoursing with equally as much pleasure and satisfaction to each other as if we had been trained up in one and the same place together, till seeming to arrive at the summit of a bank, wherefrom the most extensive and delightful prospect, ever seen by the eyes of man, came open to our view, whereon seemed to lie many elegant roads, as though branching from each other in various directions, as though for most noble large and elegant cities, towns, and villages, containing magnificent structures, (meaning churches,) with lofty steeples, palaces, castles, and other high buildings, in our sight, as, also, many beautiful lawns, fields, and country seats, as though surrounded with rural groves and evergreens, suitable enough to amuse contemplative people in their solitude; most part of which, likewise, seemed to be well stocked with the feathered creation, as also with much cattle, sheep, horses, and the like, which, while observing and discoursing on the magnificent scene, till partly satisfied with gratifying our eyes thereon, we left that topic of discourse by changing therefrom to our own concerns, of inquiring after the residence of each other, as strangers newly met together usually do, with respect to the distance and road each of us had to go, both of which seemed very long; yet, proving to one and the same point, we jointly agreed to aid, assist, and accompany, each other to the very end of it; and, with such intent, apparently descending from the bank to the rampart way, whereon we did not seem to have gone far, by the time I awoke from that most strange, uncommon, and remarkable kind of dream, wherewith my thoughts were deeply engaged, from time to time, throughout most part of the road to London, by generally comparing those sharp-pointed thorns and prickly brambles, holding them together, to a like number of painful difficulties which I had most likely had to undergo, and ought patiently to submit to, in order to avoid something worse; namely, that of slipping through the rubbish into the muddy water underneath, at such time compared to the unavoidable suit of law I was then about to undertake without being able to foresee any end or side of it, through the want of money, friends, or proper resources to go on with the suit; yet, notwithstanding these various obstacles to the business so frequently crowding into my thoughts, yet the affable young female who I had so visibly observed, voluntarily assisting at the time of my deliverance from the brambles, being viewed in the light of one truly assigned to become my bosom friend through life, by the heavenly powers above, whereto, recommending my future peace, and imploring sufficient 1 from thence, in order to fortify and support my bodily strength and mind with spirits enough to manage the concern in such a steady manner as not to decline the same till I had been rewarded with the affable young female in the end, as it was out of my power to foresee what future blessings kind Providence might have in store for me. For who could foretel, but that most delightful and extensive prospect, so lately exposed to my view, might forebode unexpected pleasures in this mortal state of life which I could not foresee, though seeming to connect with the great plenty that I constantly enjoyed while sleeping, in the height of my distress, on board the ship, thereby inducing me to place much confidence therein, and likewise hope for better days, whereto I was again strengthened and encouraged to increase my hope with comparing it to those remarkable dreams which I formerly had, and experimentally found come to pass, particularly those I so unexpectedly experienced in Lancashire, and took so little notice of, previous to the time of quitting that most delightful prospect with which the unhappy situation I laboured under had rendered me wholly unable to regain. And as Almighty God, our heavenly Father, had thought fit to bring about the change, it was become my duty to most thankfully submit to his holy will and pleasure, by cautiously endeavouring to patiently go through all those future events that might be assigned to my lot; from thence, and in that state of mind, I, according to information obtained from the people on board of the Advice, called on Mr. Collins, at the Paul's Head, in Doctors Commons, where, on finding myself in great want of cash, through the frequent expenses I was so unavoidably at, soon reduced me to the painful necessity of applying to the Lancashire gentlemen, and assisted therein by a person, who, having only his own interest in view, as appeared from that of his slyly collecting money from the Lancashire families in my name, and converting the same, for a considerable time, to his own use, previous to that of being discovered; yet, did not cause such inquiry to follow as might have reasonably been expected, through inducing me to apply to the shipwrights, conducted by such poor people as I could prevail on to go with me, from one yard to another, amongst whom a person, frequenting the halfpenny and penny book trade, happening to become one of those guides and instructors, at length prevailed on me to publish a ditty, heretofore mentioned in my narrative, the sale whereof was the cause of drawing crowds of people round me. I then had, and still have, reason to believe proved the chief cause of forcing me to sign a release that was followed by the printing of my narrative, without knowing how to sell or vend the same, till instructed therein by a sly underhand person, who engaged to conduct me on a regular journey through Portsmouth and the Isle of White to Southampton, where the designing views of this vile wretch became ripe for execution, and were actually put in force while on our way from thence to Winchester, some few days after, through pretending to have been taken suddenly ill, and prevailed on me to become seated on a low bank, close to the road side, from whence a bag of halfpence, raised by selling books on the journey, and easily carried on my back, then lying on the grass, was slyly carried off by this hardhearted wretch of a guide, and I left there, without any one to conduct me from off the open common; and here I found great reason to become truly thankful to Almighty God, our heavenly Father, whose divine goodness and mercy, in producing good from the evil designs of weak mortals, being visibly displayed in my favour, as the former deception, experienced in London, put me on a proper guard against future dangers, inducing me to deposit what trifling sum I had raised from the sale of those ditties, or otherwise, in the hands of a friend, near Cheapside, before we set off; and that taken on the road elsewhere, except the bag of halfpence, which was supposed to contain all I had: and finding myself alone, I rose up, and getting into the horse-track, continued stumbling slowly on, between two low banks, made so by the feet of horses and narrow wheel carriages, for some considerable time, till happening to get near middle leg deep, in a dirty hole, where, slipping on one side, I fell down, in the sight of a working man, who happened to be following on the same road, and, on coming up, humanely conducted me five or six miles from thence to the city of Winchester, without fee or reward, and there left me with a civilized publican, under whose roof I was comfortably succoured till the next day, when, passing through the street from thence, with a box, intending to go to London by the coach, I happened to be, unexpectedly, accosted by an old acquaintance, from Wiggan, then residing in Winchester, who being surprised thereat, and pitying my unhappy condition, sent the boy home, at the same time offered to conduct me personally to the coach inn himself, as it was not far beyond the house of a customer he had to call on by the way, and his friendly offer being accepted of, he had no sooner come into the house of such customer than a young woman was observed sitting in front, with a bundle on her lap, intending for London by the same coach, and observed by several of her own sex, then present, as well as my townsman, to have cautiously surveyed us both, from the first moment of our having come into the house, without taking her eyes off, till the cause of my journey to London had been explained and made known to all present, when the situation of that young female happening to come up in discourse, it appeared that she had been lately recommended from her mistress, with whom she had lived for some time, in Plow-court, Fetter-lane, to a lady in Winchester, with intent of her supplying the place of a favourite servant, at that time on the point of marriage, which happened, by some means or other, to be broken off; and the favourite continuing in her place, this young woman had prepared to go back to her late mistress, in Fetter-lane.

I possessed little more cash than was barely sufficient to defray the expense of coach-hire, which a genteel woman then present observing, and hearing of the loss I had lately sustained on the road, thereby supposing me to be still more embarrassed with respect to money-matters, strongly advised us to go on foot, as a protection to each other by the way; in which case, what we had would be more than sufficient for the purpose; and all present observing me to appear very agreeable thereto, the young woman seemed to approve thereof: my townsman, in particular, passing many encomiums on my late situation in Wiggan, without giving up his point, till she had, agreeably to the advice and approbation of those present, consented thereto; and we, after taking leave, set off together for Alresford, near about seven miles from Winchester; where, going into a public house, close by the road side, for refreshment, a coach drew up to the door soon after, with a driver on the box, inquiring for return passengers for London, who soon agreed to carry us, at the rate of five shillings apiece: we got up without delay, and were set down near the end of Leather-lane, Holborn, about three o'clock in the afternoon of the following day, distance, full sixty miles from Alresford, which said convenient lift afforded me a good opportunity of entertaining her with a proper account of my Gosport dream, particularly that part wherein I seemed to behold such a most agreeable young female, busily employed with endeavouring to remove the prickly thorns from behind my back, and thereby enabling me to extricate myself from the danger with which I seemed to have been so greatly exposed; as also, that of discoursing about the long journey we had to go, while on the summit of the bank, and there agreeing to accompany each other to the very end of it, hoping she would turn out to be the very identical female so visibly sent to my view in that remarkable dream, and thereby condescend to become my bosom friend through life; which, perceiving to have been duly attended to, while hearing, a favourable word or two dropped from her lips concerning it, which encouraged me to express a desire of being introduced to her mistress, then residing in Plow-court, Fetter-lane, whom I prevailed on to accept of me as a lodger, though not till she had inquired after my character and behaviour from Mr. Collings, with whom I had formerly boarded some months, and continued residing with her from the latter end of December, 1758, till the beginning of February, 1759; and, at that time, entering into a conjugal state, continued with her mistress till the beginning of May following, when our long travels first began to commence, by setting out on a journey from thence for Plymouth, by way of Bristol and Exeter, and returning through Launceston, Barnstaple, and Bideford to Ilfracomb, where, embarking for Bristol, and arriving there on the following day, we set off, ere long, from thence again, and continued pursuing our intended journey through the cities of Gloucester and Worcester to Birmingham, where my spouse was delivered of a daughter, who not living more than a fortnight or three weeks, we set off from thence about the latter end of February, 1760; continuing our route by way of Derby, Nottingham, and Lincoln, to Boston, where, having settled matters with two trustees, concerning a small legacy which had been left to my spouse by her father, we spent an agreeable ten or twelve days with her brother and sister; then, taking leave, returned through Peterborough, Cambridge, and Ware, to London, where, receiving the legacy near about a month or six weeks after, that, with the income arising from my pension, and some trifle more, acquired by selling books, with the help of which, when put together, and duly considered, was deemed nearly, if not quite, sufficient enough to put us into a small public house, whereat I might, probably, become useful in some shape or other, which was the real summit of our desires at such time, through believing ourselves more able to manage that kind of employ than any other, but to settle in Wiggan, or Boston, was undetermined; a post-letter was, therefore, despatched to my father, desiring to know how my relations stood affected, with respect to that of our engaging in a public house in Wiggan; and received for answer, that he had little or no doubt of our meeting with luck and success, as all parties seemed to rejoice at hearing of our being likely to come and reside with them; and concluded with saying, that a younger sister of mine, for whom I had no small regard, took a journey to Bristol, in search of me, near one year back, and, not succeeding therein, went to service, where she married a ship-joiner, and was then living with her husband, on St. Augustine's Bank, expressing a strong desire of seeing me in every letter which she wrote; therefore concluded a request, with begging us to call on her before we came to Wiggan; and this unexpected news changed our former design of going to Wiggan, as was intended, for a direct journey to Bristol, whereupon, finding the young couple, and enjoying their company for some days, we became prevailed on to go and reside with them in a house near Larford's Gate, which then belonged to my brother-in-law, and had stood empty for some years, through a false report of its having been haunted by the ghost of a miserly tradesman that formerly died there, and proved lucky enough to retrieve the credit of such house, as appeared from that of a good tenant coming into it about three months after; during the interval of which said time, we also became prevailed on to sell my pamphlet in Bristol, a thing never intended to have been done, till advised and persuaded to it by them; however, we had not been many days employed thereat, till I was arrested in the public street, for a debt of five pounds, at the suit of a poor woman, charging me therewith for writing letters, though she was regularly paid for them at the time she wrote them, which, consequently, induced me to bail the action, with intent to stand trial; till finding that Mrs. Wabshutt had been the sole contriver of it, and would stick at nothing to make the same appear as a legal debt, which, coming to the ears of my sister, she, for a trifling part of that sum, got a release from her; however, matters did not end there, as I was, in a few weeks after, summoned to appear before a committee, at the Merchants Hall, concerning my pension, which, having duly obeyed, I was there accused of having, according to their express words, published a false book, in order to expose the character of two innocent people, meaning Wabshutt and the doctor; to which I replied, saying: That I had published a book, but it was the truth. Then two papers were produced by a person, saying: There were two affidavits to prove it false. On hearing which, I desired to know, by whom; and where they were attested? He said, by Charles Cooper and Peter Bates, in the city of Bristol. I then desired to hear them read; when a paragraph in that of Peter Bates's was audibly read out accordingly; which, on hearing, I well knew to be entirely false; and quickly answered, That Peter Bates was not on board the vessel, but at the factory, thirty miles off, when that affair happened, and could not in justice swear thereto: but my words had little or no effect; for I was given to understand, that my pay was suspended till such time as I should behave better; whereupon I withdrew, saying: God had set me to work, and he would see me righted; which, to the best of my recollection, happened to occur on or about the 20th of December, 1760, thereby frustrating and putting an end to our future designs of going to settle in Wiggan; which I could not think of doing till the mistake had been explained, and my pension restored by the worthy committee, as, at such time, I began to suppose and believe that my friend in London had formerly deserted me, from having heard and given credit to the contents of those false papers: then recollecting having frequently heard others say, that I was reputed to have been as great a villain as ever crossed salt water, by those same worthy gentlemen, from whom I had previously received various friendly marks of goodwill and esteem, and I became likewise desirous of convincing them concerning the contents of those false papers. Then, applying for copies thereof on the following day, and having such my request absolutely refused, I resolved on having the deception thereof explained by some means or other; though, on finding myself unable to do it in Bristol, we, so far from giving up the point, took leave of our friends, and, instead of going to Wiggan, set off on the way back for London, fully bent on continuing to sell books, till sufficient evidence enough could be found to prove the falsity of those spurious affidavits, even to the satisfaction of every individual person concerned; for this reason alone I then really wished to have copies of them in my own possession, from thinking it would enable me to clear up the point much better with them than without them, as I could then produce them in the presence of my shipmates, whom I hoped to bring forward as real evidence to confute the false statement contained therein; and, luckily, hit on a plan that completely answered my desire; for, on arriving in London, I applied to a suitable person who, on hearing the same, and approving thereof some time after, wrote to a leading gentleman in Bristol, which said letter I, for my own satisfaction, put in the post myself, and is as follows: " Sir, on Tuesday I was directed to write to you by several gentlemen, at the Salutation Tavern, in Newgate-market, concerning of Robert Barker, whose parents I formerly knew. He has laid a deplorable case before me; and I thought proper to recommend him to several gentlemen, who raised him a large contribution, which is likely to be continued, if not interrupted by you, and himself proved an impostor. The reason of my writing to you is, because prosecution was proposed, and likely to take place, if not interrupted by you; therefore, I should be glad if you will give me a line, by return of post, in regard to his sufferings, false imprisonments, and what you know concerning him; and this favour will oblige your humble servant, W. M.

P.S. Please to direct to S. and M. Fleet-street, London."

Mr. M. received an answer, as desired, which is as follows: " Mr. W. M. Sir, in answer to your letter, of the 19th instant, Robert Barker sailed in a ship, to the coast of Africa, in which I was concerned; but I had not the direction of the voyage, which prevents my giving you such particulars about his behaviour as you desire; and the person who had the management is gone into Cornwall and will not return till next week, when I shall desire him to send you a short narrative of his behaviour, which I have often heard was very bad; and, if I am not deceived, there are some affidavits about it: and, for this Barker to publish a libel against the captain, after his decease, shews that he imposes on the public. I am, Sir, your most humble servant, J. L.

On having heard the above letter read, my hopes of obtaining copies of those affidavits so much increased, that I prevailed on Mr. M. to write again, as follows: Sir, Yours of the 21st of December came to hand, for which I return you mine, and the thanks of the gentlemen who desired me to write to you. Several of the gentlemen, as well as myself, are satisfied, from what you say, that the lamentable story, which Robert Barker relates, is without foundation, and a falsity caculated to impose on those who think it not worth while to make inquiry into the truth of it; and, that our suspicions of it are well grounded. You were so kind as to promise one of the gentlemen, who had the direction of the voyage, to send us a short narrative of Barker's behaviour; and you mentioned, likewise, some affidavits relating to the affair: as to the narrative you promised, with copies of some account of them, would effectually convince the gentlemen of Barker's imposition; and, I dare say, totally silence him; and would, no doubt, rid you of farther inquiries from numbers of people in these

parts, as well as in Lancashire. I am requested to remind you of your promise, and to beg the favour of you to send up the promised narrative; and, if not too much trouble, copies or extracts of those affidavits; and, for the sake of detecting an impostor, we are in hopes you will not think it an unreasonable request in, Sir, your very humble servant,
W. M.
London, 9th February, 1761.

To this letter we received the two following, No. 4 and 5.—No. 4. Sir, In answer to your favour of the 9th instant, Mr. B. who had the direction for the Thetis, is returned from Cornwall, and to whom I have shewn your two letters, and my answer to the first; and, he says: I have quoted nothing but the truth, and he will confirm the same to you next week, with abstracts or originals of the affidavits made, by which it will appear that Barker has imposed on the public. I am, Sir, your most humble servant, J. L.

No. 5.—Bristol, February the 12th, 1761. Sir, I had the pleasure of seeing the two letters you sent to alderman L. concerning Robert Barker, that pirate. The reason the villain was not hanged, at Antigua, was, because the judge of the admiralty died. The affidavits of the men against him shall be published, to the satisfaction of my unfortunate husband's friends, as soon as Mr. B. arrives home from Cornwall. The doctor that was then with my husband, at Antigua, is expected home from thence every day, and you shall have his affidavit then. I hope it will be in my power to take him up; and I shall think it a pleasure to follow the villain to Execution-dock. I esteem you as my friend, unknown, and am, Sir, your humble servant, ANN WAPSHUTT.

P.S. All the satisfaction the merchants of Bristol could give me they did, by taking three shillings and sixpence per week from him, which he used to have paid out of the seamen's hospital.

By the contents of this letter, Mrs. Wapshutt seems to have exerted all her interest and abilities in getting my pay suspended; and, whether it so happened, or otherwise, I had nothing more in view but that of convincing the worthy committee concerning my own innocence, and, in so doing, obtain a renewal of my pay, without giving offence to any individual whatever, unless writing for the affidavits, as previously described, might be deemed as such, though internally affected by my own conscience while doing that I really wished to avoid, in case of having been able to obtain them by any other means.

Printed by Galabin and Marchant, Ingram-court, Fenchurch-street, London.

No. 7, Barker's Genuine Life.

This is an exact representation of ROBERT BARKER's most wonderful Dream, concerning very material things of the highest importance.

NO. VII.

And now Mr. M. becoming anxious to see the papers, he, in order to get their promise fulfilled, wrote the following letter to Mrs. Wapshutt.

No. 6.—Mrs. Wapshutt, London, Feb. 23, 1761, I received your letter, concerning Robert Barker, and am ordered to inform you that nothing now remains, in order to put an entire stop to his complaints against your late husband, but for Mr. L. to send up copies of the affidavits, according to his repeated promise, and which, I suppose, a multiplicity of business has prevented: if these affidavits confirm what you write, you need not fear but that strict justice shall be done to Barker, who has not been seen by any of the gentlemen inquiring into the affair for more than six weeks past. I am, madam, your very humble servant, W. M.

This letter had been sent about ten days, when the following came to hand. No. 7.—Bristol, March 4, 1761. Mr. W. M. Sir, you have herewith Mr. Blake's narrative, about Robert Barker, together with sundry copies of affidavits of his behaviour, which must convince every body that he has imposed on the public; and I should be glad that the whole proceedings were properly digested and printed. I am, Sir, your most humble servant, J. L.

With this letter came a bundle of papers sufficient to make a volume, and likewise have prejudiced any unsuspecting person in Wapshutt's favour; which, having heard, I became truly sensible of; and finding the loss of both friends and income to have originated therefrom, I became the more desirous of convincing the worthy committee and others concerning the entire falsity thereof, by giving evidence, through which I might regain their former good-will and esteem as usual. Mr. M. however, seemed to think otherwise, as appeared from his own lips, saying: that none of my shipmates were then to be found, that I knew of; and without whose personal presence all I could do would be useless; then advised me to publish the whole of those papers, agreeable to the express words of Mr. J. L. with his remarks thereon; as the many contradictions and impossibilities contained therein, were, according to his idea, sufficient to convince every disinterested person concerning the sly, cruel, and underhand, proceedings of Wapshutt; that being, in his opinion, the best and readiest way of terminating such intricate business; still continuing in the same mind while writing his remarks, and despatching a letter concerning his opinion therein to Bristol, though opposed and disapproved of by me, he persisted in sending it off, and receiving a disagreeable answer, various unpleasant letters passed, to and again, between the corresponding parties, which seemed to me as though far more detrimental than useful to the point I had in view, and for such reason declined publishing the papers, agreeably to his desire, yet he continued frequently pressing us thereto; and, at length proposed letting us have the perusal of a most valuable work; saying, it would open our understanding, and enable us to pursue every thing to the best advantage, thereby encouraging us to thankfully accept the offer made, in hopes of finding such promised book answerable to the many encomiums that dropped from his lips concerning it: however, instead of finding ourselves edified by the perusal thereof, the contents of five or six pages threw us into the utmost distress and confusion of mind, through finding the manner in which we had been trained up to believe the only and true right way to salvation grossly mishandled, ridiculed, and contradicted, as though entirely folly and untrue, in such a smooth style of language as, with all our temporal genius, we could not then disprove, and verily believe that, while in that confusion of mind, those volumes would have been cast into the flames, if the papers I could not do without had not still remained in the hands of Mr. M. we, therefore, on due consideration, agreed to get them into our own possession the first convenient opportunity that offered, and soon found that it was impossible to be done, without first discoursing with him concerning the volumes lately borrowed, the contents whereof he seemed to believe and approve, as appeared from that of his steadily defending the whole in such a manner as to thereby convince us, that all we could say or do to the contrary would be of little or no avail, through hearing him go on with philosophical words, and language far above the reach of our abilities to comprehend the meaning of; and concluded with telling us, that no sensible people would ever presume to condemn such a valuable composition, wherein a most able writer had taken so much pains to promote their own interest as he had done, without first acquainting themselves with its contents throughout, which he absolutely expected us to have done at the time of putting the same into our hands, from well knowing that we should get far better through life with than without perusing it, therefore advised us to begin, as, by steadily attending thereto, we should find our own beneficial advantage arising therefrom in the end; then terminating the point, withdrew greatly affected with such additional confusion of mind as could not be removed till our rational faculties returned some time after; and then, perceiving our own weak abilities wholly insufficient to terminate a point whereon our future peace of mind, and everlasting happiness, both here and after, solely depended; then, addressing ourselves to the supreme powers above, in prayer, most humbly imploring the necessary aid and assistance of Almighty God, our heavenly Father, hoping that he, out of his infinite goodness and mercy, would enable us to judge right concerning the truth or falsity of those volumes, and that we might not be led astray from our sacred duty to him by them, or any other kind of deception whatever, as our disordered mind did not appear likely to become settled without understanding their contents properly, which induced us to read them attentively through, which having been at length done, we returned them to the rightful owner, saying: they had been attentively read, as desired, without being credited; neither would I consent to publish the papers with his remarks thereon, which he having after duly attended to, appeared displeased, at the same time expressed a wish to have them printed; and whether he had put those volumes into our hands with a view of inducing me to publish those papers, or otherwise, I cannot justly say, though true it is, that he had, through being a native of the adjoining parish to Wiggan, freely offered to transact the business for us without fee or reward; and then, finding him to expect payment for it, I begged to have his bill, which being quickly made out, to the amount of fourteen pounds, ten shillings, I offered twelve pounds, in part of payment, saying: I would bring the remaining two pounds ten, after leaving the papers with my friend, near Cheapside, who had become desirous of perusing them over; but to this he objected; saying, he could not think of parting from the papers, through fear of burning his own fingers, as the gentlemen concerned were possessed of large property; he, nevertheless, on finding me unwilling to part from the money, without he let us have the copies, with his remarks, on promising to bring them back in a week or ten days; but, instead of that, we set off without them to Leeds, where, having arrived, we crossed the country to Wiggan, and, after enjoying the company of both relations and friends for some time, we returned into Yorkshire, and continued pursuing a circular route through Hull, Scarborough, Whitby, Stockton-upon-Tees, Sunderland, and Shields, to Newcastle-upon-Tyne, and so on from thence through

Alinwick, Berwick-upon-Twede, and Dunbar to Edinburgh, distant 337 miles from London, by the direct way, and stopping four or five months there, afforded us a convenient opportunity of seeing and hearing people carry loads on their shoulders, consisting of oysters, salt, potatoes, vegitables, and other necessary articles of consumption, which they cried for public sale, while moving up and down those open staircases; but not having the pleasure of viewing them myself I counted the steps, and frequently had customers dealing freely with us 160 steps high, in the Lawn Market, and Parliament Close, wherefrom some little idea may be formed concerning the height of those lofty, stone buildings, wherefrom we took another circular route, through the city of Glasgow, Dunbarton, Greenock, and Newport-Glasgow, to Paisley, and continued pursuing our route through Saltcoats, Invine, Ayr, and Kilmarnock, to Glasgow, and from thence we returned by way of Stirling, Perth, and Dumfries, into Burnt Island, and, thence crossing the water from Kinghorn ferry to Leith, we stopped a few days in Edinburgh, to rest from the fatigues of our late tour, and discoursing of the uncommon pains taken by all sorts and conditions of people in educating their own children, especially those of the very poorest, many of whom, from the best information we could obtain, as well as our own observations, continually persevered in sparing a halfpenny or a penny per day, from the small pittance of their day-labour, to pay for schooling, which seemed to have a good effect, as appeared from that of frequently hearing more or less of those poor children read my books tolerably well at an early period of life, and others express a desire of buying them, if not prevented through want of pence, which I seldom heard without painfully reflecting on the weak manner in which my own education had been neglected. And here it may not be amis to furnish the reader with some idea concerning a far diffcrent custom prevailing between the young people of Scotland and those of England, as the young women of the former, while going drest up to any place of amusement, or other, are usually seen walking along bare footed, carrying their stockings and shoes in a bundle, and ready and complacent enough to carry their male conductors over the brooks, or rivulets of water, on their backs; and only mention the circumstance, because my spouse, though not without a kind of surprize, frequently saw them do it, with far more apparent pleasure than pain, while moving along the Scotch roads. Then leaving the capital we set off for Dumfries and Carlisle, taking a circular route from thence through Wigton, Alingfort, Workington, Whitehaven, Cockermouth, and Daren, to Perth, situate upon the main road, 22 miles south of Carlisle, where, from the continual returning through Kendal, Lancaster, and Preston, to Wiggan, still wretched, and miserably perplexed in mind, concerning the great and important point of salvation: however, those dark, cloudy, vapours, wherein we had been so involved, began to clear up, while engaged in the company and conversation of relations and friends, through happily experiencing two remarkable foreboding dreams, wherein I thought myself walking in a pleasant meadow, near a long row of poplar trees, planted above the Warebridge, and pretty near the river side, meditating on the unhappy situation of mind wherewith I had so long struggled, and could not get the better of without Supreme assistance from above, for which I thought myself fervently praying; and, while looking up, seemed to behold my own mother approach with pleasure in her looks; saying, it is well to find you thus deeply engaged with imploring assistance from the heavenly powers above, which is alone able to give it; and if you continue persevering therein, doubt not but the same will be complied with ere long: then, with a very agreeable smile on her face, disappeared. And now this most seasonable, kind, and acceptable, dream began to increase my continual hope of being made wise, and able enough to expel those gloomy doubts and fears, caused by hearing the spurious volumes, heretofore mentioned, as read by my spouse, concerning the grace and mercy held out to earthly sinners in the everlasting Gospel of our immortal redeemer Jesus Christ, which was the earnest desire of my heart; and, before we left those parts, became favourably indulged with another dream, wherein I thought myself standing erect, in the open back-door of the Eagle and Child, meaning the head inn of Wiggan, observing my uncle Hooton approaching near from the yard, whose person I seemed to know very well; as also to recollect that he had been deceased many years; and, taking his appearance for a ghost, begged him to bless me, whereat he seemed to hold up both hands, as though in a kind of surprise; saying, read the ninth chapter of John, and the fourth verse, then instantaneously disappearing from my sight, and recollecting the same, it was read by my spouse the next day, which I heard with no small degree of pleasure and satisfaction, while considering it in the light of a supernatural, or foreboding, caution concerning my own situation of darkness, which I was so very anxiously desirous of having removed; and, from that time, became strongly imprest in mind with regular hopes of such a happy change taking place some time or other; but, with respect to a temporal or spiritual light, one or both, durst not presume to say, though certain it is, that, from such time, I became far more contented and happy in mind than what I had formerly been: then, visiting Liverpool, and other neighbouring towns, reluctantly separating from those relations and friends, I set off again through Derby, Leicester, and Stamford, to Boston, where, having spent a few days with our relations there, we took another circular route through Wisbeach, Lynn, Wells, and Cromer, to Yarmouth, wherefrom we returned back to London, by way of Norwich, Ipswich, Harwich, Colchester, and Chelmsford, and there quickly found that Mr. M. the person formerly employed by me, had departed this life, and been laid under ground some few days previous to that wherein we arrived in the capital, and, on hearing thereof applied to his widow, who, on receiving two pounds ten shillings, the balance of his account, freely delivered the original papers up into my own hands; however, on finding the gentlewoman with whom we had formerly resided, in Plow Court, Fetter

Lane, to have removed from thence, and left off housekeeping, we engaged an apartment in Union Court, facing St. Andrew's Church, Holborn, of Mrs. Carrington, and, during our stay of about 15 months, formed an acquaintance with Mr. Vigors, a very worthy person, at that time keeping two hackney-coaches, in Bleeding-Heart Yard, with whom we afterwards removed to the Hat and Ton, Hatton-Wall, Hatton-Garden, which he and his family kept many years after, one or more of them being still living near it, in very good repute, continuing their friendly good-will and esteem for us to this very day; and, near about that time, I received no small consolation of mind from another most wonderful and very intelligible kind of dream, wherein I thought myself bewildered and lost, with my spouse, on a large open plain, by moonlight, wholly unable to see either hedge, tree, bush, or any thing whatever, except many sheep grasing and lying scattered here and there, as we continued moving too and again, some hours together, wishing for day-light, which at length appearing, we seemed to behold a few low shrubs and bushes at a considerable distance from us, on a rising hill from behind, which the light seemed to increase as we approached the top; and the sun, on our arrival there, appeared just rising at the horizon edge wherefrom we seemed to behold a very wide, rough, and crazy, road, as if made so through the traveling of cattle during winter, but leading to a narrow pass, enclosed on each side by thick hedges, and a quantity of high trees appearing at some considerable distance from thence, in front of a beautiful white building, visibly perceived through the leaves and branches, whereto we agreed to go, in hopes of obtaing refreshment, which we seemed to be in great need of. And here it may not be improper to mention one thing; namely, that of my sight always appearing clear and bright, while enjoying those happy dreams, as ever it was during the early period of my life; and, returning to the subject, we seemed to continue making for the narrow pass, and struggling on between the close thick hedges, till got pretty near the front of the building, where my spouse turned back in a fright, from first perceiving a monstrous kind of gigantic fiend, with a huge club on his shoulder, standing at one side, as though ready to oppose our entrance at the open door appearing in sight, which I, on observing it to be at no great distance from us, resolved to venture, notwithstanding the danger of his club; and, while edging close, to avoid the weight of that, I perceived him chained fast to a tree behind, and his grimly face so nearly resembled the looks of that ugly fiend on whose back I had formerly been forced up into the air, from the yard of my parents, yet now passed safe through the door into a far more delightful and beautiful structure that ever my eyes had beheld till then; appearing exactly four square, in height, breadth, and length, seemingly 100 yards or more, without any windows that I could perceive, though light and clear as the brightest sunny day ever beheld out of doors, having no manner of beams or pillars to support a flat roof, appearing no less white than the driven snow, in like manner as did all the walls every where, except the floor below, which seemed covered with short grass, resembling a very level kind of bowling-green, as, also, a most beautiful spreading vine running up on each side the wall and over the door, which, while admiring with a rapturous kind of delight, I seemed to hear my own name distinctly called from behind, when turning about to the sound, clearly observed a plain-dressed person standing erect at the most distant corner, in a door-way open, beckoning me to approach, which having quickly obeyed, he, with great pleasure in his looks, gave a paper into my hand and withdrew, whereon appeared my own name at full length, and, on turning up the other side, read as follows. behold the words of truth are now in the hands of thy wife; then turning towards the door, seemed to behold her entering thereat, with something in her hand, which, being eager to know the meaning of, I hastened to meet her, and happily found it to prove the Old and New Testament, which enlightening favour, obtained from above, enabled me to view those spurious volumes, which had given so much uneasiness, in their true light; and, on having awoke therefrom, I began to greatly wonder, and devise how any individual possessing those elegant talents could reasonably think of employing them in such a weak manner as it did and still appears to me. that none can judge right concerning the great and important point of salvation, unless through being enlightened therein from above, concerning those weighty events being wholly reserved for the decision of Almighty God. our heavenly father, alone, to bestow on all such as wish to earnestly receive and enjoy so great a blessing from thence.

And now, with respect to worldly concerns, those routes we had taken, through so many port-towns of Great Britain, with intent to discover more or less of my shipmates therein to no manner of purpose, induced us to carefully inspect the streets, courts, alleys, and passages, of Wapping, Rotherhithe, Deptford, and Greenwich, without finding any of them, except Peter Bates, who being prevailed on to accompany us into a public house, where we produced his affidavits, he positively denied ever having signed the same, and gave it from under his hand, in writing, before two reputable tradesmen, who likewise thought fit to sign the paper as legal witnesses thereto: and such like deception will appear fully cleared up by himself in a different part of this work; for, considering myself as in want of much better proof, he agreed to search for more shipmates in the port-towns of Kent, without success, and, while so doing, I experienced another remarkable dream, no less intelligible than the former, wherein I thought myself in London, holding the chamber-door of Mr. M. half open with my hand, observing him in a pensive mood, leaning his head on his hand, as though perusing those favourite volumes, which seemed to lye open upon the table before him, whereat I drew back, and, while endeavouring to gently pull to the door, observed him raise up his head hastily, saying: hold, hold, one word more and then I have done for ever; which, having duly attended to, I seemed to distinctly hear him go on, saying: now do I know that the son of God liveth; then both he and his favourite volumes seemed to quickly dissolve into a kind of smoky vapour, wherewith the room became so very much filled that I could neither perceive him, chair, table, or window, near which he had set, and truly mention it here in order to shew the uncommon impression made on my earthly frame of mind, from hearing those spurious volumes read, which, without the merciful interposition of kind Providence, as above, might have, probably, continued through life; and hope it will caution all others against believing in works of this kind, or suffering themselves to be led astray through the smooth style of language therein contained, as weak mortals here below may happen to neglect or forget the necessary duty of imploring aid and assistance from the supreme powers above, concerning their own everlasting peace and salvation, so freely offered to all mortal sinners, through the grace and mercy of our immortal Redeemer Jesus Christ, which those able writers, without even knowing how properly to understand or judge right, yet weakly pretend to deny, though none but such as confide wholly in wealth, money, or riches, can either approve or believe what they write. And now recollecting that one or more of my shipmates were from Ireland, we set out for the city of Chester, and thence to Liverpool, then embarking for Dublin, arrived there in fifteen or sixteen hours, and continued spending eight or nine months very agreeably, with a cabinet-maker, fronting the Liffy, on Temple Bar, while carefully searching every street, court, ally, and passage, for them in like manner as we had in London, but without success, yet received no small pleasure in finding all sorts and conditions of people residing in that elegant large capital, which, from the best ideas we could form thereof, seemed to contain near about 15,000 houses, the inhabitants behaving no less friendly, kind, and humane, than others residing in those beautiful ports, cities, and towns, through which we had formerly passed, and at length set off for the city of Cork, through Carlow, Kilkenny, Waterford, Carrick on Sure, and Clonmell, distance 111 miles from Dublin, by the direct way, and thence visiting Cove, Cove-passage, Kinsale, Bandon, New Town, Youghall, Dungarvon, and other neighbouring towns, we returned by way of St. Mallow to Limeric, distance about 33 miles from Cork, and there experienced another remarkable dream, wherein I thought myself on the banks of the river Vernew, in South Wales, just over against the spot whereon the antient castle of Mathravel once stood, viewing the clear purling streams trickle down between those rocks, in various directions, on a most delightful summer's day, close by deep water at their foot, made so by weighty falls coming down from above into it; then looking back, seemed to behold two very agreeable looking men, if not superior kind of beings, gently approaching, who, on drawing near, while viewing me with great pleasure in their looks, and pointing at the water, mildly said: wilt thou go in here and swim; then turning about, walked gently off between a large antient building on the left, and a close blooming hedge on the right, as though making for that very spot whereon I had formerly assisted Mr. Harwood in building a large barge for David Morgan, just above those rocks, and frequently reflecting thereon, without being able to comprehend the meaning of this dream, unless it was for me to acquaint the people with some particulars of those material dreams which I had so recently experienced; and how that could be done, without words, language, and abilities, suitable thereto, could not tell, from well knowing myself wholly deficient therein. yet frequently continued musing on it while on our way back through the silver mines of Rosgray and Kildare, for Dublin, distance near about an hundred miles from Limeric, and so on our intended journey to the north, from thence by way of Drogheda, Dondalk, Newry, Down Patrick, and Lisbon, to Belfast, wherefrom we made a kind of circular route, through Carrickfergus, Larn, Antrim, Ballymena, Ballymoney, and Colerain, to Londonderry, situate near about 120 miles from Dublin, by the nearest way, and thence continued through Straban, Omagh, and other small towns, to Sligo, lying in the north west corner of Ireland, about 150 miles from Dublin, and returned from thence by way of Hamilton, Inniskilling, Armagh, and Lurgan, to Newry, where, being stopped some days, waiting for a passage from thence to South Wales, in a sloop belonging to Captain Jones, at that time lying some few miles below Newry, which afforded us a convenient opportunity of making some few necessary remarks concerning the customary ways then prevailing amongst the inhabitants of those parts through which we had so lately past, whose friendly, kind, and humane, behaviour seemed to nearly resemble those of Dublin; and what surprised us considerably was, that of finding immense numbers of poor people residing in low thatched cabins, near the road side, with near about half an acre of land, more or less, annexed, and allowed rent free by the land-holder to grow potatoes for the regular consumption of themselves and families, some keeping a pig, and others two, running tame about the cabins, like as many dogs, feeding on the potato peelings, when thrown from the table; while many others, having no pigs at all, appeared scarcely able to obtain butter-milk or salt to their potatoes, yet, notwithstanding their low situation, some were ready and willing enough to follow the example generally set by their superiors, as appeared from that of freely offering part of what they had to us, or other strangers coming in; nay, so far was the general system of humanity practised amongst them, as, from the best information we could obtain, all ranks cautiously endeavoured to avoid persecuting those poor people for trifling offences, when discovered to have proceeded from extreme want; and, if all we heard concerning it be true, very reputable tradesmen had been known to have so far gained the displeasure of the neighbourhood wherein they resided, through persisting in so doing, being, in consequence thereof, obliged to withdraw, for want of trade, in order to seek customers elsewhere, and is here only mentioned from hearsay alone, as we never stopped long enough in one place to personally know any thing of the kind having happened; and, with respect to the public roads, it was a kind of rarity for us to either hear or see any waggons, or other heavily-laden carriages, moving thereon, as most part of their merchandise and other luggage was easily conveyed from place to place by single horses, on small cars, with the shafts coming nearly up to their fore shoulders, having two low wheels, resembling those of wheel-barrows, moving round with the axletree behind, whereon they usually dragged from two or three to six or seven hundred weight, from side to side, in every direction, which made those roads very smooth and level to walk on, a thing no less agreeable to us than others, during our travels through those parts: however, the vessel being at length ready for sailing, we embarked at Port Rush, some few miles below Newry, having only to add a word or two concerning the measured miles of those parts, four of them being, agreeably to the best observation we could make thereof, nearly, if not quite, equal to five measured miles in England, which, on recollection, was deemed necessary to insert, as, after a pleasant passage of three days, with light winds, we arrived at Newport, South Wales, about ten or twelve miles from Cardigan; and, during our short stay there, I experienced another remarkable foreboding dream, wherein I thought myself walking through a narrow footpath, both smooth and level, being every where surrounded with blooming trees, hedges, corn-fields, and meadwos; observing two plain-dressed figures, of nearly my own stature, standing in front of a snug farm-house, as though waiting to converse with me, who, on approaching near enough to properly distinguish their features, which seemed to exactly resemble those two beings I had formerly seen, who approached and spoke to me while standing on the river bank, as mentioned in the former dream, and now most agreeably seemed to usher me in doors, through a plain but decent furnished room into another with an open door, through which I was then desired to pass and view the landscape behind, which having accordingly done, I there seemed to behold a most extensive level plain, having no wood-trees or hedges to obstruct the sight, seemingly farther than the eye could reach, both in front and likewise on the right, appearing of a beautiful green, as if young grass were every where springing up, after the old crop for hay had been lately cut and taken clear away from thence; but, on turning to the left, I there seemed to observe my late enemy, the old gigantic fiend, by whom I formerly had been assailed, and likewise opposed, or some other, nearly resembling his shape and figure, at some distance from the place, forcibly dragging a plain dressed woman from thence, much against her will, as appeared from that of observing her struggling greatly, as though endeavouring to thereby extricate herself from his talons, but without effect, which those two friendly conductors, through whose means I had come there, seemed to view, with no small compassion in their looks; then, turning to me, said: wilt thou go to her assistance and release; whereat my spirits seemed to rise in such a manner as induced me to instantly pursue, without either dread or fear, which the huge ugly fiend observing, as I approached, seemed to let go his prey and fly over a high bank, at some considerable distance, on the left, over which he seemed to continue slyly peeping after us, as we returned towards the farm whereto we seemed to have nearly got. Just as I awoke from my dream, most cautiously reflecting on what I had therein observed, concerning the temporal frame appearing unable to avoid or withstand the alluring bates thrown out by Satan, whereby weak mortals are so frequently withheld from the enjoyment of their lasting pleasures of mind, through expecting to obtain the splendour, wealth, and riches, of this mortal state, while seldom thinking of, or praying for, the everlasting grace and mercy which is so freely offered to all true believers, by the immortal Redeemer of the human race; and who can tell what Almighty God, our Heavenly Father, has ordained to bring about for the good of all his creatures here below:

that is to say; whether or no the time is or is not approaching near, when the precepts of the everlasting gospel is ordained to spread over all the globe, in like manner as the beautiful young grass appears every where spreading up after the old crop seemed to have been cut and taken clear away.

Having, however, at length, terminated our affairs in Newport, we made the best of our way, through Fisguard, for Haverfordwest, where, from visiting Pembroke, and other neighbouring towns on that coast, we set off again through Narbarth, Larne, Carmarthen, and two or three other towns, names unknown, for Swansey, and from thence continued on pursuing our intended route, by way of Neath, Cowbridge, Cardiff, Newport, Chepstow, and the new ferry, to Bristol, where, having arrived, and enjoyed the company of our relations for some time, without any prospect of regaining my pension, for want of sufficient evidence to clear up the point, we, therefore, took leave, and set off in search of them elsewhere, but to no purpose, till the 5th of October, 1767, when, returning to Bristol again, we there happened to meet with two, namely, Charles Cooper and Randle Hunt, whom I sent for to the house of Mr. Keate, joiner, in Princes-street, where, on finding them both arrived, and confronting each other, I produced the affidavit of Peter Bates, with some other papers relating to the voyage, concerning which some idea may be conceived from the following declarations: Whereas I, Charles Cooper, did read a letter, paper, or protest, sent by several of the snow Thetis's ship's company, on the coast of Africa, to captain Fitzherbert, dated the 21st of March, 1755, and wrote in the name of our doctor, Mr. Roberts; now I, the said Charles Cooper, do declare, and am ready, if called upon, to make oath, that the following circumstances contained in that paper are false, and without foundation; first, that there were no foremast-men on board at that time but what signed the paper, as it is represented; but believe, they did not sign the paper; but I cannot think how Mr. Roberts and Mr. Wapshutt could say, some of the foremast-men were concerned, when all on board, except Richardson and Barker, are represented to sign the paper: secondly, that I do remember that I signed the paper, but did not read it, nor heard it read; I also told Mr. Wapshutt, the carpenter was not concerned in the disturbance: 3dly, that it was I, not Roberts, that fired the pistol and hoisted the signal to the ensign-staff: 4thly, that Barker did

No. 8, Barker's Genuine Life.

An exact representation of BARKER's remarkable foreboding Dream, concerning the fulfiling of a most happy event, continually hoped for by the human race.

not refuse to get the irons when ordered, but ordered his mate, Curry, to get them, which he did, and Wapshutt put them on Richardson. Signed by me, this 5th day of October, 1767, Charles Cooper. Witness, Benjamin Keate, John Young.

Whereas we, Charles Cooper, second mate, and Randle Hunt, seaman, of and belonging to the snow Thetis, in a voyage to Africa, in the year 1755, did, this 5th day of October, 1767, see, and was read by me, Charles Cooper, a paper, signed and sworn to by Peter Bates, cooper, belonging to the said Thetis snow, during the aforesaid voyage, on the 7th day of May, 1757, before Thomas Farr, a master extraordinary in chancery: now we, the said Charles Cooper and Randle Hunt, do acknowledge and declare, and are ready, if called upon, to make oath, that the following depositions, made by the said Peter Bates, are false and without foundation; first, that the complaint made against Robert Barker, our carpenter, off the Canary-Islands, is false, nor could have been made without our knowledge: 2dly, that the twelve days referred to were only ten days, and employed partly in the captain's service, partly in going up and down the river, and the rest in repairing the boat which was in distress, belonging to the Anne galley, captain Robe: 3dly, that we were on board at the time Mr. Wapshutt is supposed to be stapled down; but there never did any such circumstance happen on board the vessel at that time, nor during the voyage: 4thly, the said Peter Bates was not on board when Richardson made the disturbance on board, nor for several days after; and, that Barker did not refuse to put Richardson in irons, but ordered his mate, Curry, to hand him irons, which he did, but Mr. Wapshutt put them on himself; and, also, that he was not concerned in the said mutiny or disturbance: 5thly, the said Robert Barker did not refuse to go to the factory when ordered, but went: 6thly, that there was no David on board the Thetis at the time, and, if so, Barker was so sick and weak that he could not stand alone, much less break off his irons: 7thly, that we do not remember Barker's saying, he would take away the boat to Bonney, or Callebar: 8thly, that he the said Barker did not send a petition to Mr. Wapshutt at all, nor acknowledge his being guilty of any faults: 9thly, that the sore eyes was a disorder which all or most part of the ship's company had; but we do think the confinement, want of provisions, and clothes, were greatly instrumental to the loss of his eye-sight; and, also, in justice to the said Barker, we, the said Charles Cooper and Randle Hunt, do declare, and are ready to attest, that, during the said voyage, he, the said Robert Barker, behaved in the following manner: first, that he did his duty as carpenter on board: 2dly, that we never knew him to disobey the captain's orders, nor Mr. Wapshutt's, or any other commanding officer's on board: 3dly, that he was, during the voyage, peaceable and quiet, and by no means of a mutinous or piratical disposition: 4thly, that, when he was a prisoner, on deck, in irons, he behaved with quietness and patience till released. As witness our hands, the day and year above written, Charles Cooper. The mark ✕ of Randle Hunt.

I now conceived great hopes of success, not making the least doubt but by this time his worship's anger would be in some measure abated, and, that, by the aid of my ship-mates, the way was paved to a final reconciliation; in order to bring about which, I made a second application to the committee, where I was accused of the following articles; namely: that of having stood at the gate of the Mews, and other public places in London, with a paper at my breast, calling the trustees, whom I then stood before, all rogues and villains; which said unexpected charge threw me into a kind of surprize, never having once thought of such a thing more, but that of clearing up the point, whereby the worthy committee might become sensible of the false charge exhibited against me at the time my pay was suspended; therefore, instead of its meeting with a cool reception, from a person truly unprepared to hear such false accusation exhibited against him, I, with a kind of indignation, replied, saying: that I never called any one rogue or villain, except Wapshutt and the doctor, and that I could not avoid calling them villains still; then presenting three papers, meaning those two signed by Charles Cooper and Randle Hunt, with the other formerly signed by Peter Bates, which were received from my hand; but, in my then confusion of mind, I scarcely knew what passed, yet remember to have been asked, if they were originals, which I answered in the affirmative, and withdrew; but Mr. Keate was soon after sent for, concerning the two papers which had been witnessed by him; and, on returning from thence, gave me to understand, that the truth of both papers had been confirmed by him to the worthy committee, yet, from what had so lately happened, when before them, I conceived little or no hopes of success, and was not wrong in point of judgment, as appeared through that of finding myself the next day booked as having behaved insolently and ill, for which reason my request was rejected, and perplexed me not a little, on account of suffering myself to have been a second time surprised into an over free behaviour when admitted into the presence of my superiors, and, recollecting myself a little, I began to think it far better to give myself no farther uneasiness concerning that which could not be regained without so much difficulty, but, instead of so doing, rest content and satisfied, while endeavouring to struggle through this mortal state of life in the best manner I could without it, unless kind Providence should think fit to interfere in my behalf and restore it to me at some future period or other when least expected, therefore resolved on giving myself no farther trouble or uneasiness concerning the aforesaid petition, which having made known to those present, Randle Hunt, on recollecting himself, furnished me with the following paper: I, Randle Hunt, seaman, do declare, and am ready, if called upon, to make oath, that, being in Bristol, after my arrival from a voyage in the snow Thetis, to Africa and Antigua, captain Fitzherbert, commander, deceased, Mr. Wapshutt met me in Bristol, and asked me if I would join on his side in swearing against Robert Barker, our carpenter, that he, the said

Wapshutt, would give me a considerable sum of money, and made large promises to me. I told him, for answer, that I would not swear in a wrong cause if he would give me his hat full of gold; and would not hearken to his insinuations. As witness my hand, this 5th day of October, 1767. The mark ✕ of Randle Hunt. Witnesses, Benjamin Keate and John Young.

We then parted from each other, and continued moving along, from place to place, through various parts of the nation, as usual, frequently discoursing of the false charge which had been so unluckily exhibited against me in Bristol; and, at length, happening to accidentally mention it in the hearing of William Cusons, at that time a blind man, residing in Bear-alley, near the foot of Breakneck-stairs, Fleet-market, London, who, on paying due attention thereto, and hastily rising up, voluntarily declared, saying: that he lost his sight on the coast of Africa, in a ship belonging to the same owners as the one I had sailed in, and likewise received a pension of three shillings and sixpence a week, in Bristol, which, having been deprived of, and laid out of for many years, he had published the account, and continued selling it at the Mews-gate, and other public parts of London, for a support, ever since; and, in order to confirm the truth of what he said, instantly produced two of the above-mentioned papers, which, having been read in my hearing, threw me into a kind of surprise, from finding it nearly resembled my own case, if not the very same, whereof I had been so unjustly accused, through others, wholly unacquainted with my person, seeing him do it, and, through mistake, represented his person for mine to the worthy committee, which did not seem altogether unlikely to have happened; and, if really so, why might not kind Providence enable me to clear up that, and other false charges which have been exhibited against me, to the satisfaction of the worthy committee, by which my pension might be restored to me some time or other, in which case it would become far more useful than ever, as the sale of those books, whereon we had so long depended, was become stale, and went off so very slack, that the profits arising therefrom appeared wholly insufficient to support us, for which reason we had been long endeavouring to vend other books without success, for want of better knowledge in the business; and, whatever may have been assigned for individuals to go through, from above, I have reason to believe the following travels were assigned to our lot from thence; for, at the very time of being so greatly embarrassed for want of income, we accidentally dropped into the company of a young gentleman, who had come in the capacity of an interpreter to a family from Paris to London, expecting to go back with another, but, not succeeding therein, had been detained till he was greatly embarrassed for want of cash, and, on becoming acquainted with the particulars of our business and declining trade, strongly advised us to have my narrative translated into the French language, at the same time assuring us, that, in case of going over with it, we should find the inhabitants equally polite, friendly, and kind to strangers, as any others residing in these parts; and, as the books would be entirely new amongst them, had no doubt of our meeting with equal success; upon the whole, he continued pressing us thereto in such a forcible manner, as though notwithstanding the reason we had to believe that the chief reason he had for so doing was that of obtaining a little money from us, yet, such was our own pressing desire of increasing our income, arising from the sale thereof, as, in the conclusion, prevailed and induced us to agree on paying him two guineas for the translation, which, being at length completely finished, we set off therewith for Brighthelmstone, and embarked with captain Cellick, in the packet, about nine o'clock at night, being the 11th of October, 1769, and, shortly after sailing from thence for the city of Dieppe, found ourselves breakfasting, with two other passengers, at the sign of the City of London, then kept by madam Delarue, distant one hundred and twenty-one miles from Paris: by seven next morning, the aforesaid passengers, who belonged to an English family, then residing in the south of France, agreed to join with us in the engagement of a chaise, with two seats, drawn by four horses, wherein we, after having had our necessary concerns properly inspected at the custom-house, set off early in the morning of the following day, and arrived at Rouen, the capital of Normandy, in the evening, distant six posts, making thirty-six miles from Dieppe, for which we paid forty-eight livres, making just two Louis d'ors, each Louis d'or then passing for sixpence more than one guinea English money; and happening to meet with two or three tradesmen from Manchester, who were at that time managing or carrying on a considerable cotton manufactory in the suburb of St. Sever, scarcely a mile from thence; and, having entered into discourse with them, soon after agreed to stop and try our luck there, without risking the hazard of diminishing our little substance by venturing to a greater distance; and they inviting us to the works, afforded my spouse a convenient opportunity of crossing the river Seine, over a curious bridge of boats, after our two travelling acquaintances had taken leave, and set off on their intended journey the next day; this bridge is paved in the middle, for wheel-carriages to pass, and, likewise, for foot-people on each side, which, rising and falling with the tide, and opening in the middle for large vessels to pass through occasionally, made her to view it in the light of the most convenient bridge which she had ever seen before, as vessels of burthen, at that time, appeared coming up near the city, which was very close built, and exceedingly well filled with inhabitants, having narrow streets plentifully supplied with good water from the neighbouring hills, wherewith the walls of the city were partly surrounded, on three sides, leaving it only open to the river on the south, along side of which is a pleasant walk of some considerable length, below the custom-house, having in all thirty-six parishes, thirty-five public fountains, and many squares, with several hospitals, and fifty-six religious houses, which, from being the seat of parliament for the province of Normandy, has, in course, many curiosities, the particulars whereof being two numerous for this work, I must, therefore, content myself with only pointing out such of them, as, from the observation of my spouse and others, appear most likely to afford pleasure and satisfaction to all curious travellers. While inspecting the beautiful curiosities contained in many of those elegant, venerable, and magnificent, structures, with their baso-relievoes, paintings, monuments, tombs, and statues of their kings and princes, wherefrom all the information I obtained, found worthy of observation, was, namely, the Palace where the parliament held their assemblies, and the cathedral, dedicated to our Lady, wherein great variety of them may be seen, with a bell of 36,000 weight, if the account we received concerning it be true. The archbishop of Rouen was then allowed to annually pardon a condemned criminal; as, also, the church of St. Owen, belonging to the Royal Benedictine Abbey, with that of Notre Dame de la Ronde, the Jesuit's college and church of St. Goddard, with the convent of the Carthusians, near three miles out of town; and that of the bare-footed Carmelites, are, according to the account I received, all greatly admired by curious strangers; neither ought the statue of the Maid of Orleans, erected to her memory, by the French, in the square de Vaux, be forgot, as the English are said to have burnt her there for a witch, on account of her having contrived a way for the French to gain some advantages over them, while in possession of those parts; and the strong stone palace, or rather castle, having eight round towers, formerly built by king Henry the fifth of England, as it is said, and had strong walls, with deep ditches, full of water, from whence the custom-house and exchange may be seen. The city is governed by a mayor and six aldermen, chosen once in three years; they, likewise, have an exceeding pretty play-house, near which great curiosities may be seen, at the house of the procurer-general of Rouen, which has a very good trade, as ships of near three hundred tons burthen may load and discharge at the quay; and is, likewise, plentifully supplied with butcher's meat, fruit, and vegetables, in a great variety of markets, very well stocked therewith, all of which my spouse had a convenient opportunity of viewing. After having removed from the sign of the City of London, a very good house of entertainment, wherein we had slept the first night and engaged a private apartment, with the assistance of a female interpreter, who continued explaining matters betwixt me and a printer, till the proper bargain of having the book put in hand had been struck between us, on condition of our being allowed to publish and sell the same, both there and elsewhere, by the existing laws of France, which he, in order to convince me of, prevailed on the aforesaid interpreter to conduct us into the presence of the lieutenant of police, at the Town-house, where she gave us to understand, as though it came from his own lips, that we were not only allowed to freely publish and sell it there, but, likewise, in all the cities, towns, and villages, throughout France, which afforded my spouse another opportunity of viewing both city and neighbourhood, during the space of eight or ten days, accompanied by me and the female interpreter, while the abovementioned book was printing; and, when passing through the city, happened to cast her eyes on a man hanging by the breast, with a rope fast to the gallows, fixed in one of the public markets, looking pale, as though his death had been natural; whereat she turned to the interpreter, expressing a wish to know the reason of it; and received for answer, that he had been previously hanged by the neck with another rope, slackened time enough to let the blood settle from his face, while the hangman had been closing his distorted features, and tightening the other rope from below his armpits to the gallows, by which he was ordered to hang three days in the public market, as an example to others, for theft, which, as she said, was the crime for which he had been executed, and is here given by way of novelty, as we had never heard or seen any thing of the kind happen before; however, the books were no sooner finished printing than paid for, and likewise advertised for sale, with better success than could have been reasonably expected by people unacquainted with the language of the country, as the inhabitants, on finding the price fixed in the advertisement, and we unable to answer what they said, easily paid the money, with a pleasant kind of smile on their looks, and thereby affording us no small satisfaction of mind during the space of ten or fifteen days, till thrown into confusion by a message sent from the lieutenant of the police, to our lodgings, requiring us to appear in his presence, at the Town-house; which caused some uneasiness to the people of the house, from their not being able to make us truly sensible of the particulars, for want of a proper interpreter, as the female one had concealed herself, and was not to be found, which reduced us to the necessity of applying to one of the workmen from Manchester, who, though not so well acquainted with the French language as interpreters generally are, yet, on being acquainted therewith, accompanied us to the Town-house, and there found that our permission for selling those books had been limited to a given time, which we had exceeded, without applying to the lieutenant of the police for a renewal thereof, and been, consequently, summoned before him to know the reason of it; but this oversight was, however, attended with no farther injury to us, except that of becoming greatly perplexed in mind, which was partly removed soon after by the printer, who, on being sent for, said he had prevailed on the woman to lead us into this trifling error, through fear of losing a ready-money job, as she had, previously, given him to understand, that in case of any obstacle, likely to oppose the free publication of such book through France, we proposed returning to England without doing it; and, as he well knew that no such thing was likely to happen, thought no harm in what he had done; which explanation settling the business, we were permitted to continue selling our books there without interruption; and soon came to understand, from the lips of our Manchester friend, that all strangers, coming into any city or town of France, were under the necessity of previously applying to the ruling magistrates of the place for leave to vend or sell their trading articles, a thing every where expected and approved as a compliment of respect justly due to the ruling magistrates of the place, and likewise approved by all strangers, from having their most humble request freely granted for a limited time, and again prolonged, if necessarily applied for at the expiration thereof, which we afterwards found to have in no ways been exaggerated as, though Rouen, a close built city, appearing small to the view of strangers, yet, from the best ideas we could form thereof, seemed to contain near ten thousand houses; whereof we, instead of penetrating farther inland, returned to the city of Dieppe, with the carrosse, a large unwieldy kind of vehicle, having two doors on each side, and room for sixteen passengers within, for which we paid ten shillings, meaning five shillings apiece, French money, twenty of them being just equal to one Louis d'or, and took this step with a view of embarking for England, while trading on the sea coast, if found necessary; but that not proving the case, we applied to the magistrates for leave to break trade; which said request being readily complied with, we sold our books throughout the whole city. It has a commodious harbour, situate on the north-east coast of Upper Normandy, very well peopled, containing many seamen, but has not water enough to admit of large shipping: is of a triangular figure, and strongly fortified, being separated from the ocean by a long wall and very deep ditch, appearing to our own ideas near about half the size of Rouen; the streets are wide and level, adorned with good houses, built brick, carrying on a pretty snug trade in lace, ivory work, and various kind of toys; has a great plenty of good water, from being well supplied therewith from many handsome fountains; the two churches of St. James and St. Remise are said to be the most remarkable; there are various religious houses for both sexes, with two colleges, one belonging to the Jesuits, and the other to the fathers of the oratory. In this city a pleasant prospect of the neighbouring parts may be taken from the top of the governor's castle; and, on leaving Dieppe we set off with the carrier, in a sort of cart, drawn by six horses, near two hours previous to the appearance of day-light, wherein my spouse became no less sick than what she had been while on the passage from Brighthemlstone to that city, and found no small difficulty in prevailing on the driver, by motions, to let us come down from that strange kind of vehicle, when day-light began to appear, which was for length more resembling an English waggon than a cart, and all the goods therein contained bound fast together with ropes, in order to prevent their slipping asunder with the motion, which seemed to resemble that of a ship at sea, by swinging up and down through the uncommon length of the pole, and distances of the draught-horses from the axletree, whereof some farther idea may be conceived, through finding that he was reduced to the actual necessity of replacing both our weights with a number of stones, in order to balance the cart, and therewith arriving in Abbeville the next morning early, distance thirty-nine miles from Dieppe. This city is in itself pretty large, containing twelve parishes, is situate in a low, marshy, part of the country, but strongly fortified, with a castle, bastions, and ditches, called the Maiden-city, because they say it was never taken by an enemy. It is the capital of the country of Ponthieu, lying on the main road from Calais to Paris, in the province of Picardy, about fourteen miles from the English channel, wherewith it connects by the river Somme, up which vessels come into the middle of the town, which has several good manufactories; namely, such as woollen cloths, coarse linens, sail-cloths, soap, guns, and pistols, the latter of which are said to be greatly approved by the French, wherewith they trade pretty largely, both in corn and wool, having several monasteries, and a college, wherefrom we set off for Montreuil, on foot, distance about thirty miles from thence, situate on a hill, in the province of Picardy and county of Ponthieu, by the river Canche, nine miles from the English channel, from whence it is supplied with merchandise in pretty large boats, and divided into two parts, called the Upper and Lower Town, separated from each other by a single wall, having eight parishes, well fortified, and defended by a citadel, being the seat of a bailiwick, having two antient abbeys of Benedictines and one of monks, with the other of nuns; also, a good hospital, a seminary of learning, a convent of Carmelites, and another of Capuchins; it is called a royal bailiwick, belonging to the jurisdiction of Amiens: very good entertainment to be met with at the sign of the Court of France. Hence we pursued our intended journey to Seaforde, a little market-town near the sea-coast, fifteen miles from Montreuil, where, finding only one church, with a beautiful chapel belonging to a monastery of Benedictines. We pushed on for Boulogne, the same day, distant nine miles from Seaforde. This is a pretty well peopled sea-port, in the province of Picardy, being the see of a bishop of Rheims, and capital of the district of Boulogne, situate at the mouth of the little river Leone, which forms the harbour, about ten or twelve leagues from the Kentish coast; but not having water sufficient enough to admit of large vessels into it: is much frequented by English smugglers, and divided into the Upper and Lower Town; the former of which is very well fortified with thick walls, and a strong citadel upon a hill; it is reckoned very healthy, and adorned with a handsome square, having a town-house remarkable for its clock; likewise a cathedral, dedicated to the Virgin Mary; several monasteries, a seminary for the education of ecclesiastics, a very good hospital and college of the fathers of the Oratory; but the Lower Town is chiefly inhabited by merchants, traders, seamen, and others, running along the harbour, and defended by a mound, which partly shelters it from the wind. It has a seneschal jurisdiction, with a court of admiralty, being governed by a bailiwick. Here they have a good inn, called the Red Lion, where good English was then spoken, and strangers well entertained, with great civility; wherefrom we set off for Calais, distance twenty-one miles from Boulogne. Here we met with some hundreds of our own countrymen, causing excellent employ to the Dover packet, as, at such time, few or none arrived in Calais without full cargoes, till the first of January, by which time their numbers were greatly increased, through expecting to have the benefit of the insolvent act, then before parliament; but, from its excluding those out of the nation after the first of December, 1768, they were all completely disappointed; and many of them having been curious enough to visit the interior parts of the country, had thereby so diminished their cash as to have been reduced to great difficulties for want of it, and others to the painful necessity of begging their passage home. Calais is a convenient sea-port, in the province of Picardy, being the capital of Paysreconquis, and situate on the sea-coast, twenty-one miles from Dover, and a hundred and ninety-two from Paris, by way of Boulogne, Abbeville, and St. Amand; it is of a triangular figure, one side facing the English Channel, and the other two looking towards a large plain, surrounded with ditches, being well fortified with nine royal bastons, besides those of the citadel. As it is the frontier of France towards England, no art or labour seems to have been spared to make it strong. The citadel commanding the place and country is said to be as large as the town, surrounded with deep ditches filled with sea-water, and capable of inundating the neighbouring country. The town is divided in two parts, the largest of which has eight principal well-built streets, running from the market-place, with only one beautiful church and several convents, having, likewise, several good inns, whereof the Silver Lion is reckoned the best, and the inhabitants every where affable, kind, and very obliging to strangers; from thence we continued on for Gravelines, a sea-port town of the French Netherlands, in the province of Flanders, situate near the mouth of the river Aa, about eight miles from Calais, and twelve from Dunkirk, being exceedingly well fortified, with a castle, six bastions, four half-moons, and a horn-work; as, also, very strong walls and deep ditches. The town-house and parish-church are good buildings, with two handsome tombs in the latter, and, likewise, several religious houses for both men and women, and amongst them one for English nuns, dedicated to St. Clair; but the town seems thinly inhabited for want of trade, as there is not water enough to bring ships of burthen to the place; from whence we set off, by the canal, for St. Omer, a large city, well peopled, of the French Netherlands, situate in the province of Artois, twelve miles from Gravelines, and eighteen from Calais, having many long spacious streets, with good buildings, and is the see of a bishop, suffragan on the arch-bishop of Cambray, having a very handsome cathedral, with several churches, and many religious houses, whereof the magnificent abbey of St. Berthieu is reckoned the most beautiful, and Jesuit's College, said to be little or no ways inferior to any of those in Oxford or Cambridge, being, likewise, reported to have a thousand sluices in and near the town, wherefrom the country may be inundated for two leagues every way. They have a large lake containing several floating islands, which, with the ornamental trees of St. Omer, are said to make it look very beautiful in summer time, having likewise seventy-nine villages depending on St. Omer, and governed by a head bailiff, who holds his court twice a week for that purpose: from thence we set off, by water, for Dunkirk, which is a large sea-port town belonging to the French Netherlands, in the province of Flanders, on the English channel, at the mouth of the river Colne, near about twenty miles from St. Omer, having many handsome long streets, with good buildings, and five open squares, planted with trees; also, a great number of religious houses, with two for English nuns, and a Jesuit's College, near the town-house, which is said to contain many curiosities, as doth, likewise, the church of St. John, with a very high steeple; from the top of which, in case what I heard them say concerning it be true, the English fleet, while lying at anchor in the Downs, may be seen, through perspective glasses, and signals given to their privateers, through which numbers of English traders are easily brought into that and other French ports during war time; but, not having sufficient water enough to bring large vessels into the harbour, is said to make no small addition to the strength of their fortifications, where the arsenal concerns for the garrison and magazine are likewise deemed worthy the notice of strangers, the city having many pleasant walks planted with beautiful trees near, and, also, very good trade. It is governed, after the manner of Flanders, by a burgomaster, or mayor, eschevins, or aldermen, and a pensionary, or recorder: from whence we continued pursuing our journey by the canal to Ferns, a small town of the Austrian Netherlands, situate on the river Colm, in the province of Flanders, about ten miles from Dunkirk, and eight from the sea, having handsome streets, and good buildings, well fortified, with a strong castle and thick walls, being the capital of a little district; they have their famous collegiate church, called St. Waldburgh, and manufactories of various sorts of cloths, wherewith they have, likewise, some trade, carried on by the canal and river, on which we set off from thence in the passage-boat for Ypres, a large city of the Austrian Netherlands, in the province of Flanders, situate on the river Ypres, in a flat country, near about sixteen miles from Furnes. It is very strongly fortified, by art and nature, as the adjoining country made be laid under water from their sluices for several miles round, which makes it to be considered as one of the strongest places in all Europe, being, likewise, very well peopled, having many wide spacious streets, with a very handsome fountain, near the market-place, which is reported to be the largest in all Flanders, with the most elegant freestone buildings, of two hundred yards in front, said to have been erected by the English, who had formerly carried on a large trade in wool there, but then contained the city archives, admirably adorned with statues of the earls of Flanders and dukes of Brabant; the cathedral, being a noble gothic building, contains many beautiful paintings, and other curiosities: they have six other churches in this city, and a great variety of convents for all orders, with a Jesuit's college and very handsome church, containing beautiful paintings well worth the notice of strangers. It is the see of a bishop, suffragan on the archbishop of Mecklinburgh. They have still considerable manufactories of silk, woollen, and linen cloths, the latter of which, being sent to Holland for bleaching, takes the name of Holland, having a party of Scotch Highlanders stationed there at such time, calling it a barrier-town, with thirty villages depending on it, and sending members to the states of Flanders. From thence we set off for Menin, a small town of the Austrian

Netherlands, in the province of Flanders, situate on the river Lys, ten miles from Ypres, having only one pretty long street, tolerably well built, though forming a barrier-town, as we learned from a few Dutch soldiers, meaning Scotch Highlanders, conversant in our own language; at the same time lying in Menin, wherefrom we pursued our intended journey to Lisle, being the distance of eight miles, a very large, wealthy, and, opulent, city, and the capital of French Flanders, called the Island, or Little Paris, because it is very beautiful, having many little rivers running through and about the city; as, also, a great number of wide, spacious, streets, running from the market-place, one of them being near a mile long, and the Change is said to resemble the Royal Exchange of London, with four gates, opening to the market-place, which, with the regularity of the fortifications, are said to nearly, if not wholly, exceed all other cities of Europe for beauty, having, likewise, many pleasant open squares; as also fifty churches, whereoff the principal one, dedicated to St. Stephen; which, with that of St. Peter, and those of Notre Dame de la Trille, the church of St. Catharine, and that of St. Morris, are all greatly admired for the monuments, tombs, and beautiful paintings, contained in them, and that of St. Druan being reckoned to excel the rest for elegant paintings: there are various other churches and convents, with an elegant hospital, said to be worth seeing. They have large manufactories of linens, silks, and cambrics, wherewith they carry on a sufficient trade to give the city, near seven miles in circumerence, a good face of business, having strong walls, and defended by two citadels. They have regular stage-coaches going from thence to many large towns of Flanders, and some twice a week from the Rue Royal to Paris, wherein passengers pay twenty-five livres, and three sous a pound for baggage, distant 150 miles from thence, according to the best account we then obtained; and having at length terminated our affairs there, we set off from thence for Douay, another large opulent city of the French Netherlands, situate on the river Scarpe, in the province of Flanders, about 12 miles from Lisle, in a pleasant part of the country, very strong by art and nature, said to be capable of inundating the adjoining country to a considerable distance from their sluices. It has six gates and as many capital streets, running from them to a venerable town-house in the market-place, where the rulers of the city and members of the provincial parliament usually assemble. It is said to be admirably adorned with statues, representing the earls of Flanders, which are said to be worth the inspection of curious travellers. Douay, having thirty villages depending on it, has, likewise, a university, containing fourteen colleges, amongst which is a seminary of learing for English Roman catholics, as, also, a considerable number of convents and monasteries, and amongst them one of Franciscan friers for the English, and another of Benedictine monks. On leaving that university we pursued our intended journey to Arras, another large opulent city, meaning the capital of Artois, situate on the river Scarpe, in the province of French Flanders, about thirteen miles from Douay: it stands on a hill, and divided in two parts, called the town and the city, whereof the former is by far the largest; both together having upwards of a hundred churches and chapels, where the following are said to be the most remarkable for their architecture, monuments, paintings, and other beautiful embellishments, well worth the observation of curious strangers, especially that of the cathedral, with the church of the bare-footed Carmelites, and royal abbey of St. Vedast, being of the order of St. Benedict: it is thought to resemble a palace, and its church, for monuments, pictures, sculptures, tombs, and the like, to far excel the rest, though too numerous to particularise here. It is the see of a bishop, which prelate is said to be the temporal and spiritual lord of the place, and prseides in the assembly of the states. The town is well built, having wide streets, and two market-places, the largest of them being long, spacious, and piazzas like those of Covent-garden; but the town-house stands in the little market-place; and tapistry being first made there caused them to become famous thereat; having, likewise, manufactories of linens and woollens, wherewith they still carry on a tolerably good trade, the place being very antient and well fortified, with a castle, and two ditches supplied by water from the little river Crinchon, which, at some trifling distance from thence, falls into the Scarpe, and was thought so very strong by the Austrians, while in their possession, as to place the following superscription over one of the gates; saying, "The French will "never take Arras till the mice devour the cats;" they, however, took it, and altered the superscription; saying, "The Austrians will never retake "Arras while the cats devour the mice." If the explanation, which I heard come from the lips of an interpreter, while on the spot, was right: and from thence we set off for Cambray, another large opulent city of the French Netherlands, and capital of the Cambresis, situate on the river Scheldt, 20 miles from Arras, and 117 from Paris, agreeably to the account we received in Cambray, which lies in a plentiful part of the country, being very well peopled, and defended by two citadels, five basins, half-moons, and deep ditches full of water, they being capable of inundating the surrounding country from the Scheldt, which makes it to be looked upon as one of the strongest fortified cities in all those parts, having a very large market-place, sufficient enough to draw up the whole garrison of the place in battalion, and ornamented with various large elegant streets, which terminate there; as, also, a most elegant town-house, and the great church of the blessed Virgin is deemed a handsome structure, and said to be internally ornamented with rich chapels, basso-relivos, marble tombs, statues, and other curious things, worth notice; and the steeple of this church, which is 600 steps high, built of freestone, has a famous clock which chimes every half hour, marking the hour of the day, and the year, having little brass statues to come out and strike the hour of the day by knocking with their hammers, which was, according to the account we heard there, contrived and made by a shepherd, who, from saying, that he would go into France and make a finer, induced the magistrates, or rulers, of the place, to put out his eyes, in order to prevent it. They have nine parishes in the city, containing various other churches, many convents, and three abbeys, whereof the elegant church of St. Sepulchre, an abbey of St. Aubert, are deemed very well worth the inspection of curious strangers. The archbishop, having both temporal and spiritual jurisdiction, being called the Duke of Cambray, wherein they have a considerable manufactory of fine linen, known by the name of Cambric, which they are said to have brought to such an amazing height of perfection as to produce some pieces of twenty-two Flemish or Dutch ells in length, weighing no more than six, seven, or eight, ounces, wherein they were at such time carrying on a very good trade to England and elsewhere. From Cambray we proceeded on for Bouchain, a small but capital city of the district called Ostervant, in the province of French Hainault, situate on the left bank of the Scheldt, eight miles from Cambray, very well fortified, on the side of a hill, and divided into the upper and lower town, by the water passing through, both having the church and town-house standing in the former: both, were strongly defended by two high cavilears, or, forts, commanding the adjoining country. About here we had the pleasure of conversing, in our own language, with a party of Irish brigades that were at this time garrisoning Bouchain, where, having only stopped for a day or two, we set off on our way from thence to Valenciennes, a large populous city in the French Netherlands, being the capital of French Hainault, situate on the Scheld, twelve miles from Bouchain, and upwards of thirty from Lisle, nearly surrounded by the little river Rouen, which passes through the large streets by several channels. It is strong, and defended by a citadel, in a delicious flat country, capable of being overflowed, and the approaches of a besieging enemy rendered very difficult. Their streets are in general crooked, and the houses ill built, being narrow withal, and well peopled, which makes it to look very much crowded together; but, notwithstanding that, Valenciennes hath within its own walls many elegant structures, whereof the great church, dedicated to the Virgin Mary, supported by three rows of marble pillars, under which you may walk round the same; as, also, the cloister and church of the regular canons of St. Austin are said to be exceedingly beautiful, as well as the church of the Cordeliers, with that of St. Peter, near the townhouse, are, for their elegant tombs, monuments, statues, beautiful paintings, baso-relievos, and other curiosities, said to be greatly admired by all that have seen them; as is likewise the town-house, with that called La Salle de Comté, and many others. They have a large open market-place, and considerable manufactories of woollen, stuffs, camelots, fine lawns, and jar-raisins, wherein they seem to carry on a very good trade, through having proper rulers appointed to conduct and manage those different branches of business in Valenciennes, which was at that time governed by a provost and lieutenant provost, twelve aldermen, two counsellors, and three recorders, and this was the last city which we visited while in the French dominions. It may not be amiss to acquaint the candid reader with some little account of the treatment we usually experienced and received from the native inhabitants, which was every where friendly, kind, obliging, and humane, exactly agreeing with the account received from my countryman, previous to the time of returning from the city of Rouen, as afterwards appeared through that of never having had our business once stopped or delayed by the ruling magistrates or other, residing in any of those cities and towns through which we had passed; but, on the contrary, allowed us to trade freely for a limited time, and humanely condescended to prolong the grant when desired;

and, with respect to the large inns, that the want of the knowledge of the language obliged us to frequent, till able to make good our own journeys on foot, wherein their charges proved much less than could have been reasonably expected, as they seldom charged any more for a roasted goose or turkey, when served up from the spit to the table, with good sauces, than two livres eight sous, just equal to two shillings and two pence English; and half that sum for a duck or fowl; but, with respect to bread, butter, and cheese, that was served up in halfpenny or penny worths, when called for; and wine, charged at the rate of twelve sous a bottle, just equal to sixpence halfpenny English money, except in the province of Normandy, where, through having none of their own growth, some kinds of wine were charged half-a-crown a bottle, and made ample amends for with cider, for which we only paid three or four sous a quart; and, with respect to firing, that was made up in long fagots of thick and small dry wood, placed across iron dogs, on wide hearths for such purposes, and charged at the rate of six sous a piece, when called for to burn in the bed-chamber, each fagot making a hot scorching fire for two hours at least. There is, however, one thing in particular which I ought not to omit, and that was, on coming to any strange inn, or public house, with cold provisions in a bundle, you are agreeably received, and very well used, with or without, whether on foot or otherwise, so that, notwithstanding the expense we had first been at in that strange and hazardous undertaking, such reasonable mode of travelling, with that of experiencing a free trade every where, had enabled us to make good the whole, and something more, at the time of leaving the French dominions, a thing we had been chiefly prevailed on to do through the advice and persuasion of Dutch people, met with in Ypres, Minin, and elsewhere, some of them being conversant with our own language, and all agreeing in the same mode of representing the inhabitants of those parts in such a friendly, kind, and favourable, light, as that with the beauty, wealth, riches, magnificent cities, towns, and villages, we heard them extolled in such a manner as to exceed all other nations on the face of the globe, for their beautiful appearance, which, at length, induced us to agree on visiting those parts; and, with such intent, we set off for Mons, that being the capital of the province of Hainault, in the Austrian Netherlands, situate on a hill, near the confluence of the rivers Trouille and Hane, eighteen miles from Valenciennes; and, on applying to the magistrates for leave to break trade, as usual, but without success. This unexpected disappointment unluckily happening, for the first time, caused no small uneasiness of mind, which the interpreter observing, strongly advised us to call on a corresponding friend of his, well versed in our own language, at that time keeping a public house in Brussels, through whose interest with count Cobenzel, then governor of the low countries, a license might be easily obtained to trade freely through those parts, without farther loss of time, as such like favours were frequently granted to strangers on particular occasions; and his most welcome recommendation having been gladly accepted of, we prepared for the journey; yet, ere we leave Mons, think it may not be improper to give some account of that elegant city, which has six gates, thick walls, and deep ditches full of water from the aforesaid rivers, which, from the interpreter's account, made no small addition to the strength of its fortifications, as the neighbouring country may be overflowed to a considerable distance from them occasionally, having wide spacious streets, ornamented with good buildings, and three elegant structures, resembling palaces, near the large open market-place. They have, likewise, a considerable number of churches, monasteries, convents, and two seminaries of learning, namely, one under the direction of the Jesuits, and another under the secular clergy, whereof those mostly admired for their sculptures, paintings, monuments, tombs, statues, and other curiosities, are the town-house, and other structures, near the great market-place, as, also, of the great church, with that of the Jesuits and famous college of St. Gertrude, having thirty canonesses, all descended from the nobility, each lady keeping her own carriage; and, when in the choir, appeared clothed in white, having liberty to marry, and leave the society at pleasure; with various other curious structures, far more numerous than I am able to particularise; and their manufactories of woollen stuffs appeared considerable, in which they were then said to carry on a very good trade; from whence we set off on our intended journey, wherein finding ourselves delayed by the weather, we stopped all night in a village, several miles short of Brussels, where, from the customs, manners, and various words, I heard, resembled the Lancashire dialect, which caused me to form an idea of their ancestors having descended from Lancashire parents, at some remote period or other; and how far I was deceived or mistaken therein will, hereafter, appear, as, on finding ourselves well received by the Brussels publican, we took up our abode under his roof, and was soon after brought into the company of two neighbouring tradesmen that were of his own acquaintance; one of them gladly engaging to translate my book from the French copy into Flemish, and the other to print the sheets as they came from under his hands, so that, with the help of ready money, and the aforesaid publican acting as interpreter betwixt us, a bargain having been struck, the job was begun, and finished in a more expeditious manner than could have been reasonably expected; after which his design of inducing us to spend more of our little substance with him than what appeared necessary soon became visible enough to comprehend the meaning of, through putting our intended application to the magistrates of for some considerable time, and would have, probably, done it much longer, but for a stranger accidentally entering in at the door, and hastily accosting the publican by his own name, in plain English, afforded us a convenient opportunity of entering into discourse with a person, who, on being made acquainted with the real cause of our uneasiness, proved good-natured enough to explain the particular meaning of the landlord's design, and afterwards found the means of having us brought into the presence of count Cobenzel, then governor of the Low Countries, by whose orders a grant was made out, from under the seal of the city, allowing us to trade freely there, which also enabled us to do the same in every city and town through which we had occasion to pass during our stay in the Austrian dominions; and here it appears necessary to point out some admirable things and ways of that elegant city in such a concise manner as my short limits and slender abilities will admit of: it is of an oval shape, or figure, both large and populous, being the capital of the province of Brabant, and of all the Austrian Netherlands, situate on the little river Seine, 186 miles from Paris, 30 from Ghent, and 24 from Antwerp, being well fortified, with strong works, and double walls, six miles round, wherein genteel hackney-coaches might be then hired from Gatetate, near two miles, for one skilling, worth about seven pence English money; and, with respect to provisions, meaning such as wine, beer, fruit, and vegetables, they were so low and reasonable, that strangers might dine off seven or eight dishes, in the capital inns, or eating-houses, at the rate of eighteen or twenty pence a head; and common people satisfy themselves very well for sixpence, or less, in many parts of the city, which has seven long, spacious, streets, adorned with good buildings, terminating in the great mar ket-place, with as many gates, leading to seven public places of amusement, namely; one for hunting, another for shooting, a third for fishing, a fourth for springs, a fifth for pasture-grounds, a sixth to shady walks, and the seventh to pleasant gardens. The whole city is well supplied with great plenty of good water, from upwards of 20 fountains, whereof Neptune with his tritons, spouting water from the horses' nostrils, is looked upon as something very curious. Near the middle part of that elegant town is the town-house, which is such a noble structure as to fill up one-fourth part of the great market, and their halls, belonging to the different trades, all of a uniform height, taking up the remaining parts, are said to form one of the most beautiful squares in all Europe, which, with the numerous magnificent mansions of their princes and nobility throughout the city; in particular, the governor's palace, situate on a hill, fronting the park, containing uniform rows of trees and pleasant walks, resembling St. James's Park, in London; and, in case what I then heard was true, the whole may be seen from the beautiful gardens of the Duke de Beaunonville, and to that delightful prospect the churches, convents, monasteries, being likewise very numerous, make no small addition to the prospect, whereof those mostly admired for their elegant structures of divers kings, princes, and others, with their magnificent tombs, monuments, baso-relievos, beautiful paintings, and other curious embellishments, are the town-house, with the governor's palace, as, also, those of the prince Delinge, Dukes of Aremberg and Artois, with the palaces Epicnayberg, Ruebernprey, and Egmont, with the Great Church, dedicated to St. Gudenta, likewise that of the Jesuits, with another dedicated to our Lady, having, amongst their nunneries, two for English, one established by cardinal Howard, in the reign of king Charles II. There is a beguinage, walled in like a town, with an elegant church and many streets, wherein it is said that each female has her own convenient apartments, in order to improve the art constantly practised there, of making fine Brussels lace; there are other manufactories of tapistry and camelots, wherein they are said to carry on a very good trade; neither ought the noble playhouse, said to be one of the largest in Europe, containing rows of lobbies, or boxes, with fire-places in them to lock up, for the nobility to engage and keep the keys themselves for the use of their own families and friends; in particular, that of the prince Delinge, which is said to have looking-glass instead of wainscot, in which he may sup, by a good fireside, with a select party of friends, observing the whole play, which they frequently do, without being seen by the actors or audience; there are, likewise three priories, in a very large wood, containing 16,526 acres of ground, near the city, wherefrom it is mostly supplied with fireing.

On leaving Brussels we set off for Lovain, a city of the Austrian Netherlands, delightfully situate on the river Doel, in the province of Brabant, thirteen or fourteen miles from thence, being nine miles round the walls, but not very strongly fortified, through having a castle intersected with vineyards, large gardens, and other waste ground not built on, yet said to contain 126 streets, nine market-places, fourteen mills, and sixteen stone bridges, with several handsome palaces, and a venerable town-house, as, also, many beautiful churches, amongst which the great church of St. Peter, and that of the Jesuits, are the most remarkable for their beautiful paintings, statues, and other curiosities, where, according to the report we then heard, the manufactories of this city were so very large and extensive, as to have formerly employed 150,000 weavers, in 4,000 weaving houses, where, in order to avoid danger, a bell was usually rung every night, by way of caution, for the women to keep the children out of the way, through fear of being run over by the weavers at the time of their leaving work; till the weavers, and other tradesmen, happened to revolt, in the year 1380, against Waineslaus, then duke of Brabant, when some of the ringleaders were punished, and the rest banished, in such immense numbers, as when the van was entering the city of Brussels the rear had scarcely moved from the gates of Louvain; after which both trade and houses fell into decay, for want of inhabitants to occupy them, and at length became a heap of ruins, appearing like nothing but rubbish during the period of forty-five years, or thereabout, when John, the fourth duke of Brabant, in the year 1425, formed it into a university, containing sixty colleges, which are said to nearly resemble those of Oxford and Cambridge for their architecture, and amongst them one for English Dominican Friers, as, also, three for the Irish, namely; one of secular priests, another of Franciscan Friers, and a third, Dominicans. The Dutch have, likewise, a college here for the Roman catholics; and, when all the students are properly initiated, make oath, that they believe all the articles of the church of Rome; and the governor of the university, being styled Rector, is said to be allowed full jurisdiction over all the students, with respect to offences, which are most generally tried and terminated by him or his orders, frequently permitting the most capital sentences to be expiated with pecuniary fines. The weavers made for England, and were well received.

The trade of Louvain was, during the time of our continuing there, said to chiefly consist in beer, called Peterman, which was brewed there and sent all over the country, wherefrom we made the best of our way to Mechlin, another large opulent city, being the capital of the lordship of Mechlin, in the Austrian Netherlands, situate on the rivers Dile and Demer, in the very heart of Brabant, 12 miles from Brussels, 11 from Lovain, and 12 from Antwerp, being a large well-built city, forming several islands, made from the water of the river Dile, over which they have convenient bridges, though not very strongly fortified. The streets are wide, beautiful, and neat; have a large open market-place contiguous to the town-house, being divided into seven parishes, every one of which having a handsome church, and the cathedral, called St. Rombaud, having a very high steple, from the top thereof a most delightful prospect may be taken; and, with respect to their many beautiful churches, and other religious houses, the monastery of the Franciscans and convent of St. Clare are said to be the most worthy of notice, though many others are beautifully embellished with paintings. There are few or no streets here without containing more or less elegant structures of the nobility, through Mechlin being more frequented by them than any other city in those parts; and the beguinage resembling a little walled town, having several streets and a very handsome church, said to contain a thousand maids, all chiefly employed in making fine lace, wherein they far excel those of Brussels and other parts. In the foundries of this city they cast a number of bells, mortars, and large cannon, wherein they trade largely, as well as in beer, lace, corn, blankets, and thread: from whence we proceeded on for Antwerp, another elegant city, being the capital of the marquisate of Antwerp, a province of the Austrian Netherlands, situate on the east side of the river Scheld, 12 miles from Mecklin, 23 from Louvain, and 24 from Ghent; it is large, beautiful, and well built, in the form of a crescent, on a level, marshy, ground, having wide, beautiful, streets, inclosed by a strong wall, and basins of about seven miles round, near a hundred feet thick, the top of which is planted with double rows of trees, at the top forming a very pleasant walk, wherefrom a delightful prospect of the neighbouring country may be taken. The buildings are magnificent, and the whole appearing very uniform, make no small addition to the beautiful scenery, and, by the fabulous account we received from the lips of an interpreter, concerning the original obscurity of this city, which took its first name from the giant Antigoney formerly having a castle there, and robbing strangers as they passed, many of whose hands he is said to have cut off and thrown into the river, with a kind of triumphant warp, thereby giving it the name of Handwarp; but, since perverted and changed into that of Antwerp, which it still retains, exhibiting a visible representation of its antient splendour, while styled the grand mart of Europe, in which elevated situation, chiefly gained through foreign trade and merchandise, wherein it is said to have continued gradually increasing, till a strong citadel, with five basins, and double ditches, full of water, commanding the river, city, and country; but only one door of entrance, though there is room enough within to accommodate three thousand troops, where, through causing his own statue to be erected, trampling on the conquered states of the Netherlands, which the inhabitants looking upon as a thing intended for the purpose of holding them in awe, it gave such umbrage to the wealthy merchants there, as induced no small numbers of them to remove from thence to Amsterdam, which was nothing more than a small fishing-village at that time, which their steady attention to commerce rapidly increased till it arrived at what it now is; namely, the splendid capital of all the Seven United Provinces, while the famous city of Antwerp was falling into a gradual decay, though real marks of its antient greatness may be easily perceived by the commodious Exchange, wherefrom the model of the Royal Exchange, in London, is said to have been taken. And farther ideas of its extensive trade may be observed in the house of the Hans-Towns, called Easterlings, which was built, in the year 1468, for the accommodation of merchants coming from the Baltic, when trade was flourishing, containing three hundred lodging-rooms for them, on the middle floor, with convenient warehouses for dry goods above and wet goods below, whereto I may likewise add, what common report has thrown out, concerning the river, as if really true: four or five hundred sail had frequently gone out, and as many come in, the same day, containing room enough for between two or three thousand ships of burthen to lie safe and snug at the same time in near twenty feet of water, when the tide is out, and ten or twelve more when up, exclusive of six or seven canals, running into the city part, which makes it to be considered as a very convenient sea-port, where, in the grim statue of giant Rumbold, with his gauntlet erected, in a throwing posture, on the top of the gate, leading to the key of Antwerp, having seven gates, with as many long streets, terminating at the cathedral, near the central part of the city, containing two hundred and twelve in all, whereof the main street is more spacious than others, from being widened for six coaches to go abreast of each other; and, also, contains the most capital inns, which are generally frequented by the nobility. Near about the centre part is the great market, where the noble town-house, with the fish and Friday market, for the sale of jewels, may be found at no great distance from the former. This city is well known to have more venerable churches, convents, and monasteries, than any other in the Netherlands, whereof those most generally admired for their beautiful paintings, sculptures, monuments, tombs, statues, and other curious embellishments, are the rich abbey of St. Michael, with the Jesuit's church and college; as, also, the St. Augustines and Dominicans, with that of St. John, as well as the English nunnery; and, amongst their numerous religious houses, for both men and women, they have all, or most part of them, something peculiarly worth seeing; but what far excels the rest is the cathedral, three hundred and sixty feet high, from the steeple whereof may be seen the cities of Ghent, Mechlinburgh and Louvaine, as well as the Zealand-isles, on a clear day, whereto great numbers of the inhabitants were said to have emigrated during the civil wars of the Low Countries, that broke out in the year of our Lord 1576, and their taxing all the ships going up and down the river Scheldt contributed to diminish the trade of Antwerp, which has twenty-two squares embellished with lofty buildings, as are, likewise, most of the streets; with court-yards and gardens adjoining to their houses, which assists to shew the antiquity of it; and here it was that a native of these parts, wholly unacquainted with our language, then commanding a vessel of his own in that harbour, happening to cast his eyes on one of our hand-bills, wherein finding both my christian and sirname to exactly agree with his own, proved curious enough to find us out, and, after having had some little discourse together, with the help of an interpreter, produced an old family-writing, therein pointing out and mentioning one of his fore-fathers having purchased a spot of land from his own brother, in the year of our Lord, 1380, a person of the same name, who, after selling it, removed from Louvain to England, but into what part thereof he remained still ignorant, therefore expressed a strong desire of being made acquainted with the place of my nativity, thereby enabling him to inquire after the family, in case of taking a trip to those parts, which I could not enable him to do with any degree of certainty, otherwise than by first acquainting him with an antient affair, said to have taken place in the days of one of my fore-fathers, when the proprietor of a plot of land, spread over with considerable quantities of linen yarn to bleach, in or near the parish of Billinge, about three or four miles from Wiggan, through which an affrighted hare happened to pass in his sight, while pursued by the hounds in full cry, but at such a distance as afforded him time enough to collect together his people, and others, with sticks, clubs, and things necessary to beat them off, whereat the sportsmen appeared displeased, and are said to have insisted on pursuing the regular scent of the hare, which being resolutely opposed by the rest, a battle ensued, wherein the proprietor and his people, coming off victorious, obliged the sportsmen to go round and put their dogs into the scent of the hare at the other side of the ground, and thereby avoided the injury likely to have been sustained in case of the dogs passing through the yarn, which gave him the bye name of Turner, which becoming the general topic of discourse, it spread in such a manner as to have been communicated from father to son, even from generation to generation, till those branches of the family residing in Wiggan, Billinge, Hay, and thereabouts, were scarcely known by any other name except that of Turner, though never made use of in writing by any, and without some knowledge thereof it would be nearly impossible to hear any account of me, or those relations I may still have residing there; but, let that prove how it may, the captain seemed very well pleased therewith, as appeared from that of his having accompanied us with an interpreter, near two miles on the road from thence to Breda, before he took leave; and then proceeding on, we ere long past a couple of stone pillars, fronting the public road, near about sixty or seventy feet apart from each other, having the arms of Austria and Holland placed thereon, to mark out the boundries of the two nations: and happening to enter a most beautiful kind of village, near about one hour after, induced my spouse to express a wish of stopping to view it, instead of pushing on to Breda that night, as intended; for which piece of curiosity we paid dear enough, through having been charged four or five times more than ever we had paid for one night's entertainment since our first landing in the city of Dieppe; and, with respect to the village, every house therein seemed to have been newly built, from their having no kind of spots, smoak, or soil, on the walls or windows, that she could perceive, nor yet any kind of dirty rubbish lying on the smooth level ground below; each street having two uniform rows of trees, very beautiful to the eye. And, on leaving that village, an interpreter, to whom we had been recommended from Antwerp, through his interest with the rulers, obtained leave for us to trade three days in Breda, being the capital of Dutch Brabant, situate on the river Marne, in a low marshy part of the country, about thirty miles from Antwerp, nineteen or twenty from Bergen-op-Zoom, and nine or ten from the sea, having a strong castle and numerous garrisons, surrounded by the said river Marne, in form of a moat, and the curtains of the other strong works flanked with fifteen bastions, planted with canon, and fourteen ravelins; being of a triangular form, with strong gates at every angle, having uniform rows of trees planted on the walls surrounding that large populous city, containing smooth level streets, and clean well-built houses, appearing equally beautiful to behold, as the village heretofore describes; and what made some addition to the beautiful scene, was that of various canals running through many different parts of the city, which has a noble large town-house, in the market-place, greatly admired for the regularity of its apartments and sumptuous furniture; as is, likewise, the great church, for its lofty spire, the steeple of three hundred and sixty-two feet high, internal monuments, mausoleum, and other curiosities, deemed very well worthy of observation. On the journey from hence we crossed a water of near two miles broad, in a ferry-boat, and paid one guilder for it, making one shilling and nine pence three farthings English money, lying in the way for Dort, another large opulent city, in the province of Holland, situate upon an island, in the river Maese, sixteen miles from Breda, where, after paying five per cent. duty at the custom-house, for the stock in trade, sent by water from Antwerp, we, on applying to the magistrates, with an interpreter, for leave to break trade, were refused, and, consequently, obliged to stop a day or two upon expenses, before we could leave it conveniently; and, during that time, happened to meet with a well-meaning inoffensive kind of person, from London, with his spouse and three or four small children, reduced to much distress, by weakly giving ear to and believing the false insinuations of a person from Holland, concerning the encouragement given to English tradesmen at the Hague, wherein money was to be gained faster, if not a fortune, much sooner than in London; but, instead of meeting with such expected success, he blamed himself greatly for having declined and left a comfortable situation of business, which he had formerly carried on, as a stay-maker, in the parish of Bloomsbury, for another of the same kind at the Hague, established there in the name of his brother-in-law, meaning the same person that induced him to such a strange undertaking, apparently, with no other view but that of stripping him of all he had, and, after succeeding therein, turned him and his family out of doors, since which he had, according to his own account, been near two years, working for sixteen stivers a day, that being all he could earn to support them in the city of Dort. And hope the candid reader will pardon or excuse this digression, which seems to require a word or two more in its proper place, concerning their happy change of situation, as it came to our knowledge previous to the time of leaving those parts. And here it may not be amiss to give some account of that opulent city, being the capital of a district, called the bailiwick of Dort, and the first in dig-

Printed by Galabin and Marchant, Ingram-court, Fenchurch-street, London.

No. 10, Barker's Genuine Life.

A representation of BARKER and his Spouse on a travelling journey from Dort to the beautiful city of Rotterdam, in Holland.

nity amongst all the other States of Holland, and looked upon as very strong, by reason of its situation between the rivers Maese and Mereuve, both very wide in that place, and, likewise, surrounded on the south and east by a large lake, called the Biesbos, through which it had been formed into an island by an inundation happening to break down the banks of the Maese and Mereuve, thereby deluging such a large tract of land as to have unexpectedly overwhelmed seventy towns and villages, wherein 100,000 people are said to have lost their lives, during the year of our Lord, 1421, since which they have rebuilt most of the town, and securely repaired the banks in such a cautious manner as to prevent any misfortune of the kind from happening again. The city of Dort is large and populous, the streets are broad and well paved; the high houses are built of brick. Its situation being well adapted for commerce, they carry on a very large kind of trade, in different sorts of wines, especially Rhenish, which it sends throughout Holland, and other parts of the country; as, also, in corn, wood, and coals, brought down the rivers Maese and Rhine. Fresh salmon is, likewise, said to have been formerly taken in such immense quantities, that the servants were fed with it till they became so very much cloyed with it, as to make one general rule of agreeing with their masters and mistresses, when going to a new place, not to eat fresh salmon any more than twice a week. They have many handsome churches and public buildings, whereof those deemed most worthy of observation are the great church, with the Exchange, town-house, public hospitals and library. From thence we set off for Rotterdam, a very opulent city in the province of Holland, situate on the banks of the Maese, twelve miles from Dort; it is both large and populous, having ten gates, four towards the river, and six more on the land side. The streets of this city are broad and well paved, most of them having canals planted with high trees on each side therein, containing a sufficient depth of water for large ships of burden to load and discharge neir cargoes fronting the merchant's own doors, thereby giving it the appearance of both city, fleet, and forest, through beholding the tops of trees and chimneys uniformly intermixed with vanes of shipping throughout many parts thereof, the town having three fish-markets, with the great market, hog-market, and new market, the whole place being of a triangular form, containing a very antient town-house, with large chambers, well finished, as, also, four Dutch churches, for their established religion, with two English churches, one for the established worship and the other for the presbyterians, one Scotch church, two Armenians, one Luthera, two Antibaptists, four Roman Catholics, and one Jewish synagogue, whereof those deemed most worthy of observation are the great church and that of St. Lawrence, as the tower-steeple of the former is said to have leaned on one side, and been set up straight in the year of our Lord 1655; and the latter containing monuments and statues of various Dutch admirals, from the top whereof may be likewise seen most part of their cities and towns throughout South Holland; and, with respect to the numerous streets contained in the city, the Harengolcit is looked upon to be the most elegant and spacious, through having stately houses lately built of stone, extending from the new to the old head, near about half a mile in length, by which the city canals are filled and supplied with shipping from the river, between which they have a beautiful row of houses and lofty trees, forming a kind of mall for people of condition to walk and amuse themselves with viewing the ships at anchor, and others moving up and down the Maese, which is, near about that spot, one mile and a half in breadth, and a great deal more frequented by English than Amsterdam, as, on breaking up of frosty weather, two or three hundred ships may be observed sailing down the Maese together, and probably make good their passage home before those lying in Amsterdam have got clear of the Texel; and here my spouse, at times, amused herself in the open streets, by stopping therein, for the purpose of acquainting me of the manner in which she then observed servant women dressed in long side hoops, spread quite over with linen cloths, having some large white wooden squirts in their hands, and through them spouting water on the smoky soil, or spot, appearing visible on the walls or windows, in order to remove it from thence, which great numbers of British subjects at that time residing there, from both England, Scotland, Wales, and Ireland, most generally agreed in telling us, that it was a prevailing fashion amongst the Dutch, wherein the native inhabitants seem to find no small pleasure in doing it, as appeared from that of their seeming glad to hear how far the external part of their houses and public buildings excelled those of other nations, in point of beauty, for the eyes of strangers to behold, and there my spouse found a convenient opportunity of being admitted into that chamber wherein Erasmus, a great Dutch philosopher, drew his first breath, in the year of our Lord, 1467, after previously surveying the handsome brass statue erected on a marble pedestal, representing him dressed in a fur gown and round cap, with a book in his hand, upon the great bridge in the market-place, and at no great distance from that small house wherein he was born. The people employed in the glass-house of Rotterdam are said to be extremely ingenious and expert in the art of making various kinds of trinkets, toys, and enamelled bowls, which are sent to India and there exchanged for other merchandise of different kinds. The exchange and magazines for refitting out of shipping are reckoned good buildings, as is, likewise, the college of the Admiralty, named the college of the Maese, being the chief of Holland and all the United Provinces, where too the lieutenant-general admiral of Holland is obliged to go personally and sail down the river in a Rotterdam ship before he can take command of the Maese fleet near Helvoetsluice, though chiefly built in a dock or basin, to the eastward of Rotterdam, where great numbers of shipwrights are generally employed in building them; and we, in due time, set off for Secdam, a pretty snug village, containing many distilleries, situate near about seven miles from Rotterdam, wherein the best kind of Hollands gin was made, as, also, a considerable quantity of fishermen employed in making nets; and from thence we set off on our intended journey for the Hague, which being only called a village, yet is a most beautiful and opulent one, situate near about six miles from Secdam, and nine from Rotterdam. Being very large, populous, and, for a place without walls, considered to be, in point of size, elegance, and beauty, equal, if not far superior, to many cities enjoying the privilege of sending members to the assemblies of the states, which it is not allowed to do, though containing the seat of government, and, consequently, deemed the capital of all the Seven United Provinces; it is thought to contain five or six thousand houses, and near fifty thousand souls, being situate in a most delightful part of the country, surrounded by numerous cities, towns, villages, elegant mansions, woods, groves, shady walks, avenues, and various other rural amusements, allowed by my spouse to far excel every thing of the kind she had ever seen before, which, together with their high stately buildings, wide spacious streets, and many open squares, containing walks under shady trees, so that, look on which side you will, nothing but gentlemens seats, beautiful gardens, shady walks, pleasant meadows, fields, and most delightful kind of villages, every where strike the eye, especially the house in the wood, a very elegant rural kind of palace, situate near the way to Scheveling, and both much resorted to, by reason of that village being situate near the banks of the open sea, just two miles from the Hague. It is the seat of the States-General, and where those members, representing the cities, towns, and other provinces, reside; as, also, ambassadors and envoys from foreign princes, by reason of the supreme court of judicature and public affairs being carried on there, and foreign ambassadors admitted to an audience. Near the middle part of this opulent village stands the court, a very large antique village, moated on three sides with a fish-pond, lying on the front of three bridges, to draw up, and a large building in the middle, resembling Westminster Hall, where, on the walls and roof may be seen colours, drums, and other things, placed there as trophies of victory taken from their enemies during the time of war. At one side of this court the prince of Orange, then Stadtholder, was said to reside, and the States-General, with the nobility and members representing the cities and towns, usually met to form their supreme courts of justice, and transact the national business in various apartments thereof, which may be viewed when the States are not assembled; and some of them being very plain, others appear sumptuously adorned with pictures; but as my short limits were not sufficient enough to particularise one tithe part thereof, I must content myself with pointing out some few of those said to be most worthy of observation, which the chamber wherein the States-General assembled; and that called the Chamber of Truce, wherein ambassadors have their public audience of the States: besides these beautiful apartments, there are several others belonging to the province of Holland, deemed worth seeing, as is, likewise, the platform in the great hall, placed there for the purpose of drawing the state-lottery on, and with respect to the venerable church, magnificent palaces, stately buildings, and noble structures of various kinds. The house, or palace, in the wood, with the old palace, which formerly belonged to king William, and the house belonging to the head officer commanding the horse belonging to the Prince of Orange, and state-prison near it, are most generally shewn to curious strangers, as well as a remarkable hotel, near the end of the mall, called the Opsdam; and there are many charitable houses prepared for the support of old men, women, and children, with several good hospitals, all of which are said to be very well endowed, and truly worth seeing; as is, likewise, the cloister-church, great church, English church, and others, including the Jewish synagogue, without forgetting the military magazines, town-house, and many other noble structures, which I am reluctantly obliged to omit for want of room, as an English captain, whose ship then lay at Rotterdam, from whence he had come with his spouse, to shew her the beauties of the Hague, where she unluckily happened to miscarry, which no sooner came to the knowledge of the avaricious publican, under whose roof they slept, then he raised the rent of their apartment to four or five times the sum agreed on, at the same time obliging them to have all their provisions dressed in the family below, charging sixpence for a kettle of boiling water, and every other article in that imposing manner, through which he became so much affected as to risk the health of his spouse by removing her from thence to Rotterdam much sooner than was intended, all of which we had the opportunity of frequently hearing come from his own lips, through having then lodged within a few doors of the house, and became so alarmed thereat, as to follow them to the house of a British publican, with whom he had formerly resided in Rotterdam, who, on being made acquainted with our designs of stopping there for some length of time, readily promised to engage a private apartment for us to reside in, but, instead of so doing, continued shuffling us off, from time to time, by one frivolous excuse or other, till we began to think of his having little or nothing more than his own interest in view, through well knowing that my spouse was far advanced in her state of pregnancy, therefore, in order to avoid any imposition from happening, I ventured to set off by myself into the Scotch Dike, a long street containing many British inhabitants, from both England, Scotland, Wales, and Ireland, when happening to fall into a public house, where several people had been for some hours enjoying themselves together without breaking up, and, on hearing the purport of my business, they unanimously agreed to engage me an empty room for three months, which having been accordingly done, I, agreeable to their advice and instructions, paid down the whole rent, and, after having taken a receipt for it, put the key in my pocket, from whence I was by them conducted to the shop of a broker, where those articles appearing necessary to furnish it having been collected together, and a suitable catalogue made out, with their valuation properly annexed thereto, I paid down the money, taking a receipt from the broker, wherein he promised to refund the same when returned, after having deducted the sum agreed on for the use of it, and likewise such part thereof as may appear injured, broke, or missing, at the time; where, having thus settled matters concerning the furniture, it was then conveyed into the aforesaid apartment, under the inspection of those lucky friends who gave me to understand, that in case of not being secured that way, I might have experienced little or no less, if not far more impositions, than what the captain had lately done at the Hague; but whether it might have really happened so or not, we entered on the room, wherein my wife was delivered of a daughter in the month of October, 1759; and, on having got very well recovered therefrom, we, on returning the furniture, received back the sum due from the broker at the time appointed. We then sailed down the river with a recommendatory line from the aforesaid publican to a corresponding friend of his in the Brill, who, on being applied to, shewed us into a room, for which he demanded fifteen guilders a week; but that having been objected to and refused, we applied with another recommendation brought with us to a different person, by way of caution, who soon furnished us with a better apartment for three guilders a week in the Brill, which is the capital town of the Island of Voorn, in the province of Holland, situate on the river Maese, twelve miles from Rotterdam, and five from Helvoetsluyts. It is well fortified with strong walls, and regular old buildings, having wide spacious streets planted with trees: the ground-pavement of the longest street therein was at that time regularly white-washed from end to end, with pleasant walks of trees on the ramparts; and the great church, having a high steeple, serves for a land-mark to sailors, it being a good harbour near the mouth of the river Maese, and the island whereon it stands not more than five miles broad, and twenty long, from whence we set off in a post-waggon for near about four miles and a half to the water-side, where we crossed the river in a boat from thence to Mislinsluyts, a most delightful town or village, situated on the opposite bank of the Maese, six miles from the Brill, and six from Rotterdam, containing immense numbers of fishermen, who carry on a very good trade in salmon, cod, and herrings; where, having staid two or three days, we set off for Delft, a very complete city, in the province of Holland, surrounded with pleasant fields and meadows, five miles from Mislinsluyts, six from Rotterdam, and three from the Hague. It is of an oblong figure, inclosed by old walls, near about two miles in circumference, and defended against inundations by three dams, or dikes, holding the third rank in the assembly of the States of Holland, and said to contain near five thousand houses, well filled with genteel inhabitants to the full number of twenty thousand, if not more, therein containing large manufactories of earthen ware, called delft, wherewith they carry on a very good trade, as also in cloth and cere, being likewise frequented by wealthy merchants leaving off business in other parts, and choosing Delft for their retirement, which has two churches for their established religion, as also a French church, with another for the Lutherans, and two Roman Catholic chapels, if not more; from whence we set off for the Hague, where, having settled matters with a printer there, we continued persevering in our intended journey in a trick-scoot for Leyden, a very large opulent city of the province of Holland, being the next in size to Amsterdam, situate near the mouth of the old Rhine, nine miles from the Hague, nine from Delft, and six from the ocean, containing fifty islands, made so by the water running through them from the Rhine, over which they have 145 bridges, though several of them may be sailed round in boats. Having likewise many windmills, some part of them contrived and erected for the purpose of giving motion to the waters, which are said to be so very much stagnated during still and hot weather, through want of circulation, as to make the place unwholesome, though containing wide spacious streets, embellished with uniform rows of trees, stately buildings, and broad marble slabs at the bottom, appearing so very smoothly polished, as induces us to adopt the prevailing fashion of the people, namely, that of wearing double cloths quilted together in such a manner as to wear over the shoes, in order to prevent slipping in a deep snow, which then happening, afforded no small amusement to the inhabitants, who continued slipping thereon with torches in their hand by night on various kinds of slays raised up and made convenient enough for them to sit, each of them being drawn by one horse garnished with little bells, therewith making a tinkling noise as they passed the house in great numbers, and that to such a late hour as we could get little or no sleep before midnight. Leyden being a university, having two colleges, said to contain near two thousand scholars wearing swords instead of gowns, and dieting with the inhabitants; each student, when approved and above the age of twenty, being allowed the privilege of having a tun of wine annually, meaning eighty stopes, each stope containing three bottles, and half a barrel of beer monthly; wherein those colleges are to be seen many curious skeletons of men, beasts, and other remarkable curiosities, produced from the wonderful effects of natural causes; and from the Bourgh top, a large stone building, erected near the middle part of the city, being upwards of six hundred feet in circumference, with fruit-trees and hedges, forming a kind of labyrinth, thereon, which we ascended by fifty steps, while the snow laid on the ground, where I had the satisfaction of hearing the picturesque scene described from the lips of an interpreter, concerning Catwick, as also the neighbouring villages, corn-fields, meadows, beautiful gardens, and uniform rows of trees, both within and without the walls, having forty towers thereon, and 180 spacious streets in the city, with many canals planted with trees on each side, having stately buildings in many parts, embellished with noble structures and venerable churches, which, though truly desirous of viewing, I was obliged to afford myself the satisfaction of hearing that prospect compared with the bloom of spring by the interpreter, who gave us to understand, that the uncommon fertility of those parts were such as to partly supply Amsterdam with corn, fruit, and vegetables, from thence; as also how the mouth of that large noted river called the Rhine, formerly discharging itself into the ocean within a few miles of Leyden, had been choked up, when the Zuyder-Zee and Zealand-Isles were formed by an earthquake, happening in the ninth century, saying the very high spire of the great church, formerly serving as a land-mark to seamen while passing Catwick, before it dropped to the ground in the year of our Lord 1509; yet many curiosities, antiquities, and monuments, are still to be seen in the body of that church, as also in St. Pancrasis, our Lady, called Notre Dame, and the new church, as well as in their elegant town-house, colleges, hospital, and charity-houses, one of them being then said to contain nine hundred children, all kept very clean; and with respect to their manufactories of woollen cloths, serges, and camblets, they were, through encouraging strangers, driven out from their own country by the wars or religious persecutions, arrived at such a height of perfection, as to be deemed nearly equal to those of England, as appeared, from large quantities of them being regularly sent to the Baltic, Germany, Russia, and more distant parts. Leyden having eight gates, near one of which we passed in a trick-scoot, while on our way from thence to Haerlem, another large well-peopled city in the province of Holland, situate four miles from the sea, and twelve from Leyden, is walled round, having eight gates, but not strongly fortified, though said to contain seven or eight thousand houses, and near about forty or fifty thousand inhabitants, having many wide spacious streets and canals in the middle of them, planted with uniform rows of trees on each side, like many other cities, towns, and villages, of those parts, having likewise four Dutch churches, for the established religion, one French church, five Anabaptists, one Armenian, and one Lutheran, with several private houses or chapels for the Roman Catholics; whereof those mostly admired for their external and internal curiosities are the church of St. Bavo, in the steple whereof are two silver bells brought from Egypt, during the crusade of Pope Innocent, in the year of our Lord 1245, and the very elegant town-house, their manufactories of fine linens, ribbons, tapes, and curious fine thread for the best lace, as also, velvets and silks, wherein they trade largely to Amsterdam, Leipsic, and Hamburgh; and, agreeably to the information we received, the art of printing was discovered there, and the first book taken from the press deposited in the town-house of Haerlem, for travellers to inspect; but, let that be how it may, we set off from thence in a trick-scoot for Amsterdam, being the chief city of the province of Holland, and likewise of all the United Provinces, situate on the river Amster, and an arm of the sea, called the Wye, some trifling distance from the Zuyder-sea, being thirty-six miles from Rotterdam, and seven from Haerlem, where, taking up our abode with a publican well versed in our own language on the Guilder's Quay, towards the latter end of January, 1770, and continuing there for near about four months, affording us a convenient opportunity of observing many sly under-hand dealings carrying on there to the uncommon prejudices of English seamen and others, in such a very sly artful way as even to prevent them from suspecting any danger, till too late to evade the trap or snare laid for them, some of which happened in our personal presence, and to the best of my recollection was nearly as follows: it happened through two English ships coming into the harbour of Amsterdam, namely, one from the Bay of Honduras and the other from Naples, both of which finding it necessary to discharge part of their hands therefrom, no less than seven of those seamen were recommended to the aforesaid publican for suitable accommodations, during their stay; and all proving weak enough to become very much disguised in liquor, while enjoying the company of each other, which the designing publican taking the advantage of, thought fit to bring seven girls of the town into their company, saying, they were servants out of place; at the same time affording them such a convenient opportunity of success, as thereby to gain the desired point of becoming bed-fellows to the seamen, who, in order to reserve their money, deposited what they had in the landlord's hands, amounting to eleven or twelve pounds each man, as we frequently heard come from their own lips; and the girls, well knowing the farce which they had to act, designedly kept them all in their cups for the space of fourteen or fifteen days, even till the aforesaid publican had produced their separate bills, wherein bringing each man debtor to him, which made them to look at each other in a very serious manner, as now becoming sensible of their folly and weakness; at the same time, appearing unwilling to part from their girls, while expressing strong fears of being distressed for money in a strange place, which the landlord observing, like a person expecting the consequent result likely to follow, began to cheer them up, saying, they had no need to part from their girls, or fear being distressed for want of money, while a good ship, bound to the East-Indies, was at that time in want of hands; so that, in case of all taking a voyage in her, they might go together, and each man, at the time of properly entering to go the voyage, receive a bounty of 200 guilders, and two months pay, at the rate of 20 guilders a month, to fit him out, with an additional bounty of 150 guilders more when he returns to Amsterdam, which said alluring bait was no sooner thrown out than greedily swallowed, as appeared from those seven men speedily entering on the voyage, and receiving their proper notes for 200 guilders each man, passable in Amsterdam, at the return of the ship's books from the Cape of Good Hope, all of which the landlord purchased at the rate of 110 guilders, making just ten pounds sterling for each note, which keeping in his own possession by way of security, the seamen continued in their cups for the space of ten or twelve days longer, even till the second bill was laid before them, stating all their cash to have been expended, which, on being mentioned, the girls disappeared, and they found themselves under the painful necessity of going on board, after having discovered that the 200 guilders promised as a bounty, was to be deducted from their wages, and that they had twenty-two months duty to perform, without expecting any thing more than the 150 guilders given as a bounty, at the time of their returning to Holland, which happening to occur in our presence, while residing under the same roof, makes it incumbent on me to explain the particulars, by way of caution to his Majesty's subjects, with some other material events, as they came to our knowledge; but, ere I proceed therein, I think it may not be amiss to give some account of that large, elegant, and opulent, city, which is fortified with a strong wall and deep ditches, having twenty-six basins, eight gates, and a very elegant stone bridge over the Holstein, having eleven arches, near the foot whereof that river enters the city, and there, dividing itself into many parts, form a great number of islands, all planted with trees, near many long, wide, and spacious, streets, having canals planted with trees on each side in the middle, and every where embellished with handsome brick buildings, through which no wheel carriages are allowed to pass, excepting those of physicians and strangers, through fear of shaking down the houses, which are chiefly built on long piles of wood drove into the morass, or quagmire, whereof some idea may be formed of the town-house, a most elegant structure, being 282 feet long, 235 broad, and height of the roof 116 feet, which had been erected and wholy supported on 13659 vast piles of wood driven into the morass, contiguous to each other, at a prodigious expense, wherein almost every capital part of the city business was then said to be transacting with so much regular decorum, as to excite the notice and admiration of curious strangers; and, with respect to churches, their own, for the established religion, were eleven, with three for the English, two for the French, and one for the German; whereto I may likewise add twenty-seven Roman Catholic chapels or places of worship for them, with two Jewish synagogues, being allowed, agreeably to their own way of tolerating all religious worship; whereof those churches mostly admired for their paintings, monuments, tombs, and other curiosities, are the new and old, with the east, west, north, and south, churches, as also the English and French churches, with some others; and their hospitals, which are numerous, are good buildings, and kept very clean; they have likewise many alms-houses for boys and girls, some of them containing from five to eight or nine hundred, and others from that number to fourteen or fifteen hundred children, all of which are said to be chiefly supported by collections made from door to door twice a week throughout the whole city; and whenever those collections happen to fall short, the deficiency thereof was said to be made good by the city, which the natives allowed to be half the size of London, and in the enjoyment of more wealth; but let that prove how it may, they seem to appear exceedingly fond of money, and according to the best ideas we could form thereof, it seems to contain near about 35000 houses within the walls, and 5000 more without, where, happening to continue till the setting in of spring, it afforded me a convenient opportunity of hearing the cuckoo daily sing, as it flew from tree to tree, in the public streets, no less frequently than what I had formerly heard in the country parts of England, or elsewhere; and with respect to the Exchange, India-house, magazines, arsenals, and building yards, they are all deemed well worth the inspection of curious travellers, through carrying on a very large trade to and from the most distant parts of the globe, whereby they gain immense great wealth from corn in particular, through bringing it from those parts where it was bought very low, and depositing it in their own granaries till a suitable opportunity of exporting it to some other nation, where, by so doing, they might expect to gain double or treble its value, in order to become rich, and thereby gratify their own avaricious dispositions, though bread was continually much higher during our stay in Holland than in any other nation through which we had passed; and with respect to the aforesaid publican, under whose roof we had slept, and cautiously endeavoured to acquaint the British seamen with the disasters likely to succeed their own weakness and folly, if continually pursued, but to no manner of purpose, yet continued in so much favour with the aforesaid publican as to obtain a line of recommendation from thence to a corresponding friend of his in the city of Horne, a large sea-port in North Holland, situate on the Zuyder-Zee, eighteen miles from Amsterdam, and surrounded by a strong wall, containing five gates, inclosing many spacious streets, embellished with handsome brick buildings, capable of being inundated to a considerable distance by the sea-water at pleasure, and likewise several venerable churches, with a most noble town-house, said to be inferior to no one in all those part for elegance and beauty, excepting that of Amsterdam; and through being situated in a fertile part of the country, is likewise said to export large quantities of butter and cheese of their own making from thence, and likewise to obtain riches by feeding lean cattle sent from Denmark and other parts, which, with that of their dealing much in timber and ship building, as also in that of carrying on a very extensive trade to the East and West Indies, Greenland, Baltic, and other distant parts of the globe, which enabled us to obtain some little information concerning the unfortunate seamen, through a considerable number of them happening to be at that time confined under the same roof, but in such part thereof as we were not allowed to approach in order to converse with any one of them; yet, by the best information we could obtain, they would be imprisoned there till a ship was got ready for their embarkation, and likewise that all publicans and others concerned in those vile actions were branded with the odious name of soul-sellers, wherefrom it appeared that such underhand dealings were no less obnoxious to the natives than others; and let that turn out how it may, we obtained a recommendation from him to his corresponding friend in Inkheison, another large sea-port of North Holland, situate on the Zuyder-Zee, ten miles from Horne, and twenty-eight from Amsterdam, where on applying to the publican, or soul-seller, with the recommendation, who happening to hear the sound of English voices at the door, came hastily up some few steps from a narrow passage below, and was followed from thence by two others, the last of which having the resemblance of an English seaman, and his face besmeared with blood, as though he had been struggling for liberty without success, as appeared from that of the other suddenly pushing him down the steps, and with the assistance of others below securing him in a room adjoining the passage, while the publican had been directing us to a Dutch house near, wherein we slept for the night without hearing a single word of English spoke, or having been allowed to come inside of his own doors; and what appeared still more strange and surprising was, that of our having been the very next day ordered to quit the town without delay, and that by a person wearing some aspect of authority, but without being able to assign any other reason for it than that which occurred in our personal presence, while in front of the soul-sellers house on the night before; and in order to evade any farther difficulties or uneasiness of mind, we thought it best to comply with his peremptory commands; through which I am only able to say, that several wide spacious streets in Inkhuson were cut through, having canals and trees on each side, ornamented with good buildings, and a very large town-house, partly surrounded by water, as it came open to the view of my spouse, while going on our way back to Horne, and so on from thence to Alkmaar, the chief city of North Holland, situate about three miles from the sea, ten from Horne, and twenty from Amsterdam, in the midst of pleasant gardens, fields, and groves, having smooth level streets, well paved, and beautifully embellished with neat churches and a town-house, whereof the great church, town-house, and neat hospitals, easily attract the notice of strangers, being then said to carry on a good trade in butter and cheese of their own making, whereof we could say but little, through not being allowed to trade there, for which reason we left Alkmaar several days sooner than we intended, and accordingly set off from thence for Serdam, a sea-port town of North Holland, situate on the north dam side of the Wye, seven miles from Amsterdam, and about fifteen or sixteen from Alkmaar, containing larger magazines of timber and naval stores for building than any other place through which we had ever passed, having upwards of 4000 windmills, and a far greater number of wooden bridges over canals, leading to the habitations of number of shipwrights, under which both might pass for miles together; and some of them being versed in English, spoke to me at times, saying they annually built 300 vessels in Serdam, and had it in their power, after receiving two months notice, to have a man of war of force ready for launching every week throughout the whole length of the following year; but whether true or not, I can say no more than what occurred to our own observation concerning the place, which seemed to be near about twelve miles long, appearing for the most part rich and wealthy, which those few with whom we had the opportunity of conversing with agreed in saying, it was chiefly acquired by the trade of ship-building. From there we at length returned to Amsterdam; and there preparing for another journey, set off for Tergow, another opulent city in the province of Holland, situate on the banks of the rivers Gow and Isell, thirty miles from Amsterdam, fifteen from Leyden, and twelve from Rotterdam, being large, populous, and well fortified by a wall and ditch, capable of inundating the surrounding country in such a manner as to leave only two ways of approach along each bank of the Isell, which are so well defended by fortifications, as to make it nearly impossible for any hostile army to approach the city; on the outside of which there are groves, avenues, pleasant walks, and gardens, resorted to by many families withdrawing from the hurry of business, with intent to spend the residue of their days in a healthy place of retirement. The town-house in the large triangular market is looked upon as a noble structure, and the painted glass windows of the great church is said to be far more beautiful than any thing of the kind which can be observed elsewhere. The trade going on within and without the walls of Tergow chiefly consists in ropes, flax, bricks, tiles, and very handsome tobacco-pipes, greatly approved of throughout those parts; wherefrom we set off for Dort, distant fifteen miles; and soon from thence to Williamstadt, a small sea-port, in the province of Holland, situate on the sea or water, called the Hollands Deep, twelve miles from Dort, which, though small, is well fortified with seven bastons, and a double ditch, being a very good harbour, on what is called the Rovert, having a market, town-house, church, and magazine of arms. Hence we proceeded on for Steinbergin, a town of Dutch Brabant, situate near the sea, eleven miles from Williamstadt, very strongly fortified, in order to defend the opening of a canal to Bergin-opsoom, by which it is regularly supplied with military stores and provisions. Howbeit, passing near a gentleman's seat, while on our way thither, we happened to be called to, in our own language, by a person from his garden, who, joining us on the road soon after, proved to have lately come from Burnt Island, near Leith, in Scotland, as gardener to General Stewart; whose seat we had just then passed; and, shortly after entering into discourse with us on the topic of leaving Scotland, said, that they had met with a short but stiff passage from Leith to the Texel, wherein he had been very sick; that observing the anchor let go, and v scoot coming alongside, the captain whereof calling out in good English, desired to know if they had any passengers bound to Amsterdam, in which case they might go up without delay, as the vessel could not get up for some days to come, which he was glad to hear, through having become very desirous of joining his master's family; and with such intent removed from the ship into the cabin of the scoot, with his box and effects to the value of forty pounds, or thereabouts, where the captain continued regaling him with a few glasses of wine till others came down below; and after their exchanging a word or two with the captain in Dutch, or some other language unknown to him, he opened the door leading into the hold, and ordered him to go in there, which having refused to do, he was then pushed in by main force, and their tied neck and heels, even continuing in that painful situation till the vessel drew near to Amsterdam; then taking off the bandage, he was conveyed to the landing-place, and soon from thence, under a safe guard, to the captain's own house, and there severely cudgelled from time to time for several days together, till he at length, for the preservation of his own life, agreed to change his clothes for a jacket and trowsers, and in that disguise ship himself for the East-Indies, as a native of Denmark,

Sweden, or some part of Germany; but instead of so doing, he, on being interrogated concerning such material point, without making any reply thereto, presented a letter to the gentlemen present, directed for General Stewart, which had till then been concealed from the vile wretch, who changed colour thereat, appearing much chagrined at hearing a word or two spoke in Dutch, which, though not understood, was viewed by him as a kind of reprimand given to that barbarous wretch, while the letter was returning, as he was taken back to the house without delay from thence, where, receiving his own clothes in exchange for the seaman's apparel, which was left in the place from where they took it, he was, during the dead part of night, conducted through various intricate streets of the city, and then left to seek his own fortune, without either money or friends, or even knowing a single word of the language; but General Stewart being well known, and gratefully respected every where, the direction of his letter raised friends sufficient, enough to help him on from place to place till he reached his master's seat, who, having been acquainted with the particulars of such vile action, after some few days repose, sent him back to Amsterdam with recommendatory letters to the ruling magistrates of the place, requesting them to afford him all the necessary aid, which in their power lay, tending to detect the cruel villain, and prosecute him to the utmost rigour of the law, if possible, where, having searched two or three days for him, assisted by the serjeant as interpreter, and a proper city officer, to no purpose, till coming to the spot whereon they landed from the Texel, and, recollecting it again, soon found the house, wherefrom the wealthy culprit was brought into the presence of the magistrate, and would have probably got clear but for the trowsers-pocket, wherein he had left a knife and comb, through forgetfulness, at the time of receiving back his own clothes, and the magistrates, on hearing it mentioned, sent him back with a proper officer to inspect the pocket, who, on finding the knife and comb still therein, brought them all into the ruler's presence, who considered it as amply sufficient to prove the crime, whereof he was then convicted, and sentenced him to be flogged on a public stage fronting the town-house, and then burn-marked in two places on his back with a hot iron, though said to have actually been worth more than 20,000 Dutch guilders, for which reason it was very much discoursed of at the time of our arrival in Amsterdam; and afterwards coming to a proper knowledge thereof from the sufferer's own lips, thereby inducing me to give it a place here, with no other view but that of shewing the danger which unsuspecting strangers are liable to, while in those parts, though contrary to a message sent from the Stadtholder to the India-House, wishing them to reject all British seamen from going out in their employ, agreeably to a request made to him for such purpose from the Court of London, which, in order to evade, they artfully ship them as subjects of other nations, entering their names on the ship's books, and for such let them accordingly pass. If the above information should happily enable any of his Britannic majesty's subjects, more or less, to avoid the snare laid for them, while in Holland, my real end and meaning will be thereby most amply gratified; and now having arrived in Bergen-op-zoom, we took a glass at parting in a house frequented by him and his fellow-servants. It is a town of Dutch Brabant, situate on a kind of hill, surrounded by a morass, twenty miles from Antwerp, twenty from Bredau, seventy-five from Amsterdam, and one mile and a half from the eastern branch of the river Sheldt, from whence it has a regular communication by a canal, strongly fortified with innumerable redoubts, forts, hornworks, and palisades, along the dike, in the midst of which is a fortified village, enabling them, with the necessary aid of those strong works of Steinbergen, to bring succour into the place, without the besiegers having it in their power to prevent it, which, with the natural strength of its numerous fortifications on the land-side, makes it to have been looked on as wholly impregnable, though taken by the French in 1747, which, from the opinion of the people residing there, happened more through treachery than otherwise; and, though a marquisite, holding a tract of land, with some villages and islands, under its jurisdiction, it is not very large, yet is well built, and the market wide and spacious, having some open squares, a palace, and a venerable church, wherefrom we set off for Tholen, the capital of an island bearing that name, in the province of Zealand, six miles from Bergen-op-zoom, a pretty snug city, well fortified, with seven basins, and a strong fort, commanding a pass at the opposite side, making it to be considered as one of their strongest frontier-towns, in the province of Zealand, having a good magazine at the mouth of the harbour, and another for powder, with an antient town-house, and a venerable church, admired for its architecture and manner of building, in the form of a cross. The inhabitants live chiefly by husbandry, and brewing mead, the chief liquor used in those parts;

from whence we set off in a sailing scoot for Zirick-Zee, a considerable sea-port, in the province of Zealand, situated on the south-side of the island of Scooer, twelve miles from Tholen, being a very antient city, strongly fortified with ramparts, and basins capable of inundating the surrounding country, thereby making no small addition to the strength of that well-peopled city, containing several good buildings, and the church, called the Munster, is looked upon as the handsomest in the province. Their foreign trade, agriculture, salt, and fisheries, are the four branches by which the industrious inhabitants chiefly maintain themselves; wherefrom we set off in a sailing scoot for Middleburg, the capital of the island of Walcheren, in the province of Zealand, fifteen miles from Zurick-Zee. It is a large populous city, having many wide spacious streets, embellished with near about 4000 well-built houses, said to contain near 40,000 souls, inclosed by a wall and ditch, well-stocked with fish, having eight gates, with three or four uniform rows of lime-trees, forming pleasant walks, without the walls and inside of the city, which contains many elegant buildings, and, in particular, a noble, large, antient, town-house, with six venerable churches for the established religion, one English, one French, one Lutheran, and a Roman

Catholic chapel; whereof those mostly admired for their antiquities and curiosities are the town-house, north, south, and eastern, churches, with the bank, and place, or old abbey, where the states hold their assemblies; likewise several neat hospitals and alms-houses for both old and young, whereto I may likewise add a convenient harbour of about two miles long, containing a sufficient depth of water for shipping, wherewith they carry on a considerable trade to France and Spain for wines, as also for cloths, and various other articles; in particular, coals from England, through quantities of them being consumed in Zealand, where we unexpectedly heard a widow making a great lamentation for the loss of her husband, telling us, in plain English, that he had formerly obtained considerable property by the soul-selling trade, and, at length, proved weak enough to purchase a sloop, at the request of several British tars, and, while on a passage with them for the coast of Norfolk, intending to smuggle a cargo of gin there, was supposed to have been pushed overboard, as neither he nor the scoot ever returned to Middleburg; wherefrom we took a pleasant walk to Terverefeare, or Camfeare, a small snug sea-port, near about three miles from thence. It is surrounded by a wall, and fortified with basins and a ditch, having four gates, three on the land-side, and one towards the sea, carrying on a middling good trade with Dort, Ziriczee, and other parts, but contains nothing very remarkable or curious, except the great church, town-house, and large magazine of sea-stores, deemed sufficient enough to fit out a considerable large fleet of men of war from the island of Walcheren occasionally; whence we returned to Middleburg, and thence made the best of our way to Flushing, a considerable large opulent city, lying on the south-side of the island of Walcheren, near four miles from Middleburg, and strongly fortified on the land-side by a thick wall and wide ditch, with many great guns pointing towards the sea and harbour, which, from the information of others, seem large enough for 60 or 70 line of battle-ships, if not more, to lay safe therein; and the wealthy merchants of this city, being, in the province of Zealand, deemed next to Middleburg, with respect to size and riches, have very elegant habitations, many of them being, with the prince's palace and town-house, considered well worth the notice of curious strangers: from thence we returned, through a pleasant walk, planted with trees on both sides, to Middleburg, where, embarking for Sluys in a sailing scoot, and arriving there in two hours, or thereabout, we continued pursuing our destined trip from thence on the canal in a trick-scbot to Bruges, a large elegant city of Flanders, situate on the grand canal, nine or ten miles from Sluys, and near about twenty from Middleburg, containing two hundred spacious streets, adorned with large old-fashioned houses; having six market-places, near the largest of which stands a noble antique town-house, embellished with statues of the Dukes of Brabant and Earls of Flanders, in nitches, as big as life; having likewise seven parish-churches, besides the cathedral, with sixty monasteries and convents, two of them for English nuns, and one college of Jesuits, whereof those mostly admired for their internal and external curiosities are the Church of our Lady, with the sumptuous monastery of the nuns of the order of St. Bernard, as also the Dominicans and Jesuits church, with the Carthusians and the Carmelites, having a steeple near the end of the great market, said to be 553 steps high, and all wholly inclosed by a wall near five miles round, with fortifications, and seven gates, but not deemed strong enough to defend itself against a besieging enemy, and said to have originally taken its name from more than 200 bridges over the canal, and other waters, running through the streets, and said to have formerly been the most flourishing town of trade in all Europe, before Antwerp had arrived at such an amazing height of grandeur, on or about the year of our Lord, 1430, some ideas whereof may be still formed, by seventeen palaces, wherein the counsels or agents of different nations for carrying on trade usually resided, in particular the English, who are said to have made it their staple place of commerce for wool. They still carry on a pretty good trade in woollen cloths, stuffs, llhings, and tapestry, of their own manufactory; from hence we set off in the draw-boat for Ostend, a small city of the Austrian Netherlands and province of Flanders, situated in a morass near the sea-coast, twelve miles from Bruges, and twenty-five from Dunkirk, by way of Nieuport and Furnes, having a convenient market-place near the middle part thereof, and eight pretty snug streets, running in various directions, but nothing farther remarkable therein, except the fortification, said to be very strong by art and nature, wherefrom we returned on the canal, by way of Bruges for Ghent, in a draw-boat, being one of the most convenient in all Europe, through containing various apartments, wherein passengers might dine off six or seven dishes by the way, at the rate of one and eight-pence a head; and other passengers, in different parts of the same boat, for sixpence each, having good beer at three-pence a bottle, and wine for double that sum. Ghent being a very large city of the Austrian Netherlands, and capital of the province of Flanders, situate on the Scheldt and three other rivers, twenty-four miles from Bruges, formed into many islands by the aforesaid river running through the city, over which there are said to be no less than a hundred bridges, leading into wide spacious streets, embellished with high brick buildings, and three good markets, the largest of them being for corn, and serves as a Change for the merchants to assemble and transact business in, while officers and others walk amongst shady trees in the open part thereof, wherein we had not been many days before we were directed to a very remarkable kind of bridge, whereon were two brass figures, said to have been erected in the year of our Lord 1371, representing a father and son who had been equally condemned for some crime or other, and one of the two pardoned, on condition of cutting off the other's head with a sabre, which the father, with no small difficulty, prevailed on the son to perform and execute the painful task, when, behold, just as he was going to strike, the sword broke short off in his hand, which, being considered as a providential mark of divine interposition in their behalf they were, in consequence thereof, pardoned, and accordingly had both their lives saved through it. They have a beguinage here, surrounded by a wall like those of Brussels and Mechlin, but much larger, and said to contain 5000 beguines, chiefly employed in making fine lace, and attending sick people; they likewise have a beautiful town-house, with a high tower, standing near it, having a copper dragon at the top, gilt, and said to have been sent from Constantinople, by Baldwin, the 9th earl of Flanders. It is a bishop's see, suffragan of Mechlin; the churches of Ghent are very handsome, and the cathedral, dedicated to St. Bavon, elegant adorned within, having little or no less than fifty monasteries and convents, one of which is for English nuns; and those chiefly admitted for their internal and external curiosities are the cathedral, with the parish-churches of St. James, St. Michael, St. Martin our Lady, St. Saviour, and St. Nicolas, as also the abbey of St. Peter's on the Hill, with the church of the Barefooted Carmelites, and many others of the monasteries, deemed well worth the notice of curious strangers: and wholly inclosed by a wall, and other fortifications, about fifteen miles in circumference, requiring an army to defend it, though not more than one-half built on; they carry on a pretty good trade in corn, as also in silks, woollens, and linens, of their own manufactories, by means of the convenient rivers and canals; whence we pursued our journey through Alost to Brussels, distance thirty miles from Ghent; and so on from thence, by way of Nivelle, Genap, and Gemblours, to Namur, a considerable large city, being the capital of a province of that name, situate in a valley between two mountains, at the conflux of the Sambre and Maese, thirty miles from Mons, and thirty-nine from Brussels, exceedingly well fortified by a strong castle, erected on the highest mountain, which renders the approach of an enemy very difficult; it is likewise the see of a bishop, suffragan on Cambray, having a collegiate church and cathedral, with five parish-churches, six monasteries, seven nunneries, and a Jesuit's college, whereof the governor's palace and Jesuit's college are deemed more worth the notice of curious travellers than all the rest. We arrived there on the 25th of October, 1770, intending to go to Paris, till we were obliged with the perusal of some English newspapers by the colonel of a regiment of Scotch Highlanders, then garrisoning the city as on one of the Dutch frontier-barriers, wherein the Courts of London and Paris seemed to be differing about Falkland Islands, so far as to appear likely to bring on a rupture between the two nations, which deterred us from it; and, instead of penetrating into France, as intended, we embarked, with many other passengers, in a boat going down the Maese, by way of Hew, to Liege, being a large populous city of Germany, situate on the Maese, fifty miles from Brussels, and thirty from Namur, in the circle of Westphalia, on a dirty low spot of ground, formed into various islands by the Maese running two ways through it, over which are seventeen bridges, leading to 151 streets, the whole being divided into three parts: namely, the city, four miles round, having sixteen gates; secondly, the island; and, thirdly, the Outer Maese, all surrounded by hills and pleasant valleys, containing handsome houses, built of wood and brick, which form the capital of the prince bishop of Liege, so called from that of his being considered as temporal and spiritual lord of the place, containing one hundred churches, with a quantity of monasteries and nunneries, including a college of English Jesuits, and a convent of English nuns, whereof those chiefly admired for their internal and external curiosities are the cathedral dedicated to St. Lambert, with the parish-church of St. Paul, as also the Dominicans, Augustines, and Jesuits; whereto may be likewise added the palace of the prince-bishop, with the town-house, and other elegant structures, too numerous to particularize in this small tract. Liege is called the hell of women, because they follow the employ of men, working much harder than any where else; and the purgatory of men, because the women generally wear the breeches; and the paradise of priests, because most parts of the district belong to, and are under the jurisdiction of, the clergy: which is well situated for trade, by means of the river; though upwards of one hundred miles from the ocean, is navigable to Liege; from whence we set off for Aix-la-Chapelle, by way of Dendermonde, another large opulent city of Germany, situate in the duchy of Juliers, near about thirty miles from Liege, and is a place greatly resorted to, for the benefit of its hot baths, from many parts of Europe, by the quality and others, and said to have been first discovered by a Roman general, so early as in the year of our Lord 58, and afterwards formed into a bath large enough to contain one hundred of the quality, wherein it is said that Charlemaigne found so much pleasure in bathing with his nobility, having been since divided into various departments for ladies and gentlemen to bathe, separate from each other, being so very hot, when filled with water from the pumps, as to require no less than twelve hours in cooling; and others, in a village, containing, four parish-churches, near the south-gate, no less than eighteen hours before they can be endured, caused, as is supposed, by arising from the earth near several kind of minerals, namely, such as coal, lead, vitriol, and lapis caliminaris; also having medicinal waters to drink, together with those hot baths, they are said to have most beneficial effects of more numerous internal and external complaints than I have either room or talents to describe; I can, therefore, only say, that whoever comes to reap the benefit thereof finds convenient room enough to walk from the rain or wet near raffling-shops, coffee-houses, and various kinds of amusement, which are usually frequented by sharpers, assuming the different titles of counts, barons, and marquisses, with far more splendid retinues than any of those sharpers usually frequenting London, Bath, and Tunbridge. Aix may be called the inner and outward city, the former having a wall near two miles and a half in circumference, with ten gates; and the latter, four miles and a half, with eleven gates, containing very handsome clean streets, embellished with stately buildings, a large market-place, and an elegant town-house, having two cathedrals, and thirty parish-churches, with a great variety of monasteries and convents; whereof those deemed most worth-the observation of curious travellers are the town, cathedral, and great church, with many others, and now finding the high Dutch language prevail more than others, which rendered the sale of those books we had in English, French, Flemish, and Low Dutch, insufficient to support the expense of travelling, without having a translation of them printed in High Dutch, we therefore, instead of adding so much bulk to the luggage, agreed to risk the hazard of selling those we had in Holland, notwithstanding those obstructions likely to be experienced, while passing through the United Provinces, in our way back to England, and with such intent set off for Maestricht, a large town of the Austrian Netherlands, in the province of Dutch Brabant, situate on the Maese, fifty-seven miles from Brussels, fifteen from Liege, and eighteen from Aix-la-Chapelle. It is divided into two parts by the river called the Wick, and the town, over which they have a bridge of nine arches, so ingeniously contrived, that it may be taken to pieces, and put together again, without injury to it, the Wick being under the jurisdiction of the prince-bishop. Liege is said to have such extensive fortifications as to contain 12 or 13000 troops, and the whole town so well fortified every where as to be called the strong bulwark of the Dutch frontiers, having the troops at that time garrisoning the two places, which contain several wide spacious streets, embellished with uniform rows of trees, and handsome houses, built of wood and brick, as also two elegant open squares, adorned with pleasant walks, under shady trees, and surrounded with very handsome buildings, in one of which stands a most noble town-house, deemed well worth the inspection of curious strangers, as well as various churches for the established religion, Protestant, Lutheran, and Monastical, worship, where liberty of conscience is free; and the ruling magistrates, consisting of one half Protestants and the other half Roman-Catholics, are said to agree very well in ruling 12 or 13000 people, then residing inside the walls, of about four miles in circumference; wherefrom we despatched our luggage to Fenlow by water, and set out ourselves on foot by way of Romond for the same place, where, being arrived, and the frost having set in with so much intense severity, as prevented us from moving down the river, as intended, we engaged a tilted cart for the purpose of conveying our luggage from thence to Nimeguen, a large, rich, and populous, city, being the capital of the province of Guelderland, situate on the river Waal, near about seventy miles from Maestricht, by the road we came; where having been observed while passing through the gate into the city, and that being made known to the sheriff, or scoute, who was an officer of considerable authority, appointed to manage the trade of Nimeguen, he, the next day, called on us at our lodgings, procured by an English tradesman, to whom we had brought a recommendation from Maestricht; and, on being acquainted with the nature of our business, ordered us not to begin trade, or vend any pamphlets, till leave had been obtained from the magistrates, then sitting at the town-house, which induced our countryman to go as an interpreter with us into their presence; whereon finding such humble petition rejected, with orders for us to quit the place on the following day, as though afraid of our vending a few pamphlets to defray our expenses on the road, as appeared from that of his being unable to obtain leave for us to stop a few days, in order to regulate matters, after coming off such a fatiguing journey, which being made sensible of, we, instead of preparing for business, as intended, removed every article into the warehouse, wherefrom the post-waggons usually set off with goods and passengers to a village near the Maese, where we left them in the care of a book-keeper, properly directed, which prevents me from giving any farther account of that elegant city than what came from the lips of our interpreter, while passing through the wide spacious streets, embellished with handsome brick buildings, every where covered with slate; during which he gave us to understand, that it contained no less than ten churches, with eight hospitals, and a beautiful palace, from the top whereof a most delightful prospect of the surrounding country might be taken, as Nimeguen was allowed to be one of the most wealthy cities in all those parts; and, on arriving in the aforesaid village, found the river Maese so clogged with broken ice, as to hear the ferryman demanding nine ducats, making near about four pounds fifteen shillings and sixpence English money, though it would have otherwise been charged little or no more than one penny for each person; whereupon we engaged an apartment, with an intent to stop till the frost broke up, which, however, luckily happened otherwise, through its increasing with so much intense severity that same night, as enabled two men to drag our luggage over the ice on a ladder, used in form of a slay, on the very next day, for one shilling only, and we followed ourselves on foot to Grave, a small, but snug, city, in the province of Brabant, situate on a flat marshy spot of ground, close to the Maese, near about twelve miles from Nimeguen, commanding the pass of that river on both sides by a fort, and other strong fortifications, containing handsome streets, and neat buildings; where, having partly recovered from the late confused and perplexing journey, without being allowed to sell any books, excepting there, and some few in Fenlow, we set off for Bois-le-Duc, a large opulent city, being the capital of Dutch Brabant, situate on the river Pamel, about thirty-four miles from Antwerp, twenty-two from Breda, and eighteen from Grave, being strongly fortified by a wall and ditch, near five miles in circumference; from the aforesaid river, passing various ways through the town, over which they have fifty stone bridges, and ten spacious streets, centering at the great market; wherein stands a noble town-house, built after the model of that in Amsterdam, which, with the church of St. John, being deemed worth inspection, are frequently shewn to strangers. This city is well filled with inhabitants of a military turn, yet not so much as to neglect trade, as they have very good linen, woollen, cutlery, and needle, manufactories, which are all held in great esteem now. Having brought a recommendation from our English friend in Nimeguen to another residing in Bois-le-Duc, who had been in the habit of vending his own manufactured corks through many parts of the United Provinces, during a period of sixteen or eighteen years; and, on being made acquainted with the obstacles we frequently experienced in the different cities and towns, concerning the vending of our pamphlets, he voluntarily furnished us with such wholesome instructions as, through attending thereto, enabled us to get rid of the stock in hand, which might have otherwise turned out of little or no value; and, having duly attended to what he said, we thankfully took leave, and set off on the ice, with several market-people, wearing skaits, and readily pushing their necessary articles of marketing, placed on light slays made for such purpose, before them, while making for Huysden, a walled town, situate on the Maese, near about nine or ten miles from Bois-le-Duc, which, though small, is allowed to have very strong works; from whence we continued on for Worcum, and Gorcum, two small but very strong fortified towns, situate on each side the river Waal, near about one mile from each other, and nine or ten from Huysden; whence we continued pursuing our intended journey through Viena to Utrecht, a very large opulent city, being the capital of the province of Utrecht, situate on the channel of the Old Rhine, a complete day's journey from Worcum; which is well peopled, and has several fortifications, though not deemed very strong, or even sufficient enough to defend the place against a besieging army. It is large and well peopled, and in a healthy part of the country, making it greatly resorted to by the nobility and others withdrawing into retirement, having several wide spacious streets, centering in the great market-place, embellished with handsome houses, elegant buildings, and noble structures, as also four cathedrals, many churches, and other places of worship, whereof the great church is remarkable for a high steeple, from the top whereof may be seen fifty walled cities and towns, with the mall, said to resemble St. James's Park; and two canals running through the city, over which they have thirty-five bridges, and other curious things, pleasing to behold from thence; it is a place of great antiquity, and supposed to have been a Roman colony, under the name of Antonina; likewise the church of St. Mary, elegant town-house, and painter's hall, being deemed well worth the notice of curious travellers, as well as their famous universities, which are said to be much resorted to by foreigners, and amongst them some English; whence we set off in the trick-scoot for Amsterdam, about thirty miles from thence; and, while seeking employ for some few weeks there, and in the neighbouring parts, we unexpectedly heard an English publican, then residing in the younger street, openly declare he had just lost a favourite son, and narrowly escaped drowning himself, by the oversetting of his own boat, while going to bring passengers, or others, from an English vessel, just arrived in the Texel; for which he was now become truly sorry, through believing such misfortune to have been most justly inflicted on him, by the divine will of heaven, for slyly sending near 1000 of his Britannic majesty's subjects to the East-Indies, during his residence of about sixteen years in Amsterdam, which he at length considered as highly offensive to almighty God our heavenly Father, and proposed to leave it off for ever, which we have reason to believe he performed accordingly, through accidentally meeting with him and his spouse residing within a few miles of London, about three years after, though formerly reaping considerable advantage therefrom; as, agreeably to the best information we could obtain, various natives of other nations usually kept boats or scoots to bring home passengers or others from the Texel, in order to increase their own substance, like other English publicans, whose proceedings it may be necessary to evade, as those already given appear sufficient enough to furnish the candid reader with some idea concerning the under-hand tricks at such time going on there;

and, still having a quantity of books on hand, without knowing how to dispose of them to any advantage thereabouts, reduced us to the necessity of applying to an office in the town-house, where, for about three shillings and sixpence, we obtained a passevan, being a kind of protection, enabling us to pass through the Dutch territories, in our way to Hamburgh, agreeably to the friendly advice given by the worthy cork-cutter, of Bois-le-Duc, as before-mentioned; and, on being thus prepared for the journey, embarked with a fair wind, which continuing, we, after a pleasant passage of fourteen or fifteen hours, arrived in Harlingen, a large sea-port, in the province of Friesland, situate on the German sea, near about sixty miles from Amsterdam, being defended by a wall, two castles, and strong works; having five gates, four opening to the land, and one towards the sea; containing smooth level streets, embellished with neat brick buildings, and beautiful canals in the middle part thereof, and seem to trade considerably in corn, pitch, tar, fir-poles, deals, and sail-cloths, of their own manufactory; from whence we pushed on to Franeker, a small beautiful town, situate on the canal, five miles from Harlingen, having a university, well endowed and much frequented, where, staying two or three days only, we then made for Lewarden, a very large and wealthy city, being the capital of Friesland, situate on the canal, distance nine miles from Franeker, and seventy-five from Amsterdam, being three miles in circumference, and richly adorned with spacious streets, elegant buildings, and noble structures, greatly frequented by the nobility, having many venerable churches, and a beautiful palace, where the provincial members usually meet to transact business, being nearly in the heart of the province, carrying on a very snug trade with Hamburgh, and other cities of the Baltic, by means of a canal open to the sea, wherefrom we set off for Dockum, a small fortified city, in the province of Friesland, situate on the river Aa, twelve miles from Lewarden, through which goods are brought to that city by the canal, forming a convenient harbour in the German ocean, near about four miles below Dockum, wherefrom we set off for Groningen, being a large opulent city and capital of a province of that name, situate at the conflux of the two rivers Aa and Hunnes, twelve miles from Dockum, 107 from Amsterdam, and said to be near 200 more from thence to Hamburgh. The city is large, wealthy, and populous, surrounded by a wall and deep ditches, containing many wide spacious streets, six of the largest whereof terminating at as many gates, beautifully embellished with handsome houses, genteel buildings, magnificent structures, and venerable churches with a good harbour, from whence they are said to carry on a good trade with the Baltic and other parts; where having, at length, disposed of those books we purposely came to vend, we returned to Amsterdam. My spouse had, during our travels through the United Provinces, frequently observed small ringlets of straw hanging at the tops of houses in different quantities, from 50 to a 100, and now and then many hundreds, placed as close as they could well be to each other, hanging from the highest gable ends of large buildings to the ground, which, from the best information we could obtain, signifies as many crowns, accepted of as a voluntary duty, from the survivors of their deceased parents, relations, or friends; and, if really so, may be in some measure partly the cause of their becoming so extremely fond of dying rich, in order to establish their favourite offspring in the repute, credit, and esteem, of others; which is here mentioned from hearsay alone, concerning the value of each ringlet, through having no farther knowledge of it than what came from the lips of others; however, on arriving in Amsterdam, we made for the Hague, and soon, from thence, to Rotterdam, where we found the industrious English stay-maker from Dort, whose distressed situation there having been heard of, and taken into consideration, by the worthy minister and English congregation in Rotterdam church, as appeared from that of their having charitably raised money sufficient to establish him in a small comfortable situation of business, which he happened to be at such time carrying on amongst them; while his vile under-hand brother-in-law had dwindled to nothing, and was reduced to the actual necessity of quitting the Hague in distress. Now, having shipped our baggage on board of a Rotterdam trader, bound for London, we became desirous of making some farther trial of the British publican, under whose roof we had frequently slept, by giving him to understand, that we intended to go by way of the Brill, and wished him to see us in the passage-boat, to which he seemed readily to agree, and went out of the house; he returned some time after, telling us she had that moment put off from the land, without being prevailed on to stop for us, which was nothing more than we expected, through well knowing that all passage-boats were obliged to put off at the ringing of a bell, without being allowed to stop a single minute; and I only mention it to shew the avaricious dispositions of some publicans, being selfish enough to delay the voyage of strangers, in order to have a trifle more spent with them, as my spouse observed him appear displeased, while embarking for the aforesaid fishing-town, where, being disappointed of a passage, it cost us one guilder ten stivers more for a boat to Helvoetsluys, where we took a packet; and, after a pleasant passage of near two days, with light winds, we arrived safe in Harwich, and returned to London upon the 6th of July, 1771, with another in family, namely, a daughter, twenty months old, born in Rotterdam, truly thankful to Almighty God for having wonderfully blessed us with comforts of life, while passing through so many difficulties, at the same time praying for a continuance of his heavenly protection, whereby I might become enabled to remove the mistaken prejudices conceived against me by the worthy merchants of Bristol, and others, a thing which had been frequently attempted without success; and, lastly, through a seaman accidentally hearing my pamphlet read on board of a king's ship at sea, making it his business to find us out, with an intent to justify all he knew concerning the particulars of the aforesaid voyage, as may be seen in the following affidavit:

London, to wit.—Robert Barker, of the parish of St. Andrew, Holborn, in the county of Middlesex, shipwright, late belonging to Liverpool, in the county of Lancaster, but since belonging to the Thetis snow, of Bristol, in the African trade, bound to Andony, and from thence to Antigua, in the West-Indies, and back to England, under the command of John Fitzherbert, as captain, and John Evans, of the Royal Charlotte yacht, mariner, now residing in New-street, in the parish of St. Nicolas, Deptford, in the county of Kent, severally make oath, and not the one speaking for the other, on his oath saith, and first this deponent, John Evans, for himself, deposeth and saith, that he was a mariner before the mast, on board the said Thetis snow, under the command of the above-named Captain Fitzherbert, at his sailing from the port of Bristol, on or about the 22d of December, 1754, and that the above deponent, Robert Barker, was then carpenter on board the said Thetis, and that what is alleged or published by the said deponent, Robert Barker, touching the said John Fitzherbert, or Robert Wapshutt, and John Roberts, or either of them, in a paper writing, or pamphlet, just now seen, by him this deponent, containing 40 pages, and intitled, the unfortunate shipwright, or cruel captain, is true, and a just state of the case of the abovenamed Robert Barker, until this deponent's leaving the said Thetis in the month of November, 1755, without favour, affection, or partiality, to the best of this deponent's knowledge or belief through the voyage and at Antigua, until the time aforesaid, from his own observation, and from what he could collect with any propriety from any of the said Thetis's crew; and this deponent verily believes the same to be really true, and that the said Robert Barker is aggrieved by the wicked and vile misrepresentations of his behaviour to the worthy merchants of the city of Bristol, and others; and this deponent, Robert Barker, for himself, saith, that to the best of his knowledge, judgement, remembrance, and belief, of his case, set forth in the said paper writing, or pamphlet, or in any pamphlet, paper, book, or writing, with his privity, direction, or consent, wrote, printed, or published, touching the distresses arising to him from his loss of sight, or the hard usage or ill treatment he has met with on board the said snow Thetis, or otherwise, under the command of the said Captain Fitzherbert, and also what is sworn by the other deponent, is true; and these deponents, each speaking for himself, as aforesaid, severally make oath, that they do not know, nor have any just reasons to believe or suppose, that the ill treatment which the deponent Robert Barker received from the said Robert Wapshutt, and John Roberts, or either of them, as stated in the said pamphlet, did or could proceed from any other cause or causes, motive or motives, than what are, in such pamphlet, stated, alleged, or supposed.

    ROBERT BARKER ⨯ his Mark.
    JOHN EVANS ⨯ his Mark.
Sworn at the Mansion-House,
 London, the 15th day of
 August, 1768, before me,
    THOMAS HARLEY, Mayor.

And now, by what follows, the candid reader may form some idea concerning the unhappy situation of Bates at his own lodgings, while in a dangerous state of health, paying due attention to the distinct reading of his own affidavit, in the presence of his shipmates and others, saying he was become truly sorry, on account of having suffered himself to have been so grossly imposed upon, at the time of being induced to sign the aforesaid affidavit, which had made him unhappy, wretched, and miserable, through weakly subscribing his own name to that false, base, and injurious attestation, without giving it any proper thought or due consideration at the time, though well knowing the same to be untrue, and is as follows:

Peter Bates, of the city of Bristol, mariner, maketh oath and saith, that, in the month of December, which was in the year of our Lord 1753, he was a cooper on board of, and belonging to, a vessel, or snow, called the Thetis, then bound, on a voyage from the port of Bristol, to Anamaboa, on the coast of Africa, for a cargo of slaves, whereof John Fitzherbert was then Master or commander; and that, in the course of such voyage, and off the Canary Islands, one Robert Barker, a carpenter, then also on board, and belonging to, the said snow Thetis, behaved in a very daring and mutinous manner, and, upon this deponent's refusing to get him some butter, which he had no right to have, told this deponent, that if he would do as the cooper did the last voyage, the mess would never want for butter, nor any other provisions the ship afforded; and said if the ship's company would stand by him, he would take it himself; and this deponent farther saith, that, soon after their arrival on the coast of Africa, being some time in the month of February following, the said Robert Barker was ordered on shore, with four hands, in the small boat, in order to cut wood, and he set out upon that service, in like manner as he had done for several days before; but he then seemed dissatisfied, by reason, as he alleged, that he did not like to have his provisions cold on shore, but would have it dressed there, which being denied, he, the next time he went on shore, thought proper to take the boat to Andony, where Captain Fitzherbert then was, and, complaining to him of such denial, he was severely reprimanded by the captain for his behaviour, and ordered on-board again; but the said Robert Barker did not return on-board again till twelve days after, when necessity obliged him for clothes; he having been stripped naked by the negroes on shore; and further saith, that, soon after the said Robert Barker coming on-board, he, this deponent, was credibly informed by several of the said snow's company, that he, the said Robert Barker, should say, that as soon as Mr. Wabshutt, the first mate, should go to his cabin, he would fasten the scuttle-door with two ragged staples, if any of the rest of the snow's company would blow his brains out, if he offered to come up over the tafferel, or out of the cabin-door; and this deponent was likewise informed, by some of the said snow's company, that, at a time when Mr. Wapshutt was on board a vessel, called the Anne galley, then lying at anchor near the said snow, the said Robert Barker, together with John Richardson, the third mate, and some of the foremast-men of the said snow Thetis, were continually contriving and consulting how to take away the long-boat, with provisions and arms, in order to make their escape, and designed Barney hard, before the said Wapshutt's return from onboard the Anne galley, the said John Richardson went aft, and told Mr. Roberts, the doctor, that he was no more an officer onboard, and asked the people whether they were for life or debt, saying whoever were for life must jump up, and loose the top-sails, for he would cut one cable, and slip the other, which they refusing, and a waiff being made to the ensign-staff for a signal to Mr. Wapshott, he came on-board, and, on hearing the state of the said Robert Barker to put the said John Richardson in Irons, which he refused to do, and on the said Mr. Wapshutt sending word to the captain on shore of the above transactions, he sent an order for the said Robert Barker to come up to him at Andony, which with great reluctance he at last did, and when there, was by the captain's orders put in irons there for some time, to the intent that he and the said Richardson might not be together to plot farther mischief, most of the crew being then sick; but on the said Robert Barker complaining to the captain of the unwholesomeness of the country, and that it would kill him, the captain sent him on-board again, with an order to put him in double irons with Richardson, and to chain them to one of the ring-bolts on the deck which was accordingly done by this deponent; otherwise it was supposed they would slip the cables, and let the snow go on shore; and farther saith, that the said Robert Barker, after such confinement, would often persuade the said John Richardson to assist him, and he would break his irons off with the help of a david, which at that time lay on the main deck; and some time after, when the david was stowed away in the hold, he would often reflect on the said John Richardson, and tell him, if he had been a man, he would not have been in confinement at that time, but have got the boat, and been at Bonney, or Calabar; and this deponent farther saith, about seven weeks after such their first confinement on-board, the said Barker and Richardson wrote a letter, by way of petition to the said Mr. Wapshutt, who was then master or commander of the said snow, by the death of the said Captain Fitzherbert, who died about the 8th day of May then next, desiring to be discharged from their confinement, and for other relief; at the same time acknowledging their faults, with promises of amendment, which letter or petition was signed by both, in the presence of this deponent, and John Finch, the boatswain, who both subscribed the same as witnesses; and this deponent farther saith, that the blindness, contracted by the said Robert Barker on-board the said snow, he does not apprehend or believe was owing in any particular manner to his confinement, or any bad usage from Mr. Wapshutt; for, at the time of such his confinement, his eye-sight was as well as most of the said snow's company, who were all, or most of them, in some degree or other at that time afflicted with sore eyes, being a disorder incident to the country among the negroes; and saith, if the said Robert Barker's sight was lost, or worse than others on-board, he apprehends the same to be owing to his obstinacy, in neglecting or refusing to use the proper means prescribed him for a cure by the doctor of the said snow; and, lastly, this deponent saith, that, after their departure for Andony, and on their passage from Fernandipo to Annabonia, the said Richardson refusing to do his duty, and acting and behaving ill, on the doctor's, boatswain's, and this deponent's, complaint thereof to the said Mr. Wapshutt, he was, by his orders, put in irons a second time, where he, the said Richardson, remained till their arrival at Antigua.

PETER BATES.

Sworn the 7th day of May, 1757,
   at the City of Bristol, before me,

THOMAS FARR,
   Master Extraordinary in Chancery.

"Now having been well satisfied concerning the contrition of Peter Bates repenting, I, in order to avoid increasing his sorrowful distress of mind, instead of using any threats or harsh words tending that way, accompanied them with real symptoms of forgiveness, while taking leave, and wishing him a speedy recovery, at the time of withdrawing from thence, accompanied by others; and imagining him in no ways likely to remain long in this mortal state, a proper affidavit was drawn up, and jointly sworn to by them, in order to justify that which had so opportunely happened, to occur in their presence, and is as follows.

"Robert Morgan, of Crown-court, in Portpool-lane, in the parish of St. Andrew, Holborn, in the county of Middlesex, gentleman; David Dennison, of Gray's-Inn-lane, in the parish and county aforesaid, butcher; John Evans, of New-street, in the parish of St. Nicolas, Deptford, in the county of Kent, mariner, now belonging to the Royal Charlotte Dutch; and William Squire, of Great Saffron-hill, in the said parish of St. Andrew, Holborn, brasier; severally make oath, and not the one speaking for the other of them, saying that on the 16th day of August instant, they, these deponents, were respectively in company with Mr. Peter Bates, who was cooper belonging to the Thetis snow, which Captain John Fitzherbert was commander of, as admitted by him, the said Peter Bates, in the year 1754, sailed from the port of Bristol to Africa, and from thence to Antigua, at the said Peter Bates's house or lodgings in Limehouse; and that one Robert Barker, a person wholly blind of his eyes, being also present, then presented and shewed to the said Peter Bates a paper writing, purporting to be an affidavit, sworn at the city of Bristol, before Thomas Harris, a master extraordinary of the high court of chancery, on the 7th day of May, 1759, which related to the accusation against the said Robert Barker touching the crime he was alleged to have been guilty of on board the said Theus; and these deponents respectively, as aforesaid, make oath, that the said Peter Bates perused and read, at the request of the said Robert Barker, the said paper writing, or affidavit, attentively, for the purpose of informing himself thoroughly of the contents of the same, and whether his name, appearing to be subscribed or set thereto, was of his, the said Peter Bates's, hand-writing, or not; and these deponents further, as aforesaid, make oath, that after such perusal and reading, the said Peter Bates was frequently called on, and desired, by the said Robert Barker, and others in company, to satisfy them whether that name, appearing to be subscribed, was of his hand-writing or not, and the said Peter Bates, often replied it was, and insisted on it, that if the same was not his hand-writing, he never wrote his name in his life; and farther declared, that he was greatly imposed on in the signing and swearing to the contents thereof, or to that effect; and that two parts out of three of the same were false or untrue, or to that effect; and these deponents farther make oath, as aforesaid, that at the same time the said Peter Bates had before him, and inspected, a printed pamphlet or book, entitled the Unfortunate Shipwright, or Cruel Captain, consisting of forty pages, and relating to the said voyage, made by the said Robert Barker, in the said Thetis snow, which the said Peter Bates admitted he had several times read over, and was thoroughly acquainted with the contents of it; and on being required by the said Robert Barker to answer whether the matter therein contained was true or not, he often declared it was true, so far as related to the first part, being the pamphlet then before him, and which he referred to, entitled, as above, except such facts as are stated or alleged to be in his absence; and these deponents farther make oath, as aforesaid, that the said Peter Bates made such declaration in the open company of many other persons, besides these deponents, voluntarily, and was not in any ways intimidated, influenced, or deceived, into so doing, to the best of these deponents knowledge and belief.

    Robert Morgan,
    David Dennison,
    John Evans, his × Mark,
    William Squires.

Sworn at the Mansion House, London, the 17th day of August, 1768, before me,

    Thomas Harley, Mayor.

Now this and the other affidavit, sworn to by me and Evans, having been sent to Bristol by a worthy humane gentleman of Hatton garden, at that time wishing to clear up the affair, in hopes of regaining my lost pension, but without success; and, whether prevented through the relentless opposition of my late wealthy opponent, or otherwise, can only say, that such disappointment, added to the former one, mentioned in No. 8, page 208, thereby inducing us to venture on pursuing the hazardous trip to France, as briefly signified in the recital thereof; and, some time after we returned from thence, another shipmate, happening to hear of our situation, voluntarily came with them justify all he knew concerning the particulars of the aforesaid unhappy voyage, now placed in No. 4, 5, and 6, from page 89 to page 143, as may be observed in his affidavit, which is as follows:

London.—John Lee, mariner, an extra man, belonging to his majesty's ship-yard at Deptford, in the county of Kent, maketh oath, that he was acting, and employed, as a mariner and foremast-man on board the Thetis snow, under the command of Captain John Fitzherbert, sailing from the port of Bristol, in England, in the month of December, 1754, bound to Africa, until the said snow's arrival and return to the port of Bristol, aforesaid; that he well knew Robert Barker, the carpenter of the said snow, and saith, that he, this deponent, hath carefully perused and read the affidavit of one Peter Bates, mariner, a cooper on-board the said snow, who sailed with this deponent on the said voyage therein; and saith, to the best of his knowledge, remembrance, and belief, the several circumstances set forth and stated in the said Bates's affidavit, appearing to be sworn before Thomas Farr, a master extraordinary in chancery, on the 7th day of May, 1757, at the city of Bristol, reflecting on, or in disfavour of, the said Robert Barker, are false and groundless, and calculated, as he believes, merely to serve the purpose of Robert Wapshutt, a chief mate originally, but, by the death of Captain Fitzherbert, afterwards commander of the said snow, who always appeared to have, through the voyage from Africa, a great hatred and ill-will to the said Robert Barker; and this deponent saith, that he has perused, and with attention read, a pamphlet, or paper book, entitled the Unfortunate Shipwright, or Cruel Captain, consisting of forty pages, published by the said Robert Barker, relating to his said voyage in the said snow Thetis, and the ill treatment he met with therein; and saith, that such facts and transactions as are therein contained, and said to be done, suffered, or to have happened, in his presence, are true.

JOHN LEE.

Sworn at the Sessions-House,
Old-Bailey, the 11th day of
January, 1772, before me,

WILLIAM NASH, Mayor.

Now thinking myself in possession of proof sufficient to remove the mistaken ideas conceived by relations, friends, and others, through hearkening to and believing the false charges exhibited against me by Wapshutt, which I had painfully heard them frequently accuse me of in different parts of my travels, without knowing how to otherwise explain matters properly, than by an open publication thereof, but without meaning offence to any individual whatever, through believing the whole to have been assigned to my lot by the supreme powers above, wherein I ought to be content, and truly thankful to almighty God, for having supported me through so many difficult passages of life, before and since I had been deprived of sight; and likewise truly sensible of the perpetual temptation whereto my earthly frame of mind was continually exposed and subject, without knowing how to otherwise avoid and get the better of, than by endeavouring to forgive my enemies of every kind, in hopes of thereby obtaining forgiveness of my own sins, through the everlasting grace and mercy of his only beloved Son our Lord and Saviour Jesus Christ; which were the ideas conceived by me at the time of preparing those affidavits, for the pressing hopes of clearing up the affair, by offering them to the general inspection of others; and now here follows the letter sent by Wapshutt to Captain Fitzherbert, at the factory of Andoney, causing most part of those disastrous misfortunes that unhappily succeeded throughout the remaining part of that distressing voyage.

From on-board the Thetis, Friday, March the 21st, 1755, seven o'clock in the evening.

At four o'clock this afternoon, Mr. Cox, doctor of the Anne galley, came on-board upon duty; at six he went on board the Anne, and Mr. Wabshutt, wanting necessaries, being obliged to go with him, ordered our boat to be sent for him in half an hour, which was done accordingly. In a short time after the boat had left the vessel, one of the boys came aft, and acquainted me of a consultation that he had heard betwixt Richardson, our carpenter, and some of our foremast-men, which was, that they were to take away the boat and the arms, and what necessaries they thought proper. Presently after I was sensible of this affair, I heard some disagreeable words forwards, which were between Mr. Cooper and our second mate, and Mr. Richardson, third mate. I got up, and walked forwards, and asked Mr. Richardson what the matter was; he presently got up, and bitterly swore by his maker he would be commander of this vessel, in presence of all on-board. I, being out of order, went aft, and laid down on the arm-chest; in a few minutes he came, and took me by the hand, and told me I was to obey him, for he was captain of the vessel, and was to sail immediately. I stood in a pause some time, and ordered the cabin-boy to hand up some pistols, which he did; I fired one as a signal to the Anne galley, to get the boat on-board, and the mate hoisted a light at the ensign-staff in the mean time; he went forward, and ordered the people to slip the cables, loose the topsails, and hoist jolly roger; but as providence will always prevail, the people would not obey him; then he swore he only waited for the two men that went in the boat, which were William Bettey and David Cumings. Mr. Cooper, our second mate, advanced up to him, in order to secure him; he took up a scrubbing-brush, and swore if he touched him, he would be the death of him; he asked Bray whether he chose life or death; he replied he chose life; then, says he, you must combine with me; as for the second mate and doctor, after we are two hours under sail, they are to be cut up in pound pieces. At eight o'clock the boat came on-board with the chief mate; I acquainted him with what had happened immediately; he then called to Richardson, and asked what was the meaning of the aforesaid; he replied and said if he was disappointed at present of his proceedings, he would not fail to enjoy the first conveniency, and gave the mate very uncivil language. The mate ordered the carpenter to get him some irons, and a hammer; the carpenter replied he could find none; upon which the mate went and got them himself, and put his legs into irons. As witness our hands,

JOHN ROBERTS, doctor.
CHARLES COOPER, 2d mate.
JOHN BRAY, seaman.
PATRIC HOWELL, cook.
HENRY CURRY, landsman.
SAMUEL BINDING, ditto.
THOMAS GREEN, ditto.

The visible falsity of this base letter may probably put unsuspecting individuals on such a proper guard as not to sign papers of any kind till very well acquainted with their contents, from that of the worthy commander placing so much confidence therein, as to frequently decline acquainting me or Dicandoney with the particulars thereof, when desired, or even sending for and inquiring into the truth of it from any one of them except John Bray, which if he had but luckily done, the iniquitous designs of Wapshutt and the doctor might have been discovered, and the unhappy misfortunes of that distressing voyage prevented, whereof some farther idea may be conceived from the confidential letter wrote by him to Wapshutt, at the time of sending me back from thence to the vessel; which is as follows:

Andoney, the 6th of April, 175—

Mr. Wapshutt, I now send you down the carpenter; pray keep him strong in irons; for which purpose I have sent a short chain, with a strong lock, that he and Captain John Richardson might be kept chained on deck, with double irons on their legs, and single handcuffed. Richardson has wrote to me by the boat to desire liberty and pardon, but it is out of my power to grant either; for nothing but the law of his country can either acquit him or condemn him. I desire you will let him know my sentiments on this occasion. From your humble servant,

JOHN FITZHERBERT.

Now having got the aforesaid papers arranged together and printed, we diligently employed ourselves in vending them throughout the most public parts of London, still hoping to establish ourselves in a more settled branch of business. We then ventured to rent a house of Mr. Jackson, the corner of Mutton-lane, Clerkenwell-green, intending it for a chandler's shop, or some other branch of business, but without success, which shortly perceiving, we, ere long, became dispirited; and, in order to avoid wasting our trifling substance, gave it up fifteen months after; then set off into the country, and continued making different journeys of eighty or ninety miles from London, having established our infant daughter as a constant boarder with Mrs. Webb, a middle-aged widow, of mild disposition, keeping a small school in Lamb-court, Clerkenwell-green, contriving our journeys so well as to have the pleasure of conversing with them every two or three months, till our beloved daughter was between five and six years old, and become able enough to lead me by the hand; during which said period of time we had gradually increased both income and stock in trade, by adding various selling pamphlets to my own, containing principles of moral virtues, properly adapted to improve and instruct the minds of youth; wherewith both town and country having been long and well supplied, not only by us, but many others, reduced us to the necessity of removing to a greater distance; and being unwilling to leave the child behind for such known length of time, we jointly agreed to take her with us; and, by a regular pursuit of business, continued slowly increasing our trifling stock in trade, while moving from place to place, and keeping the child close to ourselves; unless while at proper schools, wherein we failed not to place her from time to time, through fear of missing the useful education whereof

I had been so weakly deprived, when near about that tender age; and, by attending steadily to trade while moving through various parts of the nation, became at length so much improved therein, as to employ a man, who, though pretty antient, continued with us for some years: and now, having drawn a sufficient quantity of pamphlets together, with intent to supply the western part of Cornwall, they were shipped at Plymouth, in a vessel bound to Falmouth, keeping no more back than what appeared necessary to supply the towns and villages through which we had to pass on the land-side, but without forming any idea of the double misfortunes that ensued, and actually commenced in Truro, through losing the use of my left thigh and leg by a violent pain at the hip-joint, descending from thence to the knee, and so on downwards, by the heel to the little toe, and thereby rendering both so very weak and helpless, that I could neither stand nor sit; and, in consequence thereof, compelled me to go to bed at the house of Mr. Trevreson, late a serjeant in the militia or regulars, but then keeping the Green Dragon public-house, to the best of my recollection, where I had not been long confined, before news was brought of the ship or vessel having overset, and filled, close to the quay of Falmouth, wherein our whole stock in trade was deluged, without hopes of recovery, until she could be freed and got up again, which providentially happened about three days after, when two cart-loads of them were, though very wet, brought to the door, accompanied by the journeyman we had formerly engaged. Now those unavoidable misfortunes, whereto the human race are generally subject at one time or other, being considered as necessary trials of faith, whereto we ought to patiently submit, and continue thankful to almighty God for having endowed us with health, strength, and judgement, sufficient enough to collect the property together; being likewise able to restore my limbs to their usual strength, and believing so, while offering most profound prayers and ejaculations, proceeding from a heart-felt sense of his everlasting goodness; in hopes of being restored to my usual strength, through his almighty power and goodness, once more I seemed to hear a low whisper in my ear, distinctly understood, saying, I will be with thee, and protect thee, while in a small bed-chamber. Having the door shut close, and hearing no other kind of sound that I could perceive, induced me to consider how and from whence it came, and to recollect another whisper of the kind, which I had perceived and plainly understood, while crossing the pavement, from Bristol drawbridge foot, to the house of Mrs. Kelley, then residing in Hanover-street, just after my pay had been suspended in the merchant's hall, saying, 'Thou art my servant, and I will protect thee'; which happened on a mild serene day, without a breath of wind stirring, people passing, or wings of birds fluttering, near enough to cause any sound, as I could learn from the information of my spouse, then leading me by the hand; and having compared them with each other, my hopes of a recovery speedily revived, through believing them to have proceeded from something more than natural; and, if really so, thought there was not the least danger of being restored to my perfect health and strength again; nay, so very sanguine were my confidential hopes therein, as to have desired my spouse, and daughter, when about fourteen years old, to engage a horse and cart for the purpose of conveying me to Bodmin, the county-town, about twenty-two miles from thence; which having been accordingly done, I was carried down stairs, and placed at full length therein a day or two after, before the neighbours, who seemed to unanimously agree with each other in saying, that I should not live to reach the end of that day's journey; happily they mistook, as I found myself able to sit up half an hour to the table on the following day, after having been closely confined to a bed for the space of a month or five weeks; and my strength continued slowly to increase, as business called us from place to place, for the space of near three months, by which time I was become free from pain, and able to walk as usual; but that was not all, for such uncommon events occurring, when in no wise expected or looked for, though some few years after, has gave me just reason to believe they could not have otherwise happened than by the kind and immediate interposition of the heavenly powers above, wherein we ought to confide, look up to, and truly remain for ever thankful, which first commenced while crossing Low Hill, on our way from Preston to Wigan, through not seeing the house wherein I drew my first breath; and happening to pass the same to some trifling distance without knowing it, and then turning hastily round, with intent to acquaint my spouse and daughter, there-

---

The manuscript, from which this work has been copied, is now found to make 14 or 15 numbers, instead of 12 as before expected, and cannot be omitted without leaving several very material points thereof unexplained; it is, therefore, hoped the same will not be disapproved.

No. 13, *Barker's Genuine Life.*

A black African trader bringing BARKER to view a pagan grove, or idolatrous place of worship, at Little London, near Andoney, some time previous to that wherein he became so unhappily deprived of sight, while lying on that coast in June, 1755.

NO. XIII.   B b b.

with, when behold a young gentleman, looking from the gate of a handsome new-built seat, happening to hear what I said, called, desiring to know if my name was not Barker: being answered in the affirmative, we were then desired to approach and accept of a little drink, which, after a seventeen miles walk, became truly acceptable; at the same time affording me no small additional pleasure in finding it belonged to a real sincere friend of mine, as I was quickly made sensible of by his son, a worthy young gentleman, conversing with us at the gate, saying, that, when attending Winchester academy some years back, he had opportunely cast his eyes on one of my pamphlets, wherein his grandfather's name appeared at full length; and, without forming any ideas concerning me, induced him to bring the same to his father, who, on perusing it over, expressed a wish to see me; but he being at that time visiting a neighbouring friend, we were told, that if we could make it convenient to call at three o'clock on the following day, I might have the agreeable satisfaction of discoursing with him, which being gladly assented to, he left the house, and continued discoursing with us concerning that and other matters near my side, even to the very door of my own brother, where he took leave in a most humane, kind, and friendly, manber, expressing a wish to see us again the next day, which being complied with accordingly, we became so very kindly received, and humanely treated, in the presence of my continual steady friend, his father, as to have likewise been favourably indulged with a recommendatory line from him to his brother, another worthy friend of mine, then residing in London, by whose united exertions in my favour, the income arising from my Bristol pension was restored some time after, in such a kind friendly manner as gave me reason to believe that those mistaken ideas conceived against me, at the time of suspending it, were removed and vanished, thereby affording much greater pleasure and delight than could have proved the case, without perceiving it: neither did their humane friendly aid subside or diminish there; for, being taken ill near two years after at the Hare and Hound, in Amots Chare, near the quay of Newcastle-upon-Tyne, and there confined to my bed, from the month of November to the middle of January following, by a perpetual slow fever, with little or no hopes of recovery, at which my spouse and daughter became perplexed and alarmed, through fear of losing me, after the man had been despatched to vend pamphlets on the way to and at Berwic-upon-Tweed, where happening to lose or embezzle the sum taken, amounting to near fifteen or sixteen pounds, instead of remitting it when expected, and greatly wanted for present use, through my spouse and daughter having kept close in-doors, with no other view but that of preserving my life, if possible; and that distressed situation of ours was no sooner made known to those most humane hospitable friends of mine at the White Lee, in Wigan, Lancashire, than the fears and doubts we had been so long struggling under were providentially removed with the necessary aid of a ten-pound note, sent to us from thence by the return of post, and followed by a second of no less value some few days after, which I then had and still have reason to look upon as a providential means of prolonging my days; for about the time, or soon after its having been made known to me, a violent sweat, declining fever, and a returning appetite, became visibly perceived, and surprising to some of those present, after having absolutely given me over as past all hopes of recovery; however, on being thus happily restored to health, and got back safe to London, with heads and hearts filled with a true sense of gratitude, yet more unexpected favours were in store for us to receive from those most hospitable friends, by whose means we shortly became enabled to establish and carry on a settled business in Hatton-yard, near Hatton-garden, and likewise, through their means, in due time became presented with a certificate from Christ's Hospital, when in no wise thought of, applied for, or expected, by us, to have been so humanely sent from them or others; yet, on its being filled up in the sixty-second year of my age, I providentially became one of those successful annuitants elected to receive and enjoy a regular income of ten pounds a year from the real benefit of that charitable institution, which having been most thankfully accepted of, unexpectedly enabled us to increase the stock, by adding more pamphlets into our collection, wherewith we carried on trade to some little advantage till the month of November, 1794, having duly carried on a regular correspondence with the relations of my spouse, residing at Boston, Lincolnshire, till that time, by the post, in such a kind and friendly manner as to have at length agreed to unite our own daughter with a nephew of my spouse for bosom friends through life together, which, in the month of November, 1794, brought him up from thence to us in town, and they were accordingly married by the minister of the same parish wherein we then resided, agreeably to the consent and approbation of every one concerned; and, after having enjoyed our company and conversation for a week, or something more, took leave, and set off together on the road to Boston, with our united prayers for their lasting peace, success, and happiness, through every part of this mortal state, leading to that everlasting peace we all hope to enjoy in the blissful realms above, through the merits of our heavenly redeemer, Jesus Christ; and now, matters having so agreeably terminated to the entire satisfaction of all parties, the young couple were taken into the partnership of his own parents, in order to assist in the managing and carrying on of their well-established business of glass, pots, and china, to which the young man had been trained up, with the addition of Spanish nuts, fruit, toys, and confectionery, which he had successfully carried on for some considerable time previous to their marriage, partly through having been well supplied with those various articles of trade, from his dealers in town, through our cautiously endeavouring to get them despatched from hence in time, and studiously continue, by way of encouragement to the young couple, through being allowed to carry on that separate branch of trade for their own emolument, even till his own parents thought fit to resign the business up to them, and withdraw into retirement, with an income sufficient enough for their comfortable support; and with respect to our own affairs, they unluckily turned out otherwise, partly through having lost the chief manager of the business; and more so, through being under the necessity of sending others to vend pamphlets for us in distant parts of the country, in order to have them disposed of before they were old and unsaleable in London, by whose weakness, folly, and neglect, in not duly remitting to us the money when taken, changed our usual prospect of obtaining a regular support therefrom into a continual decline; which being at length made known to the young people, and they becoming fully sensible thereof, most dutifully invited us to come and spend the residue of our days peaceably with them; this pleasant and agreeable invitation having been duly considered and accepted, we settled our affairs in the best manner circumstances would admit of, and joined them in the month of October, 1797, near three years after their marriage had taken place; and, on being most dutifully received, my spouse became usefully employed in the house-affairs; but that was far from being the case with me, through a want of sight while residing amongst their various sorts of brittle ware, and, consequently, at a loss for want of employ, which I had been accustomed to both in and out of doors, by folding and stitching pamphlets when at home, and aiding in their vending, whereas this brought on a kind of solitude, without knowing how to amuse and otherwise employ myself than by walking up and down a narrow passage of thirty or forty yards, going to the house and terminating at the open end in front of the cross chamber, which became most part of my usual exercise during the space of one full year or more; when, after having been at various times conducted to the house of our brother-in-law, I luckily succeeded in hitting on the way alone, and, in consequence thereof, fell into the company and conversation of other friends residing in various distant streets, who separately invited me to visit them at their own houses, which, by endeavouring to bring about, I, from habitual time and practice, became enabled to walk through most parts of the long smooth streets of Boston, wherein I usually continued amusing myself, to pass away the time occasionally from day to day, reflecting on the various passages of my former life, wherein those remarkable dreams accompanied it, which were in no ways forgotten; nor the two uncommon whispers which had been so plainly heard and well understood, both in Truro and Bristol, thereby inducing me to believe that, in case of being employed, and set to work by the supreme powers above, the same ought to be freely set about, without neglect or delay of any kind, which caused me to think of having truly been allotted to that kind of solitude wherein I might, through time, become enabled to explain the material passages thereof, in such a manner as to have written in black and white from my own lips, then believing it in no wise impossible, but that some able Christian writer might be ordained to select the most useful part thereof, in order to properly arrange and have them printed for the good of others, after my decease; and, with such intent, prevailed on my spouse and grand-son to assist each other in taking down the same from my own lips, in the morning early, while upon the pillow, retaining all or most part of what I had been musing on during my solitary walks the day before; but even without any thought of doing it myself, by reason of my age and situation, through believing that same place to have been assigned to my lot by the heavenly powers above, during this mortal state of life, and continued in that way of thinking, even for some years, till my brother-in-law had been removed from off this earthly stage, and our own daughter likewise, after having borne ten children to her spouse, and then removed, we hope, from hence into everlasting peace, on the 26th of September, 1807, on which day my spouse or grand-son had been employed in writing; and now this unexpected family change being looked upon as a thing ordained by the supreme powers above, to which we ought patiently to submit, by endeavouring to become reconciled to the unhappy loss, without complaint or murmuring thereat, and having in some measure pacified my thoughtful mind thereat, I began my usual solitary walks, frequently reflecting on those uncommon dreams, without being able to banish them from my thoughts, in particular that wherein I seemed to behold the Rivington mountains themselves changing into human beings, of such frightful gigantic size, appearing outrageously intent on crushing both church, houses, and people, which appeared like mole-hills beneath their feet, without shewing any the least symptoms of pity or compassion, till happily relieved by awaking from that most terrific dream: and the second, wherein I seemed to have been compelled to defend myself against the ugly fiend, compared to the doctor forcing me to obey his commands, without success. And the very next dream, mention in No. III. page 70, wherein, against my own will, I seemed to have been swiftly conveyed through the air, on the back of a most gigantic fiend, guarded both in front and rear, and, on each side by four more, just like himself, all of which having since been compared to Mr. M—— prevailing on me to hear those spurious volumes read attentively without being able to credit or disprove their contents, through being clouded, and no ways capable of forming a just idea of important truths, requiring spiritual aid and assistance from above, whereof I could not have been effectually convinced by any other means; and how these material points were communicated will appear in my future dreams, and, likewise, of the opposition made by Satan to all such as prefer that heavenly kind of information, which, according to my own ideas thereof, no mortal being, let his talents, acquired from natural education, be ever so great, otherwise enjoy full satisfaction of mind, concerning the great and important point of salvation, without spiritual aid strengthening him through divine revelation sent from the heavenly powers above, having been thus inadvertently misled into the perusal of those obnoxious volumes, compiled by such an able author, with no other views but those of gain or applause from those who prefer splendid wealth and riches to superior things, or he would not have therein so weakly endeavoured to oppose the everlasting gospel of our Lord and Saviour Jesus Christ, by turning each chapter and verse into a kind of ridicule, as though unworthy of due consideration from the Christian reader; but, in course, without looking up to Almighty God, in prayer, most humbly imploring supernatural aid from above, through which he might have become enabled to obtain his own salvation, and likewise promote the everlasting peace of all the human race, instead of having so weakly and most studiously therein opposed the Divine Will of heaven: and, whoever may chance to see that pernicious work, in forming a clear idea concerning the real falsity of it, may, I hope, become thereby enabled to draw good from evil, in like manner as so happily proved to have been the case with me; and how I came to perceive the efforts made by Satan to oppose the scripture truth, began from the time wherein I had that dream, as stated in No. III. page 74, and, likewise, happily encouraged to continue praying for; and the first thing, after properly gaining knowledge concerning the scripture-truths, by means of those two foreboding dreams, signified in No. VII. page 179 and 180, which having, agreeably thereto, been most favorably indulged with those intelligible dreams, as mentioned in page 182, and so on between it and 187, afforded so much pleasure and satisfaction to a grateful mind as to have never since been forgotten; and, with respect to the dream, signified in page 188, afforded me reason to think I had been allotted for the purpose of making them known to the world, unprepared as I then was, for want of natural talents, unless improved and enabled so to do by the Divine will and pleasure of the heavenly powers above; and how such uncommon ideas happened to increase and strengthen, may be observed in page 192, by means of another very pleasant dream, wherein I seemed to behold a most frightful gigantic fiend, forcibly dragging a plain dressed female, much against her will, in the presence of two amiable friends, at whose beck, hint, and words, I freely hastened to her assistance; which, the ugly fiend observing, seemed to let go his prey, and fly away from her, till on coming behind the bank, where he seemed to continue, slyly peeping, as though fully bent on seizing her again at some future opportunity; which caused me to frequently compare that plain dressed female to the primitive Christian Church, established by Christ and his apostles, for which the lord of life suffered cruel martyrdom by the Israelites; though well-known every where to have been the chosen people of Almighty God; with the promise of enjoying such a lasting kingdom as will endure for ever: and, agreeable thereto, how can any other be expected than a spiritual one, as the rest are liable to misfortunes and decay, like other temporal things on earth below; and, then comparing the law of Moses to the old crop of grass, seemingly cut and taken clear away, and the very extensive young grass appearing so beautiful in my sight, to the doctrine of the peaceful Christian church, sprung up like it, and prospering every where. For, who is able enough to comprehend and foresee more or less than what is found in the holy scriptures, made public for the beneficial good of all the human race; and the chosen people of God still expecting to be recalled, in order to enjoy their lasting kingdom in the promised land, but, without knowing how or when such like happy event may take place; and, whenever that may be, I hope they will, instead of remaining longer in the dark, clearly perceive their scattered situation to have been allotted for the salvation of themselves and the rest of mankind in general, from being made able to understand and properly converse with the natives of so many different nations. And who can rightly say, whether or no they may or may not have been ordained by the heavenly powers above to have the misty vapors removed from before their eyes, while in those distant lands, and, by clearly beholding the blind, mistaken, weakness of their forefathers, while crucifying the Lord of Life, become desirous of making atonement, by endeavouring to promote and make known a sweet sense of the everlasting gospel among the inhabitants of those numerous parts; and, by studiously endeavouring to promote the general peace and happiness thereof, as to become much esteemed and respected by the well-meaning people, as to find themselves enabled, through their means, to make for Jerusalem, in order to enjoy their endless spiritual kingdom in the promised land, by the universal consent and approbation of many other nations; which seems to be a thing far more pleasing and acceptable to the Christian mind than any temporal kingdom on the earth, though ever so wealthy, great, and splendid. Now, having reflected on these points, and others springing up into my thoughts, with no less force and presence of mind than when they happened to occur in my personal presence while enjoying perfect sight on the Guinea coast, beginning with the first slave sent on board of the Trial, by Captain Sanders, while at anchor near Malimbo, namely, a youth of fifteen or sixteen years of age, visibly appeared to have been circumcised, caused some inquiry to be made from the interpreter, but without receiving any farther information, except that of a religious sect of black people, who circumcise their male children near the river Gambia, and in no other parts that they knew of; which gave a reason for supposing them the descendants of Ishmael, or some part of them to be still residing there; and, again, upon our first arrival with the boat and goods at Andoney, where I chanced to see a little brandy poured from a glass, fronting an altar made of earth, whereon was laid the bare skull of some wild beast, resembling that of an ox, said to have been sacrificed thereon as an offering to their deity some days before we came; but, with respect to the main point and principle of religion, that still remained a secret from us, unless what in plain English came from the lips of Dick Andony may be deemed as such, wherein he said, they had wise men frequently foretelling great events, by obtaining proper information thereof from the deity alone; but, with respect to common thefts, and the like magic spells were deemed sufficient enough to discover, punish, and bring such like offenders to their proper senses; which gave me reason to believe that magic-art and conjuration was prevalent there, agreeable to the express words and language of Dick Andony, signifying king, or head ruler, of that place; whereto, having come up again, by order of the captain, some time after, and falling into discourse with a black trader, who was conversant in English, from Little London, a town or village situate within a mile of Andoney, who, hearing of some trifling things I had to dispose of in the vessel, prevailed on me to accompany him on a walk, wherein I was conducted to their grove, being nothing less than a pagan place of worship, to my view near fifty yards at its opening into the midst of a fine large wood, or forest, every where intersected with high and lofty trees, being made uniformly tapering to the other end, where stood a kind of perpendicular wall, appearing five or six yards in height, and eight or nine in breadth, which appeared as if built with the skulls of wild beasts, or animals painted various colours, by way of ornament, having the largest skull placed in the centre part, near about three feet high from the level bottom, every where covered with short grass, nearly resembling pasture-ground, from its appearing wholly open to the sight, above where such agreeable conductor appeared inclinable to furnish me with some necessary information concerning the grove; he began with saying: it was a public place of worship. And, with respect to the large skull, which I saw placed in the centre part, that was for the reception of very material things, named as necessary duties by the church and state. But, with respect to their deity, of whose height I might form some idea by viewing the wall in front, as that was exactly the same height as their deity, always standing on a pleasant hill, some few miles from thence, appearing very strong, bulky, and well made, in proportion to his stature, and, according to the best of my recollection, Boonego was the name which he then mentioned; saying: their wise men never made war, or concluded any peace, without first consulting with that idolatrous statue concerning it; appearing strongly prepossessed in believing those proceedings for the good of all natives thereabouts, from having been so artfully trained up, from an early period of their lives, as to believe nothing right but what came to their knowledge from thence by the information of those pretended wise men; and they were so very strongly prepossessed, concerning the truth of all they said, as to rush headlong into battle at their beck, without the fear of being killed, through having been persuaded to believe that, in such case, their souls were sent to enjoy immortal peace with those of their forefathers, which, according to his own ideas, seem to be the reason of obtaining information from their idol, previous to the time of declaring war, or making peace, and continued on, saying; whenever any opponents to those natives were killed, few or many, while fighting by the consent and approbation of those wise men: they were, likewise, expected to enjoy the agreeable company and conversation of their ancestors for ever, after which, having duly attended to these circumstances, I became seized with a strong notion concerning one or other of those pretended wise men, artfully concealing themselves in the inside of such image, ready to answer the questions of others, in the hearing of both warriors and leading people, approaching near the idol for that same purpose; and speaking through some kind of instrument or other, and giving such an awful sound to his words, in reply, as to be viewed in the light of coming from something more than mortal, by the weak-minded audience, who, from his words, seem to have been so grossly deceived and misled; it was this circumstance that caused me frequently to reflect and wonder how, or in what manner those pernicious principles could have been introduced, and so much approved by that many different parts of the earth, unless it had commenced from the early period of those dark and gloomy ages previous to their time of wisdom, judgement, and real knowledge, having been discovered, and approved by them, while it might have been in no wise unlikely but that some particular individuals, having more cunning, art, and ingenuity, than others might possess, might, by shewing such fanciful tricks as were incomprehensible to the rest, acquire the titles and names of wizards, conjurors, magicians, wise men, and the like; by which it does not seem wholly impossible but that such fabulous names may have originally sprung up, and spread from place to place through the weak capacity of mankind during those early days; and, if really so, why not thereby be elevated to such a thoughtless height of ambition, pride, and folly, as to have become the first establishers of those pagan idols amongst the people, and afterwards receive due homage from them, by the different names of gods and goddesses, which we still find mentioned in print, and frequently spoken of in our days; but, how those things might have first originated, whether through those means or otherwise, by casually reflecting thereon, from time to time, at length caused me to view those cruel, unnecessary, wars, so weakly instituted, and, commonly, put in force to the disadvantage of nations, things in themselves appearing so pernicious to mankind in general; but, whether first contrived and propagated by those pretended wise men, with a view of defending the various pagan principles, established by them in different parts, or not, is here left to the consideration of those far better acquainted with the various works of different authors concerning those times, than what I am any ways able to pretend to, through having only mentioned the foregoing from, that which had so accidentally occurred to me while discoursing in the pagan grove, at Little London; and, let them be how they may, studiously weighing those points led me to reflect seriously on material things, far more pleasing to a thoughtful mind, namely, those of good and evil meanings; how the whole human race became so uniformly involved in sin, and liable to the continual temptations of Satan, while assuming the shape of a serpent, and followed by the promise of Almighty God, to raise up a Redeemer of the world from among the seed of our first parents, both able and willing to effectually bruise the head of that old serpent, commonly called the devil; which, having conceived an idea of, it occurred to me, that all manner of sin and wickedness, of every kind, that was then spreading on the earth, to have originally come from, and continually increased, by the perpetual temptations of Satan ever leading the inhabitants thereof to so much prejudice of mind, accompanied with such strong desires of obtaining wealth and riches; perhaps with little or no other view but that of outshining each other in the ambition, pride, and vanity, frequently accompanying them in temporal things below, instead of praying for that everlasting peace, which they might have otherwise had far greater hopes of enjoying in the blissful realms above; and this induced me to recollect two phenomenons that appeared in my time, exactly resembling firey serpents; the former of which I had clearly seen pass over the pleasure-boat of Lord Berkley, when his Royal Highness Frederick Prince of Wales, father to his present majesty, George the Third, was dining there, as related in No. III. page 76, and page 83, and the latter passing over Manchester, when there; which my spouse missed the sight of, by being terrified at the sudden approach of light appearing near about the dusk of night, which we, nevertheless, soon became acquainted with from the lips of our own daughter, then old enough to explain all she had seen, from a window above stairs, concerning the comet, saying: it exactly resembled the shape and make of a firey serpent, with three visible globes in its body, containing the largest of them in the middle part, and one smaller one on each side, towards the tapering of the neck and tail, in her opinion, near about two yards and a half in length, as she clearly saw it pass, seemingly within a bow-shot of the window, whereat she continued observing it entering into a thick cloud, at the same time hearing a rumbling kind of noise proceed therefrom, which, I not being a proper judge of, through want of sight, give the same a place here, as it came to my knowledge from hearsay alone; and as such firey meteor was then said to have past over most parts of England, in the sight of its inhabitants, on the 18th of August, 1783, who, perhaps, may, by taking thought, and duly weighing those various changes which have taken place in their own minds, satisfy themselves, whether any part thereof came from the effective influence of that phenomenon or not, as I find myself wholly unable to form a proper idea thereof with any degree of certainty, therefore leave it, to reflect on very material things found recorded in holy writ, meaning the rod of Moses changed into a serpent, and again to a rod, by the heavenly command of Almighty God, from the flaming bush ordering him to go and work miracles therewith, in order to deliver his brethren, the children of Israel, from that grevious bondage which they were at such time experiencing from the oppressive hands of the Egyptians; and, when it became a serpent in the presence of Pharaoh, his servants, wise men, sorcerers, and magicians, inchanting their own rods into serpents, and observing them all swallowed up by what of Aaron, before their own faces; shewing, that all those pagan principles of idolatry then existing were, in due time, allotted to be swallowed up and banished from the whole face of the earth, by virtue of the everlasting gospel, whereof the established law of Moses was likewise ordained to become the necessary forerunner, as appears from that of a brazen serpent having been raised upon a pole, in the wilderness, by order of Moses, for those infected with malignant bites of numerous serpents infesting it, for their restoration to health, as a visible symbol of their having been ordained by Almighty God, to crucify the immortal Redeemer of the world, on a wooden cross, in Jerusalem, for the human race to look up to for salvation, and themselves become acquainted with the customary ways and language of those idolatrous nations: as none can foretel the unsearchable ways of heaven, concerning the chosen people of God; or say, why they have not likewise been ordained to preach up and explain a sweet sense of the everlasting gospel to the numerous inhabitants of those various nations, through which they have been so extensively scattered, for the purpose of making all sensible concerning the real truth thereof, in their own language, as expressly delivered by Christ to his apostles, and accounted for in the Gospel of St. Matthew, chapter xxiv. and verse 14; saying: this gospel of the kingdom shall be preached in all the world, for a witness unto all nations, &c. and then shall the end come; and, whenever it may please God to open the eyes of the Israelites, with respect to the promise which they seem to have so long misconstrued into a temporal instead of a spiritual kingdom, so happily ordained for them to enjoy at the appointed time, notwithstanding the shortness of the former being soon terminated, while the duration of the latter continues for ever, even from one generation to another; and, when those happy days come, what pleasure will it then be in observing its numerous inhabitants vie with each other in gladly obtaining a sweet sense of the everlasting gospel, from the lips of the chosen people, while studiously endeavouring to preach up, explain, and make known, those happy tidings to all sorts and conditions of mankind; with the additional satisfaction of observing many mighty kings and emperors of those nations becoming thereby induced to look upon their subjects, of all ranks, in like manner as parents do on their own family of children, cautiously endeavouring to promote the tranquillity, peace, and happiness, of all invading those unnecessary wars and bloodshed, originally instigated by Satan, to strengthen and increased his influence with the human race, through imperceptibly drawing them to a far greater love and esteem for that ambitious pride and vanity which they daily see practised amongst themselves on earth below, to that everlasting peace only obtained through the everlasting grace and mercy of our Lord and Saviour Jesus Christ, in the blissful realms above. Having been led to reflect on the foregoing, by means of that pleasing dream wherein I had observed the old crop of grass to have been cut and taken clear away, through comparing it to the conclusive end of the law, as a thing highly necessary to be removed, in order to make room for the everlasting gospel to spring up, resembling beautiful grass every where flushing to the extent of my view, and the plain-dressed female to the church of Christ, anxiously endeavouring to support and maintain the original principles thereof, as at first established by him and his apostles, wholly against the will of Satan; as then appeared to me from that of his resolutely endeavouring to persist in forcibly dragging her away from thence, and, when disappointed thereof, continued slily keeping on the alert, as though intent on seazing her again the first opportunity that offered; and those ideas were greatly strengthened by what I frequently heard coming from the lips of my spouse, and others, when reading the twelfth chapter of Revelations, verse the first and second, as follows: "And there appeared a great wonder "in heaven, a woman clothed with the sun and "the moon under her feet, and upon her head a "crown of twelve stars; and, she being with "child, cried, travailing in birth and pain to be "delivered:" which, having duly considered, it made no small addition to those ideas previously conceived by me, through looking upon this text as a clear representation placed there to foretel the durable church of Christ, till the whole earth should become illuminated with it; in like manner as it is by the glorious rays of the sun at noonday. And the crown of twelve stars on her head, thought to represent as many heavenly angels, ever ready to open the eyes of the Israelites, and thereby afford them a proper sense concerning those mistaken errors of judgement whereby they had been so misled, to expect a temporal instead of a spiritual kingdom, as ordained by Almighty God for them to enjoy with their understanding, open to a clear sense of the world's salvation alone coming through the everlasting grace and mercy of the heavenly redeemer, which their forefathers had crucified; and, when thus enlightened become ready and willing to vie with each other in expelling those idolatrous principles from the minds of others throughout those pagan lands, wherein they may sojourn, enlightening the minds of all with a clear sense of their own salvation, in like manner as the sun expels the dark clouds of night by gradually spreading rays of light over all the earth, to the downfall of Satan, though continually opposing the everlasting church of Christ, as appears in the fifth and thirteenth verse of the same chapter: "And she "brought forth a man-child, who was to rule all "nations with a rod of iron. And when the dra-"gon saw that he was cast unto the earth, he per-"secuted the woman which brought forth the "man-child." Verse the 14th: "And to the wo-"man were given two wings of a great eagle, that

" she might fly into the wilderness into her place,
" where she is nourished for a time and times, and
" half a time from the face of the serpent;" which, according to my own ideas thereof, signifies strength and power, as ordained by Almighty God; thereby enabling the church of Christ to rule over the whole earth, much against the will of Satan, his pretended wise men, wizards, magicians, and weak-minded rulers, seeming to swarm in great numbers through most of those parts; and, rather than give up that pagan idolatry, into which they had been so imperceptibly drawn, through length of time and habitual custom, by the original author of deceit, accompanying all manner of sin and wickedness; namely, that old serpent, called the devil, who, in order to maintain his power on earth, and prevent the same from being diminished and entirely overthrown by the church of Christ, induced weak rulers and others, whose minds he had so imperceptibly prepared, to frighten and terrify all members of the Christian church therefrom, but without succeeding therein, as appeared by the apostles and others patiently submitting to those false accusations continually exhibiting against them by his adherents, through being supported by faith and fortitude, sufficient from above, to put up with

and bear those cruel punishments, barbarous tortures, and various persecutions, at the very place of execution, probably in the midst of numerous spectators, frequently observing their patient manner of submitting thereto, after the example of our immortal redeemer, Jesus Christ, without complaint or murmuring, which, instead of diminishing the members of his church, continued gradually increasing themselves within and without the wilderness, into which they seemed to fly from the face of those persecutions; and continued so doing till happily relieved therefrom during the reign of Constantine the Great; by which time their numbers were become so very large, and well respected of all, as to alarm those numerous persecutors with strong fears of having their pernicious pagan worship wholly overturned by them; as, by the small account, which I have been able to obtain concerning those times. The reigning emperor, Constantine, the Great, seemed inclinable to espouse, promote, and establish, the primitive church of Christ throughout his whole dominions; and, if really so, thought I, why might not those Christian-like sentiments, prevailing in the bosom of such a mighty powerful emperor, bring on a general assembly of the pagan clergy, in order to set their heads together, in consulting how and in what manner to support and maintain their usual ascendency gained over the minds of the people, without which they could not reasonably expect to receive and enjoy the same respect and esteem from them as they formerly did before such important change of religion; namely, from pagan idolatry to Christianity, might, against their will and pleasure, unexpectedly take place and become general throughout those parts; and, if what little account I have received concerning it be true, which I have no reason to believe otherwise, those oracles, meaning idols, wherein they had so much confided, became altogether speechless. And, whether such uncommon and important alteration then taking place, with respect to religious matters, came from a premeditated sense of their own, to continue and increase the emperor's esteem for them, by telling him their idols were all struck dumb through the superior excellence of the Christian doctrine to their own, or otherwise, remains for those much better acquainted with antient records than what I am to determine; yet, when those bloody massacres, dreadful tortures, and cruel executions, which have since taken place in various parts of Christendom are compared with the primitive church established by Christ and his apostles, it may be clearly found that pagan principles had got into it; but how, or in what manner, whether through a premeditated plan, purposely contrived at the time of such general revolution from pagan idolatry to popery taking place, or otherwise, still requires due consideration, as Satan, the well known author of sin, is continually tainting weak mortal beings, to oppose the everlasting church of Christ, as those spurious volumns, contradicting the new testament, chapter and verse throughout, are still in being, and written in such a smooth style of language as baffled all my temporal genius to properly confute, till effectually convinced concerning the entire falsity thereof, by the supreme assistance of the heavenly powers above, thereby enabling me to conceive a clear idea concerning that able authors have given way to the alluring temptations of Satan, while prepossessed with strong notions of obtaining much temporal wealth and riches therefrom; but, without praying to Almighty God for superior aid from above, with a real desire of being made able to understand right from wrong, and good from evil, previous to the time of entering on that pernicious work, as both he and all other mortal beings, let their able talents arising from natural education be ever so great, are still liable to those continual temptations, as may be well understood by the Lord of Life freely submitting thereto while on earth, as signified in the fourth chapter of Matthew, verse eighth, ninth, and tenth; which are as follows: " Again the devil taketh him up into an exceeding " high mountain, and sheweth him all the king- " doms of the world, and the glory of them; and " saith unto him: all these things will I give thee, " if thou wilt fall down and worship me. Then " saith Jesus unto him: get thee hence, Satan; " for it is written, thou shalt worship the Lord " thy God, and him only shalt thou serve."— And this important temptation, suffered by the immortal Redeemer of the world, plainly shewing the power which Satan has of infusing evil thoughts into the different minds of all the human race; and allowed as a very material thing for the church to observe, while cautiously endeavouring to avoid and continually resist those temptations with a lively faith, hoping to obtain salvation through the everlasting grace and mercy of our Lord and Saviour, Jesus Christ, as ordained from the beginning by Almighty God; thereby enabling weak mortals to perceive and overcome the numerous snares of Satan, into which both old, young, rich, poor, high, and low, universally fall, through unnecessary pride, vain glory, ambitious folly, arrogance, and perpetual temptations of one kind or other, all together unable to obtain forgiveness thereof through any other means but that of steadfastly believing in the immortal Redeemer of the world; through whose everlasting grace and mercy salvation alone cometh, and by no other means whatever; yet, when become sensibly convinced of this high and important truth, I still found myself in continual want of necessary aid and assistance from above, and more especially so while experiencing temporal losses, misfortunes, and disappointments, when trusting to my own temporal genius, in order to remove and expel the malady without praying to heaven for supreme aid and assistance from thence; which, at times, threw me into a kind of despair, through fear of losing what little we had, and becoming distressed in strange places; being, at times, whole nights without sleep, in contriving how to keep that trifle we had together, instead of praying for supreme aid and assistance from above, and comparing those losses to trials of faith, caused by my own neglect of duty to God, whereto I ought to most thankfully submit, as few or none were wholly exempt from those kind of temptations, bringing them to a proper sense of their duty at one time or other, which might be prevented through not forgetting the regular hope of support from above. Now, having had full ten years to recollect, consider of, and duly weigh, the material occurrences of my past life, chiefly while moving through the various streets of Boston, easily experiencing the friendly good will and esteem of all, except that of now and then hearing a few thoughtless youths call me The wandering Jew, till I snubbed and prevented them from using that language, by hearing the rebukes of others, as a thing providentially assigned to my lot, for the purpose of writing this book; without which it could not have been compiled so together, previous to the death of our beloved daughter, who happened to fall sick, and after fourteen or fifteen days illness, expired on the 26th of September, 1807, to the unspeakable sorrow and grief of the family, through having left five children, from three to twelve years old, one of them born on the 31st of December, 1799, about half an hour past eleven o'clock at night, living in two centuries the first hour, and becoming so very unfortunate as to lose his sight by a cold; and what became still more grievous to him was, that of losing his hearing by a scarlet fever, near about one year after his mother's death, whereby their daughter, a fine girl, ten years old, was deprived of life, to the grief of all the rest, even me in particular; as she had been carefully trained up in the strictest principles of moral virtue; became an excellent reader of her age, and exceedingly fond of entertaining me therewith occasionally. Some time after which, family changes appearing likely to follow, induced me and my spouse to think of returning to London, with the manuscript we had taken so much studious care and pains to compile, and endeavour to publish it ourselves, in order to avoid becoming troublesome and oppressive to those for whom we had a most tender regard; and, notwithstanding that our advanced period in life had rendered us incapable, as we thought, of going through the fatigue necessarily required by such publication, yet I had been encouraged thereto by various foreboding dreams; one of which is as follows: wherein I seemed to have been alone, thoughtfully reflecting on the aforesaid writing, as though timorous and fearful of not being able to complete the same for want of proper talents in the apartment of an acquaintance, near Bargate-bridge, on a fine summer's day, with the street-door open, observing a most worthy friend, namely, Mr. Edward Lee, of Tooke's Court, Cursitor-street, Chancery-lane, approach in the most kind and friendly manner, desiring to know if I had any commands to my friends in Wiggan, as he was going to pass through that place, and, in such case would deliver them without delay; then, shaking me by the hand, while taking leave, said: "Take care that every word you write be really true; as, in such case, they will be improved by others for the good of mankind in general." Now, seeming to have heard this pleasing advice concerning the work I had in hand, come from the lips of one of the best friends I ever had reason to believe and respect, seemed to most gratefully affect my internal frame; and far more so, for not long after, while hearing a London newspaper read, wherein he appeared to have departed this mortal state of life some short time before, thereby affording me reason to believe those many unsolicited favours heaped on me during his natural life, were still continued beyond the grave, induced me gladly to follow his advice, in sticking close to the truth in every word. I might have proper time to insert, and though very much grieved at such unexpected news, my desire of continuing the work seemed to increase, by thinking myself employed therein from above, for some good end or other still unknown to me, and conscience being concerned, would not admit of delay, through fear of neglect, by stopping that which might become useful to others; but symptoms of family changes appearing still likely to continue, we also were preparing for the result that might ensue; and it was not long before we left the place, that I became indulged with another remarkable foreboding dream, wherein I thought myself duly attending to the words of a much approved teacher of many young gentlemen in Holbourn, while advising me to come up, in order to publish the work I had been set about; as, in such case, it would not only be received, but likewise improved by others for the good of many, which increased my hopes of doing good, held up our spirits, while tenderly parting from the family, without force or having been otherwise induced thereto than as above stated, which, to the best of my recollection, took place on the 26th of October, 1809; and now, being on our way to London, frequently discoursing about the course we had in view, and stopping all night in Stilton, I there experienced another remarkable cautionary sort of dream, wherein I seemed to think myself walking upon a narrow level footpath, separated from a pleasant garden, by wooden pales on the left: observing a clear gentle stream of water gliding through a narrow lane, close on the right, having a large antient building, with a high door, open behind, and a delightful green meadow in front, on a very mild summer's day, when thinking I heard something coming behind, and looking back, I seemed to behold my old enemy, the gigantic fiend, or another like him, close at my heels, as though creeping softly, with a design of slily seizing me behind; but, on finding himself discovered, by my turning quickly round to defend myself against his attack, he thereupon ran hastily back, through the open door of the building, on to an extensive plain behind the house, into which I seemed to follow. Observing him to stop at some distance, as if he was fearful of continuing too near the house, wherein I seemed to remain, carefully observing his motions from another door; which said dream caused me to expect strong temptations of one kind or other, if not oppositions from such as might disapprove of the work I had in view, thereby inducing me to pray for supreme aid and assistance from above, whereby I might become enabled to succeed therein, and, with such desire applied to the same printing-office, wherein my pamphlets had been formerly printed, for many years; and terms being agreed on with the proprietors, it was not many days after No. 1. had been finished, entered at the stamp-office, and offered to sale, than I experienced another very remarkable foreboding kind of dream, wherein I thought myself viewing beautiful clear water, appearing very extensive to the eye, while standing on the bank, observing no wind to any way disturb the same; which, having admired for some time, and then looking back, I seemed to behold the heads of two very large serpents, within a few yards, peeping at me over a bank, having all the rest of their shape and make concealed behind; and, on perceiving themselves discovered, withdrew their heads from my sight, which, being desirous of knowing more of, I walked to higher ground, and from thence seemed to behold them both lying snug together, in a kind of hole, open at the top, as though got into it with intent to secure themselves from my attack, which I dared not hazard doing, through fear of danger, by reason of their size, which appeared much larger than any thing of the kind I had ever seen before; and, then, waking from my dream, without being able to form any proper idea of, till No. II. came from the press, when, going round therewith, many of those friends who had so humanely purchased No. I. from us, then declined taking No. II. saying: "It was too childish for their perusal;" thereby inducing me to believe those incidental affairs, which had so unhappily taken place during the early period of my days, would have been far better omitted or shortened, with such a gloss over as might have become more pleasing to others; but that discovery came too late. For, want of money sufficient enough to print them over again, and likewise support us till they were finished, which led me to reflect on the aforesaid dream, by duly considering whether or no the influence of Satan had been such as to have drawn me into such like error of judgement as did not seem altogether unlike by the two serpents peeping at me over the bank, while those numbers were printing, and then consealing themselves in a hole when discovered; or, if the same had not been allowed by the heavenly powers above, to answer some good end or other still unknown to me, which seemed to be in no wise unlikely, as appeared to me, while comparing the extensive clear water to immense numbers of well-disposed people, seemingly from its appearing very smooth, in no ways ruffled or disturbed by the wind, more or less thereof, might probably think fit to peruse the work, and, through time, prevail on others to follow their example, thereby inducing us to resolve on stretching every nerve, in order to make it known to the world, and redoubled our diligence: with such intent, while praying for supreme aid and assistance from above, in hopes of experiencing better success in the end; and though few or none of the following numbers went of; yet the real necessity of our own affairs, and pressing desire I had of completing the work induced us to continue persevering therein, with strong hopes of the same becoming improved for the good of others when finished, as it appears to me that no mortal being can become fully satisfied in mind concerning a future state of salvation, without receiving aid and assistance from above; let his ingenious talents arising from natural education be ever so great; and, as all the human race are in course desirous of injoying everlasting peace in the world to come, would it not be the best for every individual to earnestly pray for knowledge and wisdom concerning the important point of salvation, which, though affording great satisfaction of mind, cannot be otherwise enjoyed than by the heavenly permission of Almighty God alone, it is therefore hoped weak mortals here below will not trust to their own temporal abilities concerning such a most important thing, which, if placed so far above their reach, without praying for supreme aid from above, as the almighty former of the universal world has not created mankind without souls to be saved, and means of attaining everlasting life, through confiding in the merits of his only beloved son, Jesus Christ, our Lord and Saviour;

nor yet of withholding some pleasing knowledge thereof from mortal beings earnestly praying for it while on earth below; who then would neglect praying for so great a blessing as that enabling them to live content and happy here below, through having a confidential hope of enjoying immortal peace in the blissful realms above for ever after. Why, then, should mankind differ with each other concerning the various forms of worship, while the scriptures are offering salvation to all true believers? Pray, does not religious worship proceed from the hearts of all, whether male or female; hoping to preserve their own souls alive? Why, then, trust a concern of such high importance to any but the Creator and Redeemer of it; in whose power alone it is to preserve and bless whom they please with everlasting happiness? So that, with respect to good or evil, by studiously attending to the former, those sanguine hopes I had of obtaining mercy and forgiveness for the numerous sins I had committed easily increased, till becoming baffled and confused, by hearing that false book, called, " The independent Whig," read throughout, which caused such gloomy vapours of the brain to arise therein, as all the temporal genius I was master of proved insufficient to remove; till looking up, and praying for supreme assistance from above, which through time produced much good; from such uncommon great and unexpected evil as signified in the various beforementioned dreams, which being considered as a most heavenly kind of reply to such humble request, to effectually expel those gloomy doubts wherewith my thoughts had been so long impressed, thereby enabling me to become happily content and satisfied, through steadfastly confiding in the scripture truths, and likewise taking those material dreams recently experienced by me for something more than nightly vapours of the brain, which I have heard others call them, saying they proceeded from temper, or causes of one kind or other, and deserving of no farther notice, though it clearly appeared to me Satan had been allowed to cause frightful dreams, and likewise that very material things were communicated to earthly mortals in heavenly visions of the night concerning their own salvation, and if duly attended to may, I hope, be of universal good to all the human race for ever after; as those real dreams I had experienced concerning temporal things coming to pass increased my hope of obtaining mercy and forgiveness, things leading to immortal peace, without which in my opinion that heavenly blessing cannot be enjoyed. And here it may not be amiss to shew the manner how I came to credit the authenticity of some dreams, through one experienced by my spouse, a night or two previous to the time we met, but concealed from me until some time after a marriage union had taken place between us, when she thought fit to acquaint me therewith, saying she had seen me in a dream with the butcher enter the door of that house wherein she was sitting with more of her own sex, advising her to save her own money by accompanying me throughout the journey, as I was allotted to become her bosom friend through life, and though quite blind we should live to enjoy many happy long years together; which through knowing us, again proved to be the sole cause of inducing her to venture at that of walking back on foot with me to London, and likewise of attending to the proposal I made her of marriage while on the road, all of which having properly heard, duly weighed, and compared with that foreboding dream which I experienced concerning her one night previous to the time of setting off from Portsmouth to London, and cautiously reflecting on both, induced me to look upon them, as having been really sent from above for the purpose of bringing us together; wherein I became still more effectually confirmed through hearing described all those beautiful cities, towns, villages, roads, groves, and avenues, we passed through in England, Scotland, Wales, and Ireland, as well as those of France, Flanders Germany, and Holland, from the lips of a most agreeable bosom friend, whose face I had never seen except in that delightful kind of dream; to which I may likewise add another, experienced by me at the Cross Keys, Stamford, Lincolnshire, in the year of our Lord, 1777, to the best of my recollection, wherein I seemed to visib'y observe Mr. Thomas Dane, shoemaker, of Wiggan, Lancashire, approach by daylight, saying thy brother is in the dust, and then disappeared without saying more, which having mentioned to my spouse, a post letter was despatched to my sister in Wiggan, Lancashire, the next day, who gave us to understand, by the return of post, that her husband had departed this life some few days previous to the receipt of such letter.

Now this and others of the kind induced me to observe and look upon such like dreams as authentic; and, if really so, why not those concerning immortality, which I verily believe will not be withheld from such as earnestly pray to understand the only right and true way to salvation, affording more tranquil peace of mind to individuals than any other thing whatever, through enabling them to live in a continual hope of enjoying the immortal blessing when called to the blissful realms above, which is a happy thing for individuals to properly consider, as appears from its having enabled me to enjoy little or no less peace of mind during a period of fifty-five long years in a state of total darkness than what some of those enjoying perfect temporal sight may have experienced, for which I always found sufficient reason to continue truly thankful to almighty God, for granting me those heavenly favours, and likewise supporting us while passing through so many distant lands, hoping those humane friendly customers seemingly displeased with the perusal of No. I. may, instead of condemning all the rest unheard, make some allowance for my defect in want of foresight in not shortening those innocent childish tricks contained therein with such a diminished kind of gloss as would have made them to appear more worthy of improvement with the rest; and should that happily take place without deviating from the truth, my real end and meaning in compiling this book would become most amply gratifying, and still more so if able to make children sensible of the loss which they are liable to sustain by neglecting their school like me to gratify the weak curiosity of others, which I most humbly hope parents, teachers, and all the human race, will effectually prevent, by training up their beloved offspring in such a christian-like way as may be of universal advantage to the rising generation; which increased by now and then hearing young people express a desire of seeing No. II. of this work.

And here it may not be improper to mention the uncommon distress of body and mind which the sudden change of conduct taking place in the minds of those under whose tuition I continued from the age of nine to twelve produced, by driving me into the company of various distressed children, who I had no idea or knowledge of before, without allowing for the loose manner in which I had been trained up, and thereby increasing the respect which I had previously conceived for my uncle, whereby I might have easily been brought to attend him at school, and by that means have improved my education like other scholars under his tuition, without flying from school through fear of appearing in the presence of an approved and well-known teacher, that was fully capable of improving both me and others, in useful and necessary education, if I had not been terrified into the company of various distressed children, chiefly miserable enough to practise, sleeping among hay and straw in barns and out-houses, and to follow gambling for halfpence and pence with each other by day and night, and likewise stealing fruit from the orchards of worthy inhabitants, who, on observing me become habituated thereto, looked on me as one of the most graceless boys in Wiggan, through which I became most generally suspected of facts never committed by me, while continuing to associate with those distressed children, whose pilfering tricks were but too often placed on my shoulders; and now this irrecoverable loss of education, while so capable of improvement, having since caused no small uneasiness of mind, thereby inducing me to have the same committed to writing while in Boston, together with a true account of those various troubles which had been so inadvertently wrought on me at that early period of life, and omitted here as things wholly inadequate to the moral edification of youthful minds, as also various passages of my natural life, interspersed with some wonderful dreams which I was subject to, and in consequence thereof committed to writing, but left out of this work through fear of swelling it overlarge, though I frequently enjoyed great pleasure and satisfaction of mind while reflecting on those nightly visions, wherein I seemed usually to behold and well know the face of my parents, relations, friends, and others, while therein; seeming to converse with them in like manner as ever I did before their deaths, thereby affording reason to think we shall know each other beyond the grave, as though the innermost secrets of my heart, whether good or evil, appearing well known to them, which helped to strengthen my faith and hopes of obtaining salvation through the everlasting grace and mercy of our immortal redeemer Jesus Christ, thereby enabling me to live resigned, content, and truly thankful to Almighty God, for having wonderfully supported me through so many difficult passages of life, before and since I became deprived of temporal sight, while passing through this and various other nations with my spouse, who he likewise enabled to pen down the whole of this book from my own lips, without any other assistance than what he of his infinite goodness and mercy thought fit to endow us with, even me in particular, with a strong memory, sufficient enough to recollect the same, wherefrom that narrative wrote by Mr. Glanfield, entitled the Unfortunate Shipwright, or Cruel Captain, concerning my sufferings on the voyage, was likewise taken, and not only translated into other languages, but likewise personally sold by us in France, Flanders, Germany, and Holland, and copies thereof; we have still by us to prove the truth of what is herein mentioned, which may perhaps be found worth inspection, with some other vouchers left in writing, concerning material things when I am no more.

And now having to the best of my weak abilities, judgement, and recollection, brought this work to a conclusion, we most humbly hope that all our friendly customers of every kind, whether residing in England or in distant parts, will please to accept of our most grateful and united thanks, which we have been long desirous of shewing and expressing in a more respectful way, especially to those unexpected steady friends at the White Lee, near Wiggan, whose friendly, kind, and humane, aid so freely coming just in the time of need, we look on as a succour truly sent from above, to prolong my days without allowing us the secret pleasure of shewing our gratitude agreeably to our own desire, therefore most humbly hope the Lord will reward and bless them with continual peace and happiness, both here and for ever after, and likewise all our friendly customers every where, which now is, and ever will be, the earnest prayers of their most obliged humble servants,

Robert and Elizabeth Barker,
No. 146, Great Saffron-hill, London,
October the 10th, 1811.

FINIS.

www.ingramcontent.com/pod-product-compliance
Lightning Source LLC
Chambersburg PA
CBHW080051190426
43201CB00035B/2163